D0290950

Florida
1st day of spring
2006

The Goddess Lives in Upstate New York . . .

... and in Camarillo, too!

Lynn (Gin) ~

To my very favorite
Buddhist nun, who
asks wonderful questions.
Happy reading and
exploring to you, always.

Love & peace,

Connie

The Goddess Lives in Upstate New York

Breaking Convention and Making Home at a North American Hindu Temple

CORINNE G. DEMPSEY

OXFORD
UNIVERSITY PRESS
2006

OXFORD
UNIVERSITY PRESS

Oxford University Press, Inc., publishes works that further
Oxford University's objective of excellence
in research, scholarship, and education.

Oxford New York
Auckland Cape Town Dar es Salaam Hong Kong Karachi
Kuala Lumpur Madrid Melbourne Mexico City Nairobi
New Delhi Shanghai Taipei Toronto

With offices in
Argentina Austria Brazil Chile Czech Republic France Greece
Guatemala Hungary Italy Japan Poland Portugal Singapore
South Korea Switzerland Thailand Turkey Ukraine Vietnam

Copyright © 2006 by Oxford University Press, Inc.

Published by Oxford University Press, Inc.
198 Madison Avenue, New York, New York 10016

www.oup.com

Oxford is a registered trademark of Oxford University Press

All rights reserved. No part of this publication may be reproduced,
stored in a retrieval system, or transmitted, in any form or by any means,
electronic, mechanical, photocopying, recording, or otherwise,
without the prior permission of Oxford University Press.

Library of Congress Cataloging-in-Publication Data
Dempsey, Corinne G.
The Goddess lives in upstate New York : breaking convention
and making home at a North American Hindu temple / Corinne G. Dempsey
p. cm.
Includes bibliographical references and index.
ISBN-13 978-0-19-518729-8; 978-0-19-518730-4 (pbk.)
ISBN 0-19-518729-6; 0-19-518730-X (pbk.)
1. Rajarajeshvari (Hindu deity)—Cult—New York (State)—Rochester. 2. Śrī Rājarājeśwarī Pīṭham (Rochester, N.Y.) 3. Spiritual life—Hinduism. I. Title.
BL1225.R274U634 2005
294.5'35'0974788—dc22 2005045085

9 8 7 6 5 4 3 2 1

Printed in the United States of America
on acid-free paper

Dedicated to Aiya and Amma
and to the devotees at the Rush temple
who have given me so much

Acknowledgments

The process of researching, thinking, and writing this book has been anything but a solo adventure. Although I can probably never properly thank all those who have contributed in substance and/or support to the following pages, I will at least acknowledge many of them here by name.

To start, Paul Younger alerted me to the existence of the Rush temple. I sometimes wonder when, if ever, I would have stumbled upon such riches without his timely suggestion. Susan Nowak helped me actually locate the temple and, after I moved to Wisconsin, regularly and warm-heartedly provided me with a second home in Rochester. I thank all the Sisters of St. Joseph for their abundant hospitality and for our exquisite Hindu-Catholic conversations in the evenings and over breakfast. A UW-Stevens Point New Faculty Grant supported my first trip back to upstate New York and student transcribers Amanda Fiedler, Angie Kind, and Dan Lesczynski gallantly helped with the tedious task of transforming taped interviews into print.

UWSP colleagues Barbara Butler, Don Fadner, Aurthur Herman, and Alice Keefe deftly helped apply my field data to larger academic conversations. I am also indebted, as always, to Ann Gold and Susan Wadley at Syracuse University for their support and wise counsel at various stages of the process. If it were not for a fellowship from the Madison Institute for Research in the Humanities, this book might never have seen the light of day, at least not for many more years. I am grateful to Dean Justus Paul for his continued support of UWSP's participation in this valuable program in spite of severe budget cuts and to my chair, Don Fadner, for his unbegrudging support of my year-long absence. I also benefited considerably from thoughtful exchanges with the other fellows at the Institute during the 2002–2003 year. Jeslie and Annupamma's warm hospitality and intense conversations were truly icing on the Madison cake during my extended visits.

Conversations with colleagues Paul Courtright, Whitney Kelting, Pratap Kumar, Vasudha Narayanan, and Selva Raj helped enrich my view of South Asian practices and perspectives in various communities in India and in the diaspora against which the Rush temple sometimes melds and sometimes stands in sharp relief. My loyal ex-student Amanda Fiedler, on site in Tamil Nadu and Delhi while I was writing, similarly helped explore and juxtapose particular practices and perceptions.

In an attempt to make this book accessible to a popular audience, I shamelessly enlisted a number of family members, local friends, and even our Austrian exchange student to read the manuscript at different stages of completion. I am grateful to Pana Columbus, Fran Dempsey, Amanda Fiedler, Terry Flynn, Nick Garigliano, Patricia Garigliano, Florian Hahn, Kathy Hoffman, Kurt Hoffman, Jean Leary, Amarnath Nagarajan, Ken Wagner, and Martha Yonke for their careful consideration and feedback. Students in both sections of my fall 2003 Religions of India course thoughtfully read and anonymously commented on the manuscript as well. I thank all of the above for their generous and astute observations and suggestions that, I believe, helped to make this a better book.

Aparna Hasling and Pathmanathan Kandaiya graciously allowed me to use some of their beautiful photos for the book and John Hartman cheerfully gave of his precious time, advice, and equipment to make sure the photos were in the best possible black-and-white condition before sending them to the press.

It has been my great pleasure and privilege to work, once again, with editor Cynthia Read and associate editor Theo Calderara and, this time around, with production editor Christine Dahlin and editorial assistant Julia TerMaat at Oxford University Press. Encouraging and challenging remarks by anonymous readers spurred me both to have confidence in my approach and to hone further some of the book's arguments. Copyeditor Margaret Case's fine polishing is, as always, unparalleled. Any shortcomings in the finished product are, of course, my very own.

At home, the three men in my life, Nick Garigliano and Jack and Sam Dempsey Garigliano, have supported my adventures with the Rush temple from the very beginning. Nick, in particular, has listened with apparent interest to the stories I enthusiastically brought home with me and has nurtured and fed my fledgling insights. All three have good-naturedly weathered the absences that fieldwork and writing periodically require.

Finally and most fundamentally, I owe a debt of gratitude to Rush temple participants, all of them, for their extraordinary generosity and patience. During the several-year period when I was most focused on interviewing temple members, Aiya used to joke that Corinne, like the goddesses born with weaponry in their hands, was born holding a tape recorder. Some people (including me) joked how crowds would scatter when they spied me and my tape recorder approaching, but the truth is that temple members were not only generous about making time to speak formally with me but also in the level of openness with which they shared their stories and their hearts. Many of those who never managed to sit for official taped interviews graced me with their trust and honesty, as well. For the plentiful sense of welcome and warmth I have received from temple participants, I am truly grateful.

It would be difficult to single out the many devotees whose kindness, support, and generosity have sustained me over the years, yet I feel I must mention a few whose support was instrumental to the researching and writing of this book. From the very beginning, Charulata Chawan has taken a hearty interest in my work and has gone out of her way to organize interviews, administer questionnaires, and engage in lengthy conversations about the process and product of research. Although her life's work is currently with the Syracuse University library, she might just consider a second career as an ethnographer. Aparna Hasling's sensitivity, moral support, and keen insight have sustained not only my work from beginning to end but also, more personally speaking, a crucial connection to the temple when geographical distance has separated us. Sudharshan Durayappah has been an invaluable source of information, analysis, and comic relief. The hours we have spent discussing the temple and its place in larger religious and academic frameworks have produced insights without which this book would not be the same. Now that I have written from my vantage point, it is his turn. Amma's stable, wise, and supportive presence at the temple is a quiet force of inestimable value. The genuine concern she has offered me and many others in her sphere of influence should never be underestimated. Her depth of spiritual and practical dedication and vision makes her truly one of a kind.

The person primarily responsible for the substance and tenor of this book—not to mention the substance and tenor of the temple itself—is Aiya, who bore my steady stream of questions and omnipresent tape recorder with patience and good humor. Not one to keep his views to himself, he regularly was candid with me about the ups and downs of being a guru, of dealing with the needs of temple participants, and of running an organization that adheres to yet stridently strays from traditional principles. On rare occasions, he would even ask my advice. The extent to which Aiya shared with me the teachings of his tradition and furthermore trusted me with his thoughts and opinions is of no small significance to me. His generosity, openness, and honesty—and my admiration for them—give significant substance to this book. More than anything, his towering faith in the Mother of us all has left me a different person than when I began this project.

Contents

Note on Transliteration

This book employs diacritical marks for Tamil and Sanskrit words, following Library of Congress style. For readers unfamiliar with Indian terms, it is my hope that the benefits of familiarizing oneself with diacritics and with more accurate pronunciation will outshine the drawbacks of the (initially) confusing array of dots and dashes.

Many of the terms used have both Tamil and Sanskrit forms. In such instances I follow temple usage and thus the Tamil form. Most typically this means adding an *m* to the end of a Sanskrit word such that *prasada* becomes *prasadam* and *linga* becomes *lingam,* etc. The glossary at the end of the book likewise lists such recurring terms in Tamil form. Place names and personal names of individuals are Anglicized, written without diacritics, to conform to their common usage when writing in English.

Basic Guide to Pronunciation

Vowels

Long vowels are pronounced differently and are given more emphasis than short ones; they are distinguished by placing a line over the vowel.

a	like *u* in *up*	*e*	like *e* in *met*
ā	like *a* in *father*	*ē*	like *a* in *lake*
i	like *i* in *pit*	*ai*	like *i* in *hike*

ī	like ee in *sheep*	*o*	like the first *o* in *potato*
u	like *u* in *put*	*ō*	like the *o* in *oak*
ū	like *oo* in *troop*	*au*	like *ou* in *shout*

Consonants

Consonants with corresponding sounds that differ most strikingly from English are

ś, ṣ	like *sh* in *shut*	*r*	is rolled like a Spanish single *r*
c	like *ch* in *chat*	*ṛ*	like *ri* in *river* (rolled *r*)

Consonants with dots beneath them like ḷ, ṇ, ṣ, and ṭ are retroflex. They are pronounced with the tongue curled back so it touches the roof of the mouth. Double consonants like kk, cc, or ll, are given greater emphasis or held longer than single consonants.

The Goddess Lives in Upstate New York

Introduction

A Temple Trip

Imagine for a moment that I have visitors whom I decide to take on a day trip to the Śrī Rājarājeśwarī Pīṭham, the "seat" (*pīṭham*) of the goddess Rājarājeśwarī. Since they have never been there before and I do not tell them where we are headed, they are in for a bit of a surprise. As we near the temple, we look out at the lovely rolling landscape of rural upstate New York and remark, depending on the season, on the deep green of the rain-drenched hills, the electric fall foliage, or the sparkling winter wonderland around us. After winding though long stretches of farmland dotted with barns, silos, and cows, our car takes a turn down a long, narrow driveway that leads toward a small, neatly painted, one-story yellow barn. We leave the car in the parking lot and, as we near the barn, we encounter a four-foot statue of Ganeś, the rotund, elephant-headed Lord of Beginnings and Remover of Obstacles. Ganeś, appropriately, is our first clue that something Hindu is afoot.[1] Carved in typical south Indian style from black granite, he tastefully wears splendid silks and gold-colored ornaments. Peering out from his clear Plexiglas shrine, he may or may not sport sunglasses to keep the sun's glare from his eyes; this also depends on the season.

Entering through the side door, we add our shoes to the rows of footwear and, because morning worship (*pūjā*) is in full swing, we hear the faint sound of chanting coming from beyond the next door. As we pass through this door and into smoky air thick with incense, we are greeted by a chorus of Sanskrit chants, the clanging of bells, boisterous Karnatic temple music (electronically piped in) and, most dramatically, an array of gleaming gods and goddesses. Upstate New

York farmland, in essence, could not seem farther away. Focusing more closely on the deities in our midst, our eyes are drawn first to the goddess Rājarājeśwarī, "Empress of Emperors," to whom the temple is dedicated.[2] She sits in regal splendor on the opposite side of the temple, flanked by (another) Ganeś on her right and a Śiva *lingam* on her left.[3] Resplendently decorated with gold jewelry, draped in silk, and heavily garlanded with flowers, these three deities are exquisitely carved from black granite. Directly to our right are the nine planets or Navagṛha, crafted in mostly human form and each accompanied by a female consort and an animal *vāhana* or vehicle. Plated in gold and nattily dressed in color-coordinated silk sarongs and turbans, the Navagṛha and their entourage stand at eye level on a square platform.[4] Although temple activity revolves around Rājarājeśwarī and her powers, the remaining deities lining the side and back walls are embodiments of the Śaiva-Śākta tradition. Gold-plated and dressed in silk, they belong to the family of gods and goddesses associated with the divine pair, Śiva and Pārvatī.[5]

Since my visitors are familiar with south Indian and Sri Lankan Tamil traditions, they recognize most of the surrounding deities, the ongoing ritual, and note the temple's distinct south Indian flavor. Yet two things immediately stand out. One is the temple's floor plan. Its deviation from south Indian norms is nearly as dramatic as discovering a glittering gang of Hindu deities in the middle of North American farm country. Rather than inhabiting enclosed individual shrines that allow for exclusive priestly access, the gods and goddesses brazenly stand (or sit) out in the open. The temple design encourages any and all visitors to approach and pay their respects. Yet official priestly ritual is also in evidence, witnessed by the ongoing *pūjā* and the remains of earlier offerings—flowers of various shapes, hues, and freshness, tucked into every conceivable granite and gold crevice.[6] The spirit behind the temple's open design is further expressed through the *pūjā* itself. One temple member—a woman—honors the deities with physical offerings of flowers, incense, water, fruit, and flame while a group of others, sitting among the congregation, chant along in Sanskrit and perform ritually prescribed hand gestures (*mudrās*) at appropriate moments. Rather than enacting the typical divide between a male priest who mediates divine blessings and devotees who receive them, the *pūjā* confuses traditional lines of temple participation.

Like this trip with my imaginary visitors—with surprises at every turn—this book's extended trip to the Śrī Rājarājeśwarī Piṭham of Rush, New York, is a study in unexpected twists and turns that define and enliven the temple and its community. The reality suggested by the book's title, that the Goddess lives in upstate New York, sets the stage for our exploration in three ways. On one level, the elaborate rituals performed at the Rush temple create an atmosphere where deities and their powers—particularly the powers of Rājarājeśwarī—are made to thrive. This commitment to enlivening divinity through ritual finds itself juxtaposed against and influenced by today's secular scientific

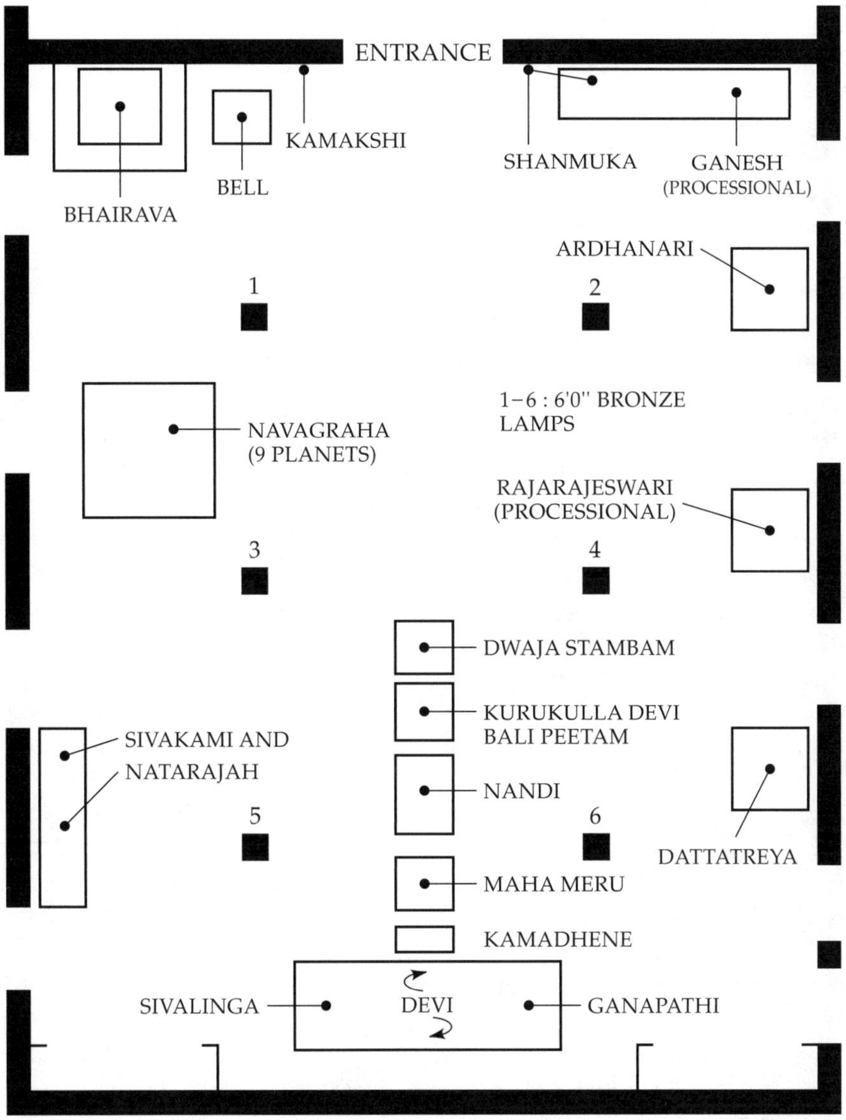

Temple floor plan sketched by Aiya, November 2003.

worldview. Second, the guru-mandated openness of temple practices—in which ancient ritual performances and esoteric teachings break through their traditional confines—brings the Goddess to life in ways unavailable, if not unthinkable, for devotees at more conventional temples. Finally, the rather everyday sense in which the Goddess lives, or resides, in upstate New York has important implications for deities and human participants alike. The dynamics of south Indian temple life as it works to settle and flourish in rural

North America—imaged by elaborately adorned deities amid U.S. cows and silos—present opportunities and challenges for all involved. These three areas of exploration, reflecting the work of the deities, the guru, and the devotees, respectively, ensure that the Goddess lives and thrives in upstate New York. They also, for our purposes, help set the book's itinerary.

The book's first part, exploring the dynamic between miraculous and scientific worldviews, highlights the workings of and faith in Rājarājeśwarī, known as Devī or Mother to her devotee children.[7] Key to locating Devī's place in Rush temple practices and in the lives of her devotees is the Śrīvidyā tradition to which the goddess and temple belong. Śrīvidyā, or "auspicious wisdom," is a tantric path that honors the great goddess Tripurasundarī and places considerable emphasis on harnessing her powers through ritual. Tripurasundarī herself transcends description, and manifests for her devotees as three different goddesses with distinct attributes—the eldest of the three, according to temple tradition, is Rājarājeśwarī.[8] The Śrīvidyā tradition, flourishing primarily in northern Kashmir and parts of south India since at least the sixth century, is today practiced most widely—and usually secretly—in south India.[9] The community traditionally responsible for formalizing its practices, guarding its secrets as their own, is the Smārta community, an elite subcaste within the brahmanical fold. Although historical and textual evidence suggest that Śrīvidyā is meant for men and women of all castes, its elitism and association with the brahman community in India and Sri Lanka is rarely challenged.[10]

The Rush temple guru, Sri Chaitanyananda, known affectionately as Aiya,[11] defies convention when he, a nonbrahman, enthusiastically brings Śrīvidyā's ritual secrets into the open. Aiya validates his work through his entrenchment within an esteemed Śrīvidyā guru lineage and is quick to point out that the true maverick in his life to whom he owes his position as Rush temple founder is his own guru, Sri Amritananda, known as Guruji. A Smārta brahman from the south Indian state of Andhra Pradesh, Guruji was a professor of nuclear physics at a Zambian university when he and Aiya first met in 1978. Aiya, at the time, was working in Zambia as an architect. Soon after they met, Guruji initiated Aiya and his wife, Amma (the Tamil term for Mother), into Śrīvidyā. Not only did Guruji break with lineage tradition by offering initiation to a nonbrahman couple, he furthermore instructed Aiya to pass on what he learned to anyone interested, regardless of their background. Six months after initiation, Aiya, Amma, and their seven-year-old daughter, Charu, emigrated to the United States, exporting Aiya's capacity as religious teacher and ritual specialist to new terrain. In the early years, students regularly met in Aiya and Amma's attic that they had converted into a shrine room. Later, their one-and-a-half-car garage became headquarters for worship and learning. Since 1998, the yellow barn surrounded by rolling hills and silos has hosted the goddess and her entourage.

Part II discusses the temple's commitment to nonconvention amid its attention to ritual precision and features Aiya as instigator of both. Aiya himself embodies this space-in-between, reveling in yet rebelling against traditional expectations for religious leadership. As teacher, counselor, philosopher, and storyteller, he fulfills the many-faceted guru role for students of all backgrounds. As ritual specialist, he likewise performs his job as temple *pūjāri* or priest with precision and gusto. Aiya veers from traditional norms when he enthusiastically shares his priestly role with others and, as a guru with blessings from his own guru, when he freely transmits Śrīvidyā's highly secretive, typically exclusive, tradition to almost anyone willing to learn. Because of Aiya's unconventional bearing, visitors to the temple in search of the esteemed priest-guru have been known to walk right past him—past the Sri Lankan Tamil man wearing trousers and a T-shirt, still youthful as he nears his sixtieth birthday, laughing loudly at a joke or comically dodging clear of someone he has just teased. Unable to find the guru they thought they came to see—somber, perhaps orange-robed and bearded, holding forth with religious platitudes—they are eventually directed back to the clean-shaven, rambunctious man in street clothes. Although Aiya's conversations regularly take philosophical turns, and although he dresses more like a typical temple priest while performing ritual, he is not always readily identifiable, based on preconceptions of holy countenance, as an influential religious leader.[12]

Part III's discussion of interchanges between foreign and domestic cultures, religions, and landscapes highlights anecdotes and reflections of community members and temple participants. Throughout the book, I often identify temple participants, by no means a homogenous group, according to their level of commitment. At the perimeter are visitors who come on rare occasions, typically propelled by curiosity or long-distance pilgrimage. These sporadic participants tend to be of Indian or Sri Lankan ancestry, mostly first-generation North Americans and their children. Closer to the core are semifrequent visitors including, for the most part, Sri Lankan Tamil immigrants and their children who live in Toronto. Although Toronto hosts several major Sri Lankan-run temples and dozens of smaller ones, Torontonians regularly make the three-hour trip to Rush. They do so for a host of reasons: to relax in the temple's idyllic rural setting, to take part in its nonconventional atmosphere and, most commonly, to reap the benefits of its elaborate rituals, gleaning the blessings of its powerful goddess, Śrī Rājarājeśwarī.

Temple members identified as inner-core devotees represent the smallest, most dedicated, segment of the temple population. Although the number of people to whom Aiya has given a mantra, and thus initiated into the Śrīvidyā tradition, is nearly impossible to estimate, the ever-shifting group of temple regulars roughly numbers about forty at any given time.[13] From June 1998 through October 2002, I formally and informally interviewed about thirty inner-core devotees, composed mostly of first- and second-generation South Asians from India and Sri Lanka, along with a handful of U.S.-born non–South

Asians. About three-quarters of this group were willing if not enthusiastic about lending their thoughts and experiences to my tape recorder and me on at least one occasion.[14] A number of other devotees who repeatedly and gladly shared with me their reflections over the years nevertheless managed to avoid—either by happenstance or design—being formally interviewed.[15] Their anecdotes and opinions, although not included verbatim, also help form this book.

The following pages incorporate exchanges with dozens of people peripherally involved at the temple—pilgrims, semiregular visitors, and Rush community members—yet the bulk of this book weaves scenes, stories, and ideas offered to me by Aiya and some of the temple's most dedicated participants. The resulting tone is thus one of an insider, largely supportive of temple practices and policies. It is by no means utopian, however. Religious dedication and community building has its challenges, and life at the Rush temple is no exception. As temple participants concluded during a number of conversations, religious movements that defy the status quo will, by their nature, be works in progress, never finished and finalized as long as the challenge is extended.[16] While providing an exciting and fulfilling ride, such movements experience their share of bumps along the way.

This excitement and tension, typically associated with challenges to convention, also can be linked to the temple's newness. The four and a half years that I officially spent chronicling events and viewpoints mark the beginning stages of Rush temple life (I unfortunately missed the grand installation ceremony by two weeks). This book thus represents a particular moment in time. It reflects on the birth of a temple and its early development, with all their attendant joys and pains. Expanding physically over the years, the building that encloses the temple is now nearly twice its original size and the number of deities and their accoutrements has nearly doubled as well. Also shifting gradually but constantly over time has been the composition of the temple's inner-core members. By the time of this book's publication, most of the members quoted within will remain, a few will have receded, and a few new and peripheral members will have become prominent. Ideas and opinions cited in the book will have, in some cases changed as well. In spite of this inevitable flux, I have found that a certain spirit—one that struck me (and my imaginary visitors) when I visited the temple for the first time—endures within Rush temple life. My hope is that this resilient spirit, constituted by and connecting the temple tripartite—the goddess Rājarājeśwarī, Aiya, and temple devotees—permeates the following chapters as well.

Although the book is largely organized according to three defining and enlivening temple junctures that feature Devī, Aiya, and temple devotees, respectively, I must add that one cannot so easily box in or distinguish these three characters and categories. Naturally, the goddess's presence and power permeate conversations and reflections throughout the book, Aiya's exuberant voice booms almost constantly, and devotees—without whom the temple and its guru would have little purpose—are never completely absent. According to Śrīvidyā theology, this kind of overlap makes perfect sense: divinities, gurus, and devotees should be difficult to separate from one another since, in the end, no such apparent division actually exists. Likewise, as we will see, the juxtaposed worldviews, practices, and religious cultures featured in the book's three parts often appear linked while seemingly incongruent, interdependent while purportedly oppositional.[17]

I emphasize junctures and interrelationships—between miraculous and scientific worldviews, nonconventional and conventional practices, and domestic and foreign sensibilities—largely because they provide a good entrée into exploring the temple's unique spirit. Moreover, classical studies of religion and culture often describe junctures—boundaries of standard space, society, and time—as sacred in their own right. For instance, ruptures in mundane space, represented most powerfully by mountains, are often given sacred qualities; people and states existing outside conventional social structures can glean religious or quasi-religious status; and intervals between seasons, daily cycles, and life stages frequently emerge as moments that allow for if not necessitate ritual performances.[18]

Sacred intersections are often also, by their nature, fraught with ambiguity and uncertainty. Moments-in-between such as springtime or the minutes between dawn and daylight "even at their worst, contain the hope of the best and, even at their best, the threat of the worst" (Bourdieu 1977: 131). "Holy men" whose transgressive lifestyles relegate them to the borders of polite society can emerge, in some cases, as the most exalted yet despised among humans (Ewing 1997: 201). Intercultural borders, opening opportunities and necessities for making and remaking identity, likewise can be a "sign of ambivalence, a permanently fraught hope. They discover over and over that the good and bad news presuppose each other" (Clifford 1997: 7, 10).[19] The junctures that structure this book likewise demonstrate, depending on one's angle, the mixed news of Rush temple intersections. "Sacred" intersections represent moments in which participants discover miracles and meaning, yet they are not without their risks and frustrations, even for dedicated insiders for whom the costs are well worth the benefits.

Part I's description of Devī's power harnessed through temple rituals and their attendant miracles unearths a number of seemingly precarious juxtapositions. It begins by describing how my exposure to the temple caused a gradual, and in some cases uneasy, shift in my understanding of ritual power—a process that unfolds both within and outside my cognitive control. Chapter 2 explores the temple's blurring of scientific and supernatural worldviews through practices in which devotees invoke and physically manifest divinity through lavish ritual offerings, concise bodily practices, and correct mindfulness. For outsiders, such external rituals can give rise to suspicions that Hindu temple practices are "idolatrous," a view rooted, in part, in British colonial attitudes. Although many North American Hindu temples compensate for these suspicions by downplaying the role of ritual power, the Rush temple enthusiastically embraces and celebrates it. Chapter 3 relates stories of miracles that reflect the precarious bridging of earthly and divine realms and offers another view into the ways Rush temple members negotiate, contradict, and ignore conventional perceptions.

Part II looks at how the temple, at Aiya's instigation, adheres to and defies religious orthodoxy and established practice. Chapter 4 sketches Aiya's insistent attempts to gain religious knowledge, blocked from him because of his caste. Once on the Śrīvidyā path, he becomes a different kind of nuisance to the status quo—his enthusiastic propagation of an otherwise exclusive tradition is all the more unnerving because of his meticulous attention to ritual detail. Inhabiting the intersection between blasphemy and orthodoxy, he is difficult to ignore. Chapter 5 describes how temple members experience this dynamic, particularly women and young people who, typically marginalized in traditional religious settings, glean great satisfaction from their participation as Śrīvidyā initiates and temple priests. Chapter 6 describes the levity and uncertainty that emerge from the intersection between convention and non-convention. When Aiya expands the boundaries of religious authority, allowing access to divinity in spontaneous and surprising ways, he also leaves a door open for potential dispute.

Part III depicts the temple as a hopeful yet fraught meeting ground between geographies and cultures, as the crossroads between South Asia and mainstream rural America and their respective religious traditions. Chapter 7 depicts the transplanting of South Asian divinity onto North American soil through the travels and miraculous appearances of Hindu deities. Intrinsic to this process is the transposition of South Asian sacred geography—typically inseparable from South Asian religions—to rural upstate New York. Chapter 8 highlights some of the ups and downs of converging ethnicities and religions as experienced by temple participants and Rush community members. Although racism and religious intolerance are typical of the South Asian immigrant experience, cultural interchange sparks unexpected possibilities and outlooks as well. Chapter 9 brings us "home," to the image of the temple most commonly described by inner-core members, all of whom have been unmoored, at some level, from their cultural or religious heritage. Although seemingly mundane, the temple as home is a concept many devotees hold most sacred. Amid its many balancing acts and incongruities, it is where participants ultimately find comfort, security, and rest.

Although I never heard Aiya refer to the temple or its traditions as sites of potent yet precarious intersections, I have been alert to occasional allusions and inferences. One such instance occurred during the summer of 2001 when Aiya, a handful of devotees, and I were eating lunch around the *homam* fire pit outside the temple. (In spring 2003 the *homam* pit became part of the enclosed temple structure.) The approximately four-by-four-foot square pit, lined with red bricks and surrounded by wooden planks, is where, during regular *homam* rituals, participants sit, chant, and lower offerings into the fire. During warm weather, the same area becomes a useful, flat place to congregate for lunch. During a lull in a rollicking series of conversations, Aiya leaned slightly in my direction and earnestly asked me the question: "Amma [although Tamil for 'Mother,' this is a common form of address for women], do you know when the best time is to draw more deeply into meditation?" Wondering what prompted his question, I shook my head while he continued, "It is the split second after you exhale and before you inhale—just after inhaling and before exhaling. If you focus on those points, you will be able to go more deeply into meditation." Still not sure why he had interjected this tidbit at me, I made an appreciative comment as the discussion veered into another direction.

Aiya's description of a fleeting moment in between—of a state of sacred potential when we have in fact stopped breathing—is more than simply handy advice for meditation. It has become part of my repertoire for thinking about ruptures and intersections and their attendant opportunities and risks. Aiya's example parallels well the idea that, particularly for the temple insider, the positive news of the interstices far outweighs the negative: the fact that someone has stopped breathing between breaths is, although undeniable, not really worth considering. For the most dedicated devotees at the Rush temple, the potential uneasiness of temple junctures is minimized in light of their potential benefits. In some instances risks are not only minimized, they are also negated—transformed into a means for celebration.[20]

PART I

Encounters with Divinity

Ritual Power and Miracles

I

Temple Entryways

One midweek summer afternoon, during a lull in temple activities, Sudharshan and I were hanging out at the small house that sits on the temple grounds. Propped up on barstools at the kitchen counter, we were enjoying a cup of sweet milky tea he had made for us and, as usual, an animated discussion. Over the years I have found in Sudharshan, an exuberant man in his mid-thirties and long-time core member of the temple, an ideal conversation partner. He and I have very similar perspectives on a range of issues and, because he also teaches religious studies at a university, he is familiar with much of the academic accoutrements I lug around with me to the temple. Between sips of tea, we discussed the various angles I might take in writing an academic book about the temple. About twenty minutes into our conversation, Sudharshan, with a worried look on his face, earnestly blurted out, "I just hope people don't think of you as a crazy person who's writing about another crazy person."

With Sudharshan's concerns ringing in my ears, I have decided to make the subject of his worry my point of entry into this book and, I hope, to diffuse his apprehension. His worry has to do with the realm of ritual power and miracles, something Aiya, the temple's head priest and guru, and his students work very hard to generate at the Śrī Rājarājeśwarī Pīṭham. In part, it would be impossible to avoid the subject of ritual power, since it is so foundational to the temple and to the Śrīvidyā tradition in which Aiya practices and trains his students. It is also central to Aiya's flamboyant style. He has gone to great lengths to develop a temple steeped in ritual activity—the bigger, the longer, the grander, the better. As he sees it, his

Divine Mother deserves nothing less than royal treatment. Miracles, signs of her grace, are logical by-products of the grand rituals performed in her honor.

Part of the conundrum, as Sudharshan frames it, is the risk that Aiya and temple participants will appear "crazy" to outsiders. Yet the job of an ethnographer, as I understand it, is often to question points of reference that label particular realities as correct or incorrect. My task is to understand and write about the temple in a way that gives consistency to a worldview not necessarily shared by other, culturally dominant, worldviews.[1] Furthermore, Sudharshan is not simply concerned about Aiya's perceived sanity (and by implication his own and that of other temple devotees), but about my own. His comment assumes I share his worldview, and in many respects he is right. It also assumes I will be forthcoming about my position when I write—which I am. Such an approach is necessary to describe effectively the cohesion of the temple's worldview and the cognitive leaps sometimes required when one works to understand—or one unwittingly gets pulled into—its framework. Such an endeavor would perhaps be risky if the road were not already so well paved by others.[2]

This first chapter's recounting of my circuitous route to and within the temple has much to do with control—or lack thereof. As I see it, good ethnography is about surprises and contradictions; it rarely if ever is what we initially intend it to be. Intellectual hypotheses and well-planned proposals give way, in the best of circumstances, to the force of relationships that are both within and outside our charge.[3] This chapter reports shifting perspectives, steered first by academic tradition, next by relationships with Aiya and temple devotees, and finally by something I am hesitant to label. It chronicles a gradual loss of certain kinds of control during my first fourteen months at the temple. Presupposing individual control is an illusion or oxymoron, the account simply becomes a description of a shifting balance of interaction and awareness. This balancing act, I might add, is something quite different from "craziness."

Burned Saris and Deflated Expectations

To begin, it seems I ended up at the temple largely by accident, although from Aiya's perspective there are no accidents. During the summer of 1998 I was scheduled to do research in Kerala, south India, at Potta, a Catholic Charismatic healing center. The project was to be a natural extension of my dissertation about Hindu-Christian interactions in Kerala. One mid-June evening, one month before I was to depart, however, I came to the conclusion that I could not go to India: I strongly resisted leaving my young children behind. True, they would be fine with my husband, but I would be miserable. The project would have to wait and the grant forfeited. In search of another research direction to compensate for the lost trip, I spoke the following evening with Paul, one of my colleagues, when he visited our home in Syracuse en route to a conference. Paul recalled hearing a Sri Lankan friend he highly respected speak enthusiastically about an innovative temple that just moved to a town outside Rochester. He encouraged me to visit the temple and find out more for myself.

One week later, with the help of my friend Susan in Rochester, I found the Śrī Rājarājeśwarī Web site and driving directions. I packed my two sons, Jack and Sam, into our car and drove an hour and a half in torrential rain to East River Road in the town of Rush, just south of Rochester, hoping to make it in time for the nine-thirty morning *pūjā*. Since the temple had no sign at the time and nothing lining the residential street stood out in a temple-like way, I drove slowly up and down several times until an elderly man taking out his recycling pointed us in the direction of what looked like a small one-story barn, freshly painted yellow. As my sons and I found our way to the side door and removed our shoes, we could hear chanting coming from the next room.[4]

Stepping into the building—a bit like stepping into a small, sparkling, and rather quirky south Indian temple—we were dramatically received by an array of deities, many of them glistening gold. Śrī Rājarājeśwarī sat in black granite splendor, flanked by elephant-headed Ganeś and the Śiva lingam. All the deities were elegantly dressed in brilliant silks, decorated with gold ornaments, and festooned with flowers.[5] My sons and I were less dramatically yet warmly received by Mohan, an energetic, middle-aged gentleman, and Dipi a slender, gentle-looking college student. Mohan was in the midst of conducting *pūjā* and smiled and nodded in our direction as Dipi set out a blue foam-filled mat for us to sit on. As we settled onto our mat, south Indian Karnatic music blasted unexpectedly from hefty speakers suspended around the room, making us jump. As the music blared, one of my sons noted that Dipi, who was sitting nearby, was operating a remote control device, surreptitiously starting and stopping the boisterous music at appropriate moments. After an hour in which Mohan honored each of the deities with offerings of flowers, fruit, water, incense, flame, and chanting—interspersed with music at which we grew less jumpy—the *pūjā* was over.

While the boys explored the temple's expansive grassy grounds, Mohan, Dipi, and I stood inside, surrounded by deities, and chatted. Mohan was not, as I had thought, Aiya. He explained that he was from Goa on the west coast of India and had been living in North America for nearly two decades. Dipi was a Punjabi Sikh born in the United States. When speaking about Aiya, the point the two men seemed most eager to impress upon me—or perhaps the point I was most impressed by—was how he, as a religious leader, maintained a healthy sense of humility and humanity. They described Aiya as a lively man who frequently cracked jokes, took out the garbage, and mowed the lawn. He encouraged full involvement at the temple regardless of gender, caste, ethnicity, or religion. The picture they painted was of someone with a truly democratic—and thus revolutionary—spirit, qualities that convinced me that the Rush temple had much to offer and was a place about which I wanted to learn more. After I met with Aiya during subsequent trips to the temple, he gave me his blessings not only to continue learning but also to write.

This unconventional aspect of Aiya and his temple agenda will have to wait until the book's next section. My current task is to deal with what, for me, was the hard part, something that complicated my early understandings of Aiya and the temple's purpose. This side of the equation, although involving a guru who challenges the status quo, features the deities themselves and the ritual worlds they inhabit. Rather than focusing on democracy and social revolution, I elaborate here upon glitz and glamor—upon the gold-plated divinities lavishly honored through temple rituals. These are aspects of the temple that seemingly contradicted the practical ideals that initially beckoned me to return again and again, and to learn.

As it turns out, I deftly avoided giving this part of temple life the attention it deserved for at least two months. At first, Aiya graciously allowed me to drill him with question after question about his unorthodox vision and the ways this affected him personally. He was, I found, funny, engaging, and a consummate storyteller. Sitting in white plastic chairs in the hall outside the temple kitchen, or in the little house adjacent to the temple, the structure of our conversations became, as time passed, less formal. Over tea or over our midday meal, Aiya and I—often joined by one or two other temple visitors or devotees—exchanged our thoughts not just about the temple but also about the latest news on National Public Radio. Although it should not have mattered, I was pleased to find little disagreement between us, whether on social, political, or even (so I thought) religious issues.

Before I allowed myself to acknowledge the religious divide separating us, I discovered a good deal of overlap as well. Since doing an MA in systematic theology in Berkeley in the late 1980s, my thinking has been influenced by a cluster of political theologies, often labeled liberation theologies, highly critical of the abuses of institutional Christianity, particularly within Catholicism. Various liberation theologies give voice to those marginalized by the Church, namely, the disenfranchised poor, women, racial minorities, gays, and lesbians. I was refreshed by the ways Aiya affirmed my own position through his commitment to a religious tradition of which he was nonetheless intensely critical. Most specifically, we were unanimously critical of the abuses of power that (from our perspective) often masked and undermined the prophetic impulses of our respective traditions.[6]

Political and religious reform were our favored and, for me, most engaging topics, yet Aiya's philosophical views on religion meshed easily with my worldview as well. His Vedāntic ideas, sprinkled throughout our conversations, fit well with my affinity for process theology, an approach to religion I also brought with me from my theology days in Berkeley.[7] Influenced in particular by Advaita Vedānta, attributed to the eighth-century south Indian philosopher-saint

Śāṇkara, Aiya maintains that the universe contains nothing but a single Ultimate Reality, or divinity. Because his Śrīvidyā tradition honors the goddess Tripurasundarī, she is viewed, in her various manifestations, as the divinity who encompasses all reality, all divinity. According to Advaita Vedānta, the common perception that we, as individuals, are separate from this Ultimate Reality and from one another is due to *māyā*, or illusion. The gradual task of breaking through the illusion of separation and of finding union with the Divine Mother is central to the temple's ritual and meditative practices.

Process theology—developed during the late twentieth century by Christian and some Jewish philosophers and theologians—echoes this perspective somewhat through its view that God's earthly presence is activated solely through our receptivity to divine will within each of us. This runs against traditional theologies that depict God as a separate entity "out there," plotting our futures and punishing our transgressions. In essence, process theology proposes the radical notion that although God is believed to be entirely benevolent, God has no "hands," and is therefore vulnerable and reliant upon creation to do—or not do—the work of divinity. In contrast to Rush temple theology, however, supernatural intervention does not figure into process theology, since it maintains that divinity cannot manifest outside the natural world and outside human assent and cooperation.[8] Hope in miracles, according to this system of thought, is not only inconsistent with the nature of divinity but it also causes people to shirk their responsibilities as God's agents on earth. Process theology thus offers a rebuttal to Marxist claims that religion is the opiate of the masses, and complements the politically minded, Marxist-influenced, liberation theologies that advocate social and economic justice and activism.

Admittedly, my ability to engage in respectful dialogue with members of various religious communities should have nothing to do with my theological baggage. When spending time at Christian and Hindu pilgrimage shrines in Kerala, south India, I felt I successfully put aside my biases, respectfully entering into and understanding a mind-set that welcomed and expected miracles.[9] Obstructing this process at Rush, however, was the discovery that Aiya initially affirmed my worldview on so many levels. At pilgrimage shrines in India, it was rare for me to find theological perspectives that coincided so well with mine—ironically in spite of, in many cases, a shared Catholic background. I was, as a result, constantly stretching my perceptual comfort zone. How convenient it was when my initial visits to Rush did not require this kind of "work." I could, on a theological and philosophical level that cut across our different religious affiliations, relax and enjoy the ride.

As I sat enjoying the common ground between Aiya and me, I probably missed opportunities to challenge my perceptual realm—perhaps from our very first meeting. It was not until late September, after I had been a regular at the temple for over three months, that I sensed a collision between our different worlds of logic. By this time I had experienced a variety of rituals at the temple—lengthy *homam* fires in which chanting and material goods were burned as offerings to the deities, *abhiṣekam* rituals where all present doused the granite Rājarājeśwarī, Ganeś, and the Śiva lingam with milk, and daily *pūjā* offerings to the temple deities. At the Rush temple, rituals are performed with gusto and, differently from other temples, in a communal fashion. Aiya encourages, even harangues, all present to chant along. In spite of my leftish theology, I enjoyed the corporate, sensual expressions of devotion of which the Rush temple is a veritable gold mine.

The inevitable impasse occurred during the 1998 Navarātri festival, a nine-day event honoring the Great Goddess's victory over the buffalo demon Mahiṣāsura—also understood metaphorically as her victory over human ego. The ritual climax of the event is, at Rush, a ceremony called a *caṇḍī homam*, a four-hour ritual involving elaborate offerings into a fire. On this particular day the large blue-and-white striped tent set up especially for festival *homams* (permanently replaced in 2003 by an extension built onto the temple) was filled with over two hundred people, mostly Sri Lankan Tamils of all ages from Toronto. Sitting at the fire's periphery was a circle of eight—four women and four men—offering designated items at regular intervals into the fire. These

Aiya and Amma offering to the *homam* fire during Navarātri festival, 2002. Photo by Aparna Hasling.

eight, along with the Śrīvidyā *upāsakas*, or initiates, sitting in the immediate vicinity, were the most energetic and confident chanters, maintaining their mood of reverent enthusiasm for hours. Leading the chanting and expertly guiding the *homam* was Dr. Viswanathan (or Vish Uncle, as he is affectionately called), a retired pediatrician from Rochester. Several hours into the *homam*, it seemed that someone had added green wood to the fire, which began to emit great billows of smoke. Vish Uncle, who I imagined was getting tired, started to cough, and I worried about him a little.

But my greatest cause for consternation amid all the ritual intensity and reverence was the burning of the saris. At fourteen points during the *homam*, a list of offerings ritually prescribed for the goddess—including material for a sari blouse, underskirt, wooden comb, mirror, gold *tāli* necklace for married women,[10] red *kumkum* powder, fruit, sweetmeats, and a mixture of 108 herbs—were wrapped up in magnificent silk saris, giant swaths of brilliantly colored cloth that I later learned were worth around four hundred dollars each. Along with this bundle, devotees who sponsored the *homam* offered to the goddess yet another exquisite sari along with more womanly items.[11]

Before each offering, Priya, a petite bespectacled devotee in her early twenties, born in Sri Lanka and raised in Canada, gathered the offerings and placed them on a large brass tray. She first walked among those sitting closest to the fire, allowing each to touch the offering, then strategically positioned herself so those sitting further away could form lines and do the same. By touching the offerings, we each offered a piece of ourselves into the packet bound for the fire. At the designated moment, after the tray had made its rounds, someone in the inner circle dropped the various feminine necessities into the fire pit. When only the sari bundle was left, the lead chanter ran ghee (clarified butter) into the fire through the joining of two wooden devices called a *hṛk* and *śṛk*, representing the union of male and female. As the ghee streamed steadily out the mouth of the *śṛk* and into the flames, those familiar with the Sanskrit *vasordhārā* chanted it loudly and very quickly—preferably in one breath. Throughout this ritual climax, all present touched the person next to them, creating a human web of contact that wound its way from the tent's peripheries to the inner circle and to the person holding the offerings, connecting us all to the sacrifice and to the Mother Goddess represented by the fire. Finally the sari bundle was offered and into the fire it went. Fourteen times.

From where I sat at the time, the idea of the *homam* was appealing to me. The offering of self, of ego, of interconnected selves to the divine, seemed to me a rich and religiously sensible gesture. I learned that the practice of touching the *homam* tray as well as the web of human contact was an innovation started by Aiya's guru, allowing a corporate offering by the congregation rather than confining it to the male brahmans who traditionally perform the ritual. This also made good sense to me. Burning actual material goods furthermore seemed ritually expedient as long as, I told myself, they were not too costly.

Prior *homams* I experienced at the temple seemed to fit these parameters. But the amount of material wealth burned to ashes at the *caṇḍī homam*—thirty-two exquisite saris in all—was more than I could comfortably digest. I wanted not to be bothered by this, but could not chase it from my mind. The next time I visited Aiya I told him so. He chuckled at my discomfort, we acknowledged our differences, and, it appeared, we put the topic behind us. I appreciated that he welcomed my honesty and did not try to talk me out of my position, but I was still baffled. How could someone with his political views, with such concern for the poor and powerless, condone throwing thousands of dollars into a fire?

After letting this issue simmer quietly and uncomfortably for nearly six months without resolution, I spoke up about it again. This time I had been at the temple long enough that the "obvious" finally became obvious to me and I could let go. One winter morning, Aiya, Dipi, and I were sitting in the little house having tea between morning and noon *pūjās*. We were in the midst of discussing a recent miraculous event at the temple (something I was warming up to), when Aiya recognized a car that had earlier pulled up outside the temple. He fled out the door and raced through newly fallen snow in his bare feet to catch its owner before she left. Dipi and I put on our shoes and followed behind.

Inside the temple, Aiya was talking with Amrit, a woman from Karnataka, south India, who owns a florist shop in Rochester and each week brings several generous bundles to the temple. Aiya had something he wanted to give her, a gold medallion that was hanging around Rājarājeśwarī's neck. After Dipi helped remove the medallion from Devī's chain and Aiya presented it to her, the four of us stood next to the nine golden planets and talked. Aiya raised the subject of an upcoming *caṇḍī homam* and Amrit asked me if I had ever been to one. When I responded that I had, Aiya quickly interjected, comically raising his eyebrows and jerking his head in my direction, "This one here is really bothered by all the expensive saris we throw into the fire." I agreed that this bugged me and added in my defense, "But Aiya, think of all the good you could do with that money!" Without skipping a beat, Aiya retorted, "But think of all the good that comes from such a powerful *homam*!"

From Aiya's perspective, no remark could have been more natural. Yet, on this particular day and in the context of my changing world, my unspoken response to his easy retort involved the startling sensation of something resolutely clicking into place. I found I no longer had to force mismatched puzzle pieces into my design because, at this point, the design itself had begun to shift. I was beginning to understand ritual power from a different angle. In a way, I had added to my thinking another type of human accountability to the one proposed by process theology—that humanity manifests divinity by doing good deeds. Viewed from the temple, divinity is manifested by doing good rituals, as well.[12]

Shifting Religious Terrain

Not long ago, academic convention was such that these kinds of shifts in perception were thought to put one at risk, particularly of losing scholarly objectivity.[13] I was interested to find that this tradition of scholarly detachment is not unknown to temple members. On several occasions, people who discussed with me my approach to writing this book have worried whether my somewhat insider perspective might jeopardize my chances for tenure and promotion in my job. When Aiya came to Wisconsin in the spring of 2002 to guest lecture for one of my classes, he "slipped" and referred to the fact that I had performed *pūjā* at his temple. Stopping in his tracks, he dramatically grimaced and said in a stage whisper to me, "Is it okay that I said that?" As I laughed and nodded and the rest of the room erupted in laughter, I was struck by Aiya's concern that I be portrayed to the outside academic world as a detached observer.

In recent years, the idea that good reporting requires personal detachment has fairly disappeared from the ethnographical enterprise. This shift has much to do with the question of whether a privileged, objective stance can exist at all.[14] Religion, nonetheless, can be a sticky matter. Even when academics propose that truth is largely a human construct and is therefore relational if not relative, certain religious beliefs are more difficult than others for a Eurocentric rationalistic audience to swallow. Contemporary anthropologists who go native by adopting "questionable" religious frameworks (and decide to write about it) often feel they have some explaining to do. Although they agree in principle that detached objectivity is impossible, some feel a need to respond to the voices of convention. Thanks to these perspectives running at cross purposes through my brain, the story of my gradual involvement at the temple, marked at first by the act of touching Aiya's feet and receiving a mantra, is inelegant, even comical, at best.

Perhaps ironically, I had decided to refrain from touching Aiya's feet during ritual out of a sense of respect. According to Indian and Sri Lankan custom, touching the feet of an elder is an everyday gesture of reverence, not necessarily a religiously loaded one. But a disciple touches her guru's feet for the additional reason that feet are the place from which blessings flow. After a guru or priest performs a ritual, his or her feet are particularly imbued with power; temple participants often treat this moment as a special opportunity to offer respect and receive blessings. If Aiya were merely an elder or perhaps simply a guru for whom feet touching was expected protocol outside a ritual context, I probably would have complied from the start. But it seemed to me that touching Aiya's feet after *pūjā* meant assenting to a cluster of beliefs I did not properly understand or accept. Maybe more important, it would also have designated me as one of his spiritual students. Doing so, in either case, would have been misleading and therefore, I felt, irreverent.

Although my decision not to touch Aiya's feet may have set me apart from the very beginning, other kinds of ritual involvement felt less inappropriate. When people crowded around Aiya after *pūjā* to receive red *kumkum* powder and *vibhuti* ash on their foreheads as a form of the goddess's blessings, I joined them. I did so because I felt my separation from the others was a matter of interpretation, a bit like the different interpretations Catholics and Protestants give to the Eucharist. While for some the blessing was literal and tangible, I understood it as symbolic, but a blessing nonetheless. While the others would bow down to touch Aiya's feet after receiving the *kumkum* and *vibhuti*, however, I did not.

Over time, although I continued to ritually and physically mark the divide between temple devotees and myself through this nonact, the actual distance between us had begun to dissipate. Not only had I started forging friendships with many of the devotees but I was also coming to better appreciate the temple worldview. More than anything, Aiya's warmth and generosity during our weekly visits, along with his broad vision and commitment, evoked in me a growing sense of gratitude and admiration. Touching his feet would have marked a personal investment already present in our interactions and in my notes, yet there was a line I physically could not bring myself to cross. I wanted to talk to Aiya about this, but as time went by I became more embarrassed, chastising myself in my field notes instead. If I did not believe in researcher objectivity, what was the problem, really? Was it my ego? Wasn't I being disrespectful in the name of respect?

After more buildup and internal melodrama than I care to admit, I arrived at Rush one late October morning, bursting with determination. The temple was empty, and as I tried to make myself useful by setting up incense sticks for the *pūjā*, Aiya breezed in with his usual cheerful welcome. He announced that today was a special day for Subramaniam (Ganeś's brother, also known as Kārttikeya or Skanda). With that he began the *pūjā*. When the ritual was nearly finished, Aiya sat on the floor and contentedly decorated a silver *kālasam* pot with an array of mango leaves, flowers, a bright purple silk sash, a string of beads, and a coconut placed on top. Once he finished, he stood up to offer me the customary red *kumkum* and *vibhuti* ash on my forehead. I received them and bent down to touch his feet, trying not to think melodramatic thoughts. When I stood up again, Aiya went about his usual routine, humming to himself and putting things back in order as though nothing new had happened. While waiting for him to finish, admiring the decorated pot, I asked about Subramaniam's celebration. He explained briefly, "Today we celebrate his battle over *ahaṃkāra*, or I-force. Today is the day he won his victory over the ego." How appropriate.[15]

Aside from the issue of touching Aiya's feet, the other variable separating me from the temple's inner-core devotees was the fact that I did not have a mantra, a form of initiation into Śrīvidyā and spiritual link to a guru. In part, the reason I did not seek out a mantra was because of my current religious affiliation. It was not that I thought doing so would be wrong; one tradition at a time simply seemed enough. As Aiya liked to say, in typical neo-Vedāntic style, all religious roads lead to the same destination, to God. Yet he would add that if one wanted to get there quickly, with the least amount of fuss, one should pick one religion, one road, and stick to it. At the same time, I would hear Aiya assuring people that acquiring a mantra simply functioned to enhance one's practice—whatever that practice might be. In light of this, nontemple friends of mine, Indian and non-Indian, Hindu and Christian alike, would often encourage me to ask for a mantra. What was the harm? Upon reflection it seems that not getting a mantra, somewhat like not touching Aiya's feet, was a line I drew to keep my head above water. It was my concession to the voices of scholarly convention (ones with whom I did not necessarily agree) warning me to keep my distance lest I get towed under.

The benefit of not taking a mantra as opposed to not touching Aiya's feet is that one avoids being visibly set apart from other temple participants—or so I thought. Late December during my first year at the temple, Aiya was leading a weekend *pūjā* workshop for devotees. He suggested I come along, bring my tape recorder, and learn some of the technicalities of *pūjā* worship. About twelve of us, devotees of all ages from across the United States, enjoyed a day of explanation, demonstration, and frequent tangents into Aiya's trademark stories. As the workshop wound down, the group sat on the floor, talking and sucking on gigantic cinnamon fireballs distributed from a plastic jar. Aiya sat in a chair at the front of the room, fireball protruding from his cheek, talking to someone nearby. I waited in an empty chair next to him and asked, when he finished talking, what day the following week would be best for a visit. Before he could answer, Priya chimed in above the other voices, "Hey, Aiya! Everyone here has a mantra except for Corinne! Why don't you give her a mantra?"

A week earlier, as we cleaned the temple kitchen, Priya had asked me if I had a mantra. When I told her I did not, she left the matter alone. I appreciated the question, since I felt it indirectly assumed I was part of the group. She brought it up at the workshop, it seems, because she thought Aiya might just give me a mantra on the spot. Now, when Aiya and I were sitting at the front of the room with the rest of the workshop participants looking on, we considered in silence—to my dismay—the question en masse. After some thought, he gave what I considered the worst possible answer, "She doesn't need a mantra, Amma. She won't be doing *pūjā*, either. All this information is just for her files."

Files! I felt I might as well have been wearing a white lab coat and looking into a petri dish. On the contrary, the temple had come to feel in many ways like "home" to me. I relished the fact that Aiya and many temple members treated me with warmth, like I belonged. This statement, although in many ways correct, was an unwelcome reminder of my position as ethnographer, leaving me, I felt, out in the cold.[16]

In March, during an interview with Dipi's parents at their home in Syracuse, his mother took a break from answering questions and asked me if I had a mantra. When I said I did not, the three of them speculated that perhaps Aiya had not given me one because I was not ready for it. He would know, they surmised, when the time was right. Feeling I was, by implication, spiritually deficient, I tried arguing that perhaps I didn't get a mantra because of my Catholic background. They gently reminded me that this could not be the case. They were Sikh, after all. I was left with the sinking feeling that not having a mantra meant I was not just an outsider, but somehow inadequate, as well. This was the last straw, and the next time I saw Aiya I asked if I could get a mantra. I was doubtlessly asking for all the wrong reasons and Aiya, with his "we'll see" attitude, let it slide for the time being.

The following month, Linda, a good friend who studied theology with me in Berkeley and currently lived in Massachusetts, came for a visit. A professor of ethics in a religious studies department, she was, at the time, considering joining a convent (and later did). During her visit, we went to the temple where she enjoyed, in her quiet, confident manner, the rich ritual atmosphere as well as a lively talk with Aiya over lunch by the *homam* pit. On Tuesday morning after Linda went back home, I returned to the temple. Although it was midweek, a large group of Sri Lankan Tamils from Toronto were milling around, getting ready to boil rice at the temple entrance as an offering to the goddess. Aiya, freshly showered and dressed for the midday ritual, scooted in my direction when he saw me, announced his welcome, and then, mysteriously in hushed tones, said, "You know, your friend Linda is not who you think she is." While I contemplated this remark, he shuddered in comic-dramatic style, "She is a very powerful person!" Knowing that the visiting devotees would interrupt us at any moment, I asked him to please make sure he told me the whole story when I came back the next day.

Brimming with curiosity—I had brought a number of visitors to the temple before and nothing like this had ever happened—I returned to a much quieter temple on Wednesday. Aiya explained that Linda had been, in her past two lifetimes, someone who had risked her life to fight injustice. Over a hundred years ago in present-day Iraq, she was martyred for her activism. Plus, to boot, she was a woman. Not sure what to make of this information, I asked what I should do—should I tell her? He shrugged, saying, "You can if you want, but she'll probably think I'm crazy." When I told him there was no way I could not tell her, he suggested, "She can come here and get a mantra if she'd like. It will help to sharpen her focus." As an afterthought he added, "Tell her this doesn't mean she has to give up being Catholic."

Early May, Linda made another trip in our direction. She was not entirely sure what to make of Aiya's reading of her past lives, but looked forward to receiving a mantra. We decided to go to the temple on a Monday, since fewer people would be there and she could talk more easily with Aiya. No one was at the morning *pūjā* except us, and as we sat crossed-legged on the floor next to one another, the event seemed ordinary enough to me. One incident did stand out slightly, however. When Aiya approached Linda with the camphor flame he had just offered to Rājarājeśwarī at the start of the *pūjā*, she was supposed to receive blessings from it—and thus from the goddess—by wafting her hands over the flame toward her body. Because I sat on the far side of her and could not demonstrate, Linda, sitting attentively, looked at the flame in front of her and then back up at Aiya, not sure what to do. He chuckled and wafted the flame's blessings over her, afterward laying his right hand on top of her head in a fatherly fashion. It briefly occurred to me that this was not exactly protocol. During the December workshop we learned that the person performing *pūjā* should not touch anyone from the time they take their pre-*pūjā* shower until the conclusion of the ritual. I thus took note of the gesture, but did not consider it again until later.

After *pūjā* the three of us went to the little house near the temple to have tea and some cookies I had made. Dipi arrived a little later, as did Sagar and Thoshi, a north Indian couple living in St. Catherines, Canada. Singha, a Tamil engineer on a break from work, came just before the afternoon *pūjā*. When midday *pūjā* was over, Aiya walked over to Linda with water blessed during the ritual, put some into her hand, told her to say a mantra, and then to drink. I was standing nearby, and he turned to me and did the same. That was how I got my mantra—without fanfare and, I suspected, because Aiya was nice enough not to leave me out. The group of us then went back to the little house and ate lunch together, sitting in a circle in the main room. After enjoying food and conversation, Linda and I, who arrived in separate cars, said our goodbyes and headed in separate ways.

Religion You Think about versus Religion You Experience

That night Linda called me from Massachusetts. Thinking she was just checking in, I thanked her for letting me know she got home safely and asked what she thought of the temple visit. Rather than engaging in light conversation, she began with a nervous laugh and then replied in a deadly serious, slightly shaky voice, "Actually I was calling for a reality check." After asking if I noticed Aiya touch her on the top of her head at the beginning of *pūjā*, she described, slowly and methodically, as if recalling them, the sensations triggered by his touch, "It was the strangest thing. I felt this intense burning, electric sensation throughout me." After stopping to think for a few seconds she continued, "It burned the strongest at the base of my spine, in the pit of my stomach, in the middle of my chest, the base of my neck, in the middle of my forehead, and on the top of my head where he put his hand." After another brief pause, she added, "The palms of my hands and bottoms of my feet also felt like they were on fire."

Stunned at the other end of the line, knowing that Linda had very little exposure to Asian religious traditions, I told her that she had practically given me the textbook description of the *cakras* located at different points along the spine starting at its base and ascending to the crown of the head. The burning palms of her hands and soles of her feet I was not familiar with. Taking this in and then continuing, Linda described how, when Aiya performed *pūjā* at the different deities' stations, she felt different *cakra* points in her body burn with the same intense electric heat. When he circumambulated the nine planets, she said she was overwhelmed with such emotion, it took everything in her not to cry. Finally, when Aiya performed his customary blessing of a life-sized picture of goddess Kāmākṣī, holding up the camphor flame in front of different parts of her body, Linda felt the corresponding areas of her body lighting up with heat. Finally, when she tried out her mantra once she got home, visions of golden light appeared behind her closed eyelids.

I must say, although Linda is one of the most level-headed people I know, I was amazed she could sit next to me during the entire *pūjā* and hide the fact that fireworks were erupting inside her body. On the phone, she seemed rattled by her experience, hoping to understand it in order to gain some semblance of control. I could tell her what *cakras* were on paper and that *śaktipat*, the descent of a guru's power into an initiate, was meant to awaken the *kuṇḍalinī* energy along the spine and open the *cakras*, yet this was something that happened to other people, primarily people I read about in books.[17] Although I should probably have known better, I had no idea Aiya could do this. Unlike me, Linda was not preconditioned to think about her *kuṇḍalinī* rising or her *cakras* opening up, let alone experience them doing so. It was as though something unknown had jumped out and grabbed her from behind. If I were less of an outsider in terms of my confidence in ritual power I might have seen this coming. But I had been grabbed from behind, too—and set down in a place quite different from where I started.

The next week, back at the temple and overflowing with questions, I was glad to find four devotees I was getting to know fairly well, two women and two men from Philadelphia, seated and waiting for morning *pūjā* to start. Mohan and his lively eight-year-old daughter, Purvaja, joined us soon afterward, as did Aiya, freshly showered and ready to conduct the ritual. Once *pūjā* finished, I seized the opportunity to ask Aiya if he was aware of Linda's temple experiences the prior week. He was not, so, as the others circled around, I described them. Everyone looked surprised and impressed except for Aiya. He nodded as I talked, as though confirmed in his initial assessment of Linda. Piquing his interest a bit was my description of how her body reacted correspondingly to the camphor flame blessing of Kāmākṣī. He noted, with some enthusiasm, how nicely this demonstrates how we are truly one and the same with the goddess.

The following week Krishna and Mangala, both doctors originally from Sri Lanka, were visiting Rush from southern California. Since they did not appear to have a particular conversation agenda when I arrived, I brought Linda up again. I first offered some background information for Krishna and Mangala and then asked Aiya if Linda's experience was typical for someone touched on the head during *pūjā*. Aiya said it was not—people generally felt a sense of love and goodness.[18] When I asked why he did not do this for everyone, he cited three reasons. One, he did not do it for those unprepared to handle its effects. Two, he did not do it for people whose channels had already opened. Three, he did not do it for those he knew would be regular participants at the temple. It was essentially a "jump start" for special visitors. I surmised that because Aiya promotes the Śrīvidyā tradition as offering the best means toward realizing union with the divine—with its attendant mantras, rituals, and meditation practices—his focus is not on giving *śaktipat*.

Finding myself stuck on the issue of predisposition, wondering how this experience could happen to someone whose worldview did not allow for *cakras*, I asked, only half jokingly, "Why *cakras* and not a stigmata? Is it because you touched her head in a temple, not a church?" Aiya laughed and took this opportunity to tell Krishna and Mangala about his favorite Catholic mystic, Padre Pio, who regularly experienced the stigmata, the bleeding wounds of Christ, on his hands. Our conversation never got back on (my) track, so I left the subject alone. The fact that Aiya laughed rather than answering my question probably meant he thought I knew better, that I was joking. He knew I was aware of the mechanics of the *kuṇḍalinī* and the *cakras*—he had, after all, charted the process for us with colored pens on posterboard during the December workshop. He probably also assumed I understood that belief can have little to do with experiencing religion—that these experiences are and are not beyond our cognitive grasp and control.

The *pratiṣṭhā* festival marking the first anniversary of the temple's consecration was Memorial Day weekend.[19] Although Linda could not make it for the entire three days, she joined the festivities planned for Sunday, including the grand chariot procession in the evening. Mid-morning Sunday we parked in a grassy area along the growing rows of cars and headed over to the temple. We passed Bruce from Philadelphia, who greeted us from his perch high atop a homemade wooden *capparam* chariot to which he was busily adding finishing touches. The project, overseen by the temple's master devotee-woodworker, Pathmanathan (known as Path Uncle), originally from Sri Lanka, was truly a marvel of craftsmanship, artistry, and electronics.[20] Aiya, who at the moment was wandering around checking on things, passed by and cheerfully announced that his daughter and son-in-law were at the festival, visiting from Irvine, California. They had surprised him that morning, making his excitement over the first anniversary celebration complete.

Inside the temple, a line of people waited to perform *abhiṣekam* to the three main granite deities and out in the tent a larger group sat around a *caṇḍī homam* led by Vish Uncle. Linda and I first performed *abhiṣekam* to the deities, since the line was not too long. After dousing Ganeś, Rājarājeśwarī, and the Śiva lingam with small vessels of milk, we went to the tent and found a place to sit fairly close to the fire. We did our best to follow along with the chanting, when possible, and I again watched as we formed a giant web of human contact and lowered exquisite sari bundles into the fire.

About an hour later, still doing my best to chime in at the right time and stay alert to the activity around me, my hands and arms started tingling. Assuming they were falling asleep, I tried to get the blood circulating by flexing them and rearranging my sitting position. No matter what I did, the tingling continued and, in fact, was getting stronger to the point that they seemed to be vibrating. A little startled and wondering at the off chance if this had to do with the *homam*, I figured that if anyone else were feeling anything it would be Linda. I leaned over and asked if her hands were tingling, actually vibrating, by any chance. Sitting composedly, she thought for a few seconds, nodded, and whispered that they were. About fifteen minutes later, my feet started tingling and, immediately assuming they were falling asleep, I tried to sit differently. This also had no effect and, as the sensation became more intense, I leaned over to Linda again and asked if her feet were vibrating too. Her immediate response was an abrupt "I don't know!" but then a few moments later she leaned over and whispered that they were, in fact, tingling. When my lips and tongue started vibrating as well, I decided maybe Linda wanted to be left alone and waited until after the *homam* to mention it. When I did, a look of surprise spread across her face. She was about to bring up the same thing. When we talked about the experience later during the festival and up to a few days afterward, the sensation returned.

The sensation also returned for both of us during the evening's devotional singing, led by Aiya and accompanied by various devotees on drums and violin. Later that night when Linda was part of a cluster of women who brought the gold-plated processional Devī out from the tent and onto the newly constructed chariot, she felt her *cakra*s burning again in full force. After the goddess was secured to her chariot, Linda and I joined a raucous procession in which, against convention, all the women present pulled the ropes fastened to the brand new colossal *capparam* chariot, leading it around the temple grounds, the festival participants filling the night with sounds of shouting and laughter.

The next time I had a chance to talk to Aiya was the following week as we stood in the parking lot before I left for the day. I began to tell him what happened—that Linda and I during the *caṇḍī homam* felt our hands vibrating,

Women pulling the Devī's chariot during the 2000 *pratiṣṭhā* festival. Photo by Aiya from inside the chariot, using Corinne's camera.

then our feet. He interjected before I could finish, "And then your tongue started vibrating too?" A little surprised (although less was surprising me these days), I told him that this was true, and could he please explain. He said that we were likely feeling the presence of Saraswatī, and perhaps at that moment in the *homam* they were invoking Saraswatī. I told him that the sensation returned when Linda and I talked about it and at other times during the evening. He thought for a moment and said he would ask the Mother, during meditation, about this. Later he offered, not as a definitive answer but as something more for me to think about, that the *cakra*s involve a complicated network running throughout the body's nervous system. They do not simply run up the spine, as most people think.

Although my own theories come and go, I cannot say I truly understand these experiences any more now than I did during my earlier conversations with Aiya. For him, the explanation that Linda and my sensations came from Saraswatī or from the opening of *cakra*s may be enough, and for those familiar with traditions that trigger such sensations such events may be quite unremarkable. But for me, although the initial shock at Linda's *śaktipat* experience has worn away and my less dramatic but equally shocking experience during the *caṇḍī homam* recedes into the past, I am nonetheless left with a set of questions difficult to dispel. Although I may be convinced now more than ever that *cakras* do not just exist on paper, that mantras and rituals do have physiological effects, and that some gurus actually can transfer power with their hands, the religious mechanics remain largely a mystery. If I have learned anything, however, it is that my job is not necessarily to understand in a way that suits me, that religious experience does not always evoke rational discourse but can be a form of understanding in itself. Perhaps it is enough to tentatively surmise—reflecting a leap of faith coming from experience rather than cognition—that it can be a good idea to burn expensive saris as an offering to the Goddess. As Aiya would suggest, just think of all the power it generates. Who am I to judge the intricacies of ritual power?

Suffice it to say, temple experiences—particularly ones I did not opt for or anticipate—have significantly rearranged my perceptive and cognitive worlds. The events and bodily experiences recounted above have helped me to take much more seriously religious approaches that extend and challenge the ideological constructs and beliefs garnered during my theology training at Berkeley.[21] I describe these events and experiences here because it is important to consider the origin and impetus for such shifts. I recount them because it is my hope that readers, especially those with cultural and theological roots similar to mine, will subsequently approach the next two chapters about ritual power and miracles with their original frameworks of logic slightly askew. This, as my friend Sudharshan would agree, is not the same as advocating "craziness."

2

Perspectives on Ritual Power

The Cost, Science, and Grace of Divinity

Aiya's Banquet Philosophy and the Price of Ritual Power

When it comes to ritual, it goes nearly without saying that Aiya is like a kid in a candy shop. His oft-proclaimed rationale for ceremonial largesse is that the Divine Mother deserves nothing but the best: "If your mother were to come to your house for a meal, would you just set out a few snacks? No! If you could, you would carefully prepare an entire banquet!" Although those around him try at times to rein in his devotional magnanimity, Aiya maintains that there is no point in restraint. Not only do abundant blessings arise from devotional abundance, nothing we offer the Goddess is ours to begin with. During one of our late morning chats in the temple house, he explained,

> If I have two ounces of ghee [clarified butter] sitting in front of me, I will offer the two ounces of ghee. If I have ten gallons of ghee in front of me I will offer the ten gallons. So Amma tells Priya and Vijitha and all these other people [including Corinne in a few months] "Don't put too much in front of him, he'll put all of it in!" Because I am like that. I don't care! I do not think that I am offering it to a fire—I am offering it to the Mother. And to me, what She has given me belongs to Her. It's not mine to begin with. So what She's given I'm just offering back.

Although Aiya expresses exuberantly and often his religious rationale for the grand treatment he gives to the temple goddess, it is also part of his personal commitment and style. In contrast, Aiya's guru, Guruji, who runs the Devīpuram temple near Visakapatnam in Andhra Pradesh, is a ritual minimalist. He currently spends most of his energy organizing social programs for underprivileged women and children. Although Aiya recognizes the merits of Guruji's work in India, he feels his own style better fits the needs of his community on this continent. Aiya maintains that Sri Lankans and Indians in North America, rather than requiring low-income housing and basic necessities, are in greatest need of cultural and spiritual sustenance. Aiya's emphasis on ritual also is consistent with Śrīvidyā's emphasis on harnessing divine power through ritual practice.[1]

Aiya does not fill all areas of his life, however, with luxury and beauty. When not performing rituals, he dresses neatly and comfortably in loose-fitting T-shirts and trousers. Aiya and Amma's home outside Rochester is modest yet functional. The little house that sits near the temple, a gathering place and temporary accommodation for regular devotees to camp with sleeping bags on the floor, provides a particularly striking contrast. The furniture in the small living room consists of mismatched chairs bought at an office sale. The cream-colored rug was, for many years, perpetually stained.[2] Although the house is kept clean, little is aesthetically interesting or pleasing about it, seemingly because Aiya cannot not be bothered. Instead, he channels his energies and funds into maintaining standards of opulent beauty in the adjacent temple and its grounds—down to the last detail.

This disparity was underscored for me one morning in early March. Aiya and I walked from the meticulously maintained temple out into frigidly cold weather, and into the little house. As he briskly headed toward the kitchen to make us tea, Aiya stopped short, muttering something about cold air leaking into the house from around the air conditioner installed in the window. Surprised to see as much as a half inch of open space over the top and to one side of the air conditioner, I laughed and suggested that it must not be *that* hard to install, why not just take it out and close the window? Making vague references to the warmer season on its way, Aiya implied that it should be left alone. As he talked he fidgeted with rags lying nearby, stuffing them into the open space. When he ran out of rags he used paper towels, completing the task when he could squeeze in no more.

In the same way that the little house is decisively a nonproject for Aiya, the temple is an eternal project. During the days when the temple was in his garage, the growing number of devotees had to compete for space with the multiplying deity images, or *mūrtis*, that Aiya commissioned from India. As the garage temple became increasingly crowded, devotees joked that soon they would be banished to the elements to make room for Aiya's gods and goddesses. When the temple moved to Rush, deities continued to arrive, as did six-foot oil lamps, a large bell, and a decorative metal flagpole and flag. All items from India were made of brass, and sent to Toronto for goldplating soon after they arrived.

Early September 1999, I happened to be at the temple the day a large wooden crate arrived from India with a shipment of four six-foot-high brass oil lamps. Mohan, his wife Rupa, Aiya, Thanga (a retired woman visiting from Chico, California), and I excitedly unpacked the exquisitely decorated lamps from their crate, noting the Indian ants and spiders that came along for the ride. After cleaning all the pieces, assembling them, and lining the lamps into two rows down the center of the temple, we stood back to admire them. Impressed by the stunning effect, I remarked jokingly to Aiya that there must be method to his madness, after all. He became very serious, mentioning that the goddess Śrī Rājarājeśwarī, whose name designates her the Queen of Kings, Empress of Emperors, deserves nothing short of royal treatment. Her temple should be a place that befits royalty.

The following week I noted that the new lamps had disappeared from the temple and asked Aiya where they went. He mysteriously replied, "to Toronto."

Rājarājeśwarī adorned with vegetable garlands, Navarātri 2001. Photo by Pathmanathan.

Aiya delivering new shipment of Indian brass lamps to the rear of the temple. Photo by author.

Remembering that he sends everything brass from India to be plated in Toronto, I commented that soon he would have to get himself plated, as well. To this he laughingly added that Kartik, a south Indian–born gentleman in his mid-twenties and longtime devotee, likes to tell people that if they sit silently for too long in the temple Aiya will get them plated. Later that day, Aiya explained that he gilds the temple lamps and deities—a rare feature for Hindu temples worldwide, winning the Rush temple much notoriety—because it is practical. It makes cleaning easier. Knowing how important a beautiful and extravagantly decorated temple is for him, I responded in disbelief, thinking he was kidding. He insisted that this was true: "In the old garage days, before I had students, I used to spend all my time cleaning brass. Once I had students I had them polishing away like mad!" Chuckling at this image, he continued, "My son-in-law claims that he had to polish a certain number of lamps before he could get his mantra."

The standard Aiya sets for the *mūrtis* of the gods and goddesses runs deeper than their gold plating. He explained this to me one day as we sat drinking tea, "I will not go and arbitrarily pick out some sculptor and say, 'Make something.' I will first study what he's been doing, what specialties he has, what his lineage is like, and then carefully go and commission it." Noting that many temples are not so careful about purchasing temple items, he added,

"That's just me, it's not everybody else. My theory is, if I'm going to build a temple that I'm going to offer to the Mother—which means that I'm going to offer it to the devotees—the temple is not the building. The temple is where the devotees' hearts melt. That's the temple service."

Although material resources are the most tangible of costs involved in Aiya's banquet philosophy, time is another cost worth mentioning. Learning, preparing for, and performing elaborate rituals are not only extremely time-consuming but comprise a never-ending process. Many temple members consider the hours Aiya and others spend learning and performing rituals their gift to them. In spite of this, some worry that Aiya's generosity to the Mother—reflected in the addition of new and more elaborate festivals and rituals each year—ends up seriously taxing him and a handful of regular temple volunteers.

The person who takes the biggest brunt of Aiya's flamboyance and generosity—indispensable to his ability to maintain his current level of ritual exuberance—is without question his wife, Amma. Although Amma holds down a full-time job as an accounts clerk in a hospital, she spends countless hours in the temple kitchen preparing food for the steady and growing flow of visitors. Accompanying Aiya to the temple most nights and weekends to work in the kitchen and occasionally to assist him in ritual performances, her quiet yet strong presence is an integral part of temple dynamics. As Aiya regularly adds rituals and festivals to the temple calendar, Amma worries that members, including herself, will have difficulty keeping pace. No less dedicated to building a place of worship than her husband, she advocates a more measured approach.

Occasionally tempered, if only slightly, by more practically minded devotees wary of the costs of elaborate rituals, Aiya reasons that the temple receives blessings in kind, commensurate with its outpouring of devotion and trust. During one conversation on the subject, Aiya offered an example of divine providence sent through an instructor at a local college. A few months earlier, the gentleman had arrived at the temple with some of his students to witness a Saturday *homam*. Noting that one of the fire offerings was honey, he afterward informed Aiya that he was a beekeeper and volunteered to bring some of his honey to the temple. Since then, the gentleman has regularly and unceremoniously delivered a five-gallon vat of honey outside the temple house. Reflecting on this, Aiya laughed and mischievously announced that he is now tempted to pour five gallons at once onto the fire, "I have nothing against that!" But, alas, he cannot lift the vat.

In spite of the fact that blessings in the form of a beekeeper regularly donating honey—and a florist donating flowers for *pūjā* and a neighbor donating wood for *homams*—and regular minor miracles that seemingly keep finances afloat, the temple occasionally finds itself strapped.[3] This is not simply because Aiya's approach is expensive to maintain. Also worked into the equation is Aiya's reluctance to ask temple visitors for money. Unlike many other temples that display large price lists in their entryway, at Rush there is no set charge for rituals performed on visitors' behalf. The cost of individualized *arcana* rituals are at the recipient's discretion; fruit and flower *prasādam* offerings are given freely to temple participants. The price of sponsored *pūjās* and *homams* is on a sliding scale. Those who cannot afford them can have them performed for free. Generally speaking, what a person chooses to donate is, as Aiya regularly puts it, "between you and your Mother."

Highly critical of temples that become inflated sources of revenue for temple boards and priests—both in India and in North America—Aiya finds the issue of money management an emotional one.[4] An incident I witnessed in which hackles were raised occurred the day the large brass lamps arrived from India. After cleaning and assembling them, the five of us returned to the little house and, when we were settled onto mismatched chairs, chatting over tea and spicy snack food, the phone rang. Because Aiya constantly gets phone calls, none of us paid much attention until we heard him say in a forceful tone, "Nothing! We don't do that here! What you give the Mother is entirely up to you. There's no fixed amount!" After he hung up the phone and noted our questioning looks, Aiya explained that someone called to ask directions to the temple and to get information about the Saturday *abhiṣekam*. After he explained the Saturday routine, gave the gentleman directions, and was about to hang up, the man interjected in a singsong teasing tone, "But you forgot to tell me something!" When Aiya asked what it was, he answered that Aiya had not yet quoted him the price of the ritual. The response to this question is what we had overheard. Frustrated by the caller's tone and assumption, Aiya remarked to the group, "It's sad, really, this mindset—that everything always has to come down to money."

Although he refuses to make money the temple's focus Aiya nonetheless encourages devotees not to cut corners, to offer Rājarājeśwarī, Empress of Emperors, her due respect. During a formal post-*pūjā* talk one Saturday in April, he related the schedule for the upcoming *pratiṣṭhā* festival and pressed the point that participants offer only the best to the Goddess: "On the second day we will do *caṇḍī homam*. Led by Dr. Viswanathan here, he will do the *caṇḍī homam*, and all the things that are prescribed will go into the fire. Here and now I am going to tell you that we are going to offer fourteen saris into the fire. If you want to donate the saris, only Kāñcīpuram silk, nothing else. Nothing else will do. If you want to offer something, you offer the best you've got. You don't offer something that you think you won't use."

A notable way Aiya refuses to compromise, indirectly costing the temple money, is his insistent conformity with ancient temple tradition by burning camphor during *pūjās*. Because camphor is messy—leaving a black residue on walls, ceilings, and temple objects—North American temples have almost uniformly replaced camphor flames with wick flames from oil or ghee lamps. Aiya will not give up camphor in spite of its drawbacks partly because its familiar blaze and smell evoke devotional emotions. It also traditionally burns without leaving a trace (although this is not true for camphor processed today), symbolically associated with the burning of the ego, an appropriate metaphor for temple practices and aims. At Rush, camphor has not only blackened the temple's walls and ceilings but has also gummed up, over time, the sound system as well as the photocopier and computer in the nearby temple office. In spite of this, along with persistent suggestions by some devotees that they switch to ghee lamps, Aiya will not be swayed.[5]

Not all extravagant rituals strain the pocketbook or temple equipment. Although elaborate and time-consuming, the *śrīcakra pūjā*, a powerful ritual at the heart of the Śrīvidyā tradition, does little to tax the temple's tangible resources. Rather than requiring expensive material offerings, the *śrīcakra pūjā* demands time and energy for its preparation and performance. As Aiya described it during a weekend post-*pūjā* talk, late May of 2002, "The *śāstra*s say that [*śrīcakra pūjā*] is equivalent to having witnessed or having performed one thousand *aśvamedha yagña*s [horse sacrifices]. What is the significance here? An *aśvamedha yagña* can only be performed by a king of kings, an emperor of emperors. Because a tremendous amount of wealth and manpower and resources are needed for that. But a *śrīcakra pūjā*, even a pauper can do it with a few leaves . . . whatever flowers are available during that season, you can collect them and do the *pūjā*." Aiya continues by describing the *amṛta*, a mixture commonly used in the *śrīcakra pūjā*, made from fifty-four ingredients, which takes about one and a half to two hours to prepare. He goes on to describe the ultimate offering during the ritual: the self in its entirety:

> Then you do *homam* inside yourself. You are offering everything to Her. You say that your good deeds and bad deeds, action, inaction, good desires and bad desires, righteousness and omissions committed are all offered. Because, as human beings, as we go about this business of living, we will be creating a lot of mischief. We will actually be doing a lot of harm without even thinking about it. So all that is offered. And in the end you say, my life, my intelligence, my body, in the waking state, sleeping state, in the dreamless sleep state, whatever I have committed with my mind, words, actions, whatever my hands do, wherever my feet take me, whatever I say. All this I offer to Her.

Whether a ritual requires thousands of dollars of Kāñcīpuram silk to be burned or gallons of honey, or whether the sacrifice is of the self—ritually speaking or in the hours spent preparing, cooking, polishing—such are the costs of powerful rituals and, by association, a powerful temple. The monetary cost of the temple *mūrtis,* carefully selected and crafted, gleaming in gold, likewise contributes to the beauty of the temple, melting the hearts of devotees and allowing practitioners to more fully enter into and be receptive to divinity in their midst. Most temple devotees, even the more practically minded, would agree that, at the end of the day, divine power is worth the hefty price.[6]

Not Just a Symbol: The Scientific Language of Sacred Power

Aiya seems to have a scientific explanation for just about everything. When describing the qualities and efficacies of costly temple images and rituals, he frequently lapses into language more befitting a physicist, geologist, or biologist than a guru or priest. A good portion of his scientific language comes from his nuclear physicist guru, Guruji, who spent the first part of his career as a researcher in India. When Indira Gandhi commissioned Indian physicists to develop nuclear arms for their country in the early 1970s, Guruji refused to take part. He moved to Zambia in 1979 and spent the rest of his career teaching at a Zambian university. It was in Africa that he and Aiya met.[7]

The meshing of science and faith, performed with alacrity at Rush, is not new to Indian or North American Hinduism. Some of its first proponents were Indian holy men who preached to U.S. audiences in the late nineteenth and early twentieth centuries. Vivekananda, founder of the Vedanta Society in New York and the Ramakrishna Mission in India, who was famous for captivating his audience at the 1893 World Parliament of Religion in Chicago, was one of the first to popularize the connection between yoga and science. Yogananda, another highly influential guru who equated yoga with science, established the Self-Realization Fellowship in California during the 1920s. These charismatic Indian gurus and their teachings struck a chord with many North Americans, and the melding of scientific and religious language sparked an interest in Hinduism across the continent (Eck 2001: 105; Bharati 1980: 256). By the mid-twentieth century, the incorporation of scientific rationality within the religious realm had made significant inroads in urban India as well.[8] Aiya and Guruji's mingling of science and religion thus coincides with a larger trend that appeals to many Indian immigrants, North American-born Indians, and Euro North Americans alike.

The connection between science and religion is rooted in teachings popularized during the mid-1800s among the English-speaking Indian elite. This movement, referred to as the Hindu Renaissance, was in many ways a response to the British Christian presence in India that branded temple *mūrti* worship as idolatrous and superstitious. Drawing on philosophically oriented Vedāntic teachings, Hindu Renaissance leaders also rejected image worship as idolatrous and framed Hinduism, instead, as an ethical spirituality. As the movement spread throughout North America, preached most notably by Vivekananda, the related philosophies of Neo-Vedānta emerged, extolling the virtues of Hinduism as a scientifically verifiable religion and stressing a unitary truth that lay beneath all religions.

The deemphasis of ritual and emphasis on yogic practices and social work have made Vedāntic and neo-Vedāntic philosophies more at home at guru ashrams than at ritually oriented temples (see Clothey 1992: 136).[9] As neo-Vedānta continues to gain currency and as ritual decreases in importance, first- and second-generation South Asians living in North America do not seem to be abandoning temple activities, however, because rituals offer important ties to tradition. Keeping apace with shifting ideologies, North American temples nonetheless tend to adjust to new expectations. For instance, although ritual performance continues, participants often see them as providing "a moral and aesthetic force" in their lives rather than a source of divine power (Waghorne 1999: 123; see also Leonard 1997: 121–22). Likewise, participants often view the image of the temple deity, or *mūrti*, as a symbolic representation of, rather than an actual host to, divine presence. Demonstrating this perspective is a visitor's guide to the Venkateshwara Temple in the Penn Hills of Pennsylvania, written in 1979. It explains, "Where the Hindu worships the idols in the shrine, he is aware that it is to God that he really offers worship. It is wrong, therefore, to characterize Hinduism as an idolatrous religion. The idols are symbols of an invisible spirit" (Narayanan 1992: 165).[10] Noting how North American Hindus are often anxious to deemphasize rituals and emphasize ethical religious expressions, Vasudha Narayanan surmises that they "are wary of being known as idolaters; early Western missionary terminology ringing in their ears" (1992: 165).[11]

The Rush temple both supports and defies current trends. Like a neo-Vedāntist, appealing to North American as well as urban Indian and Sri Lankan tastes, Aiya often uses scientific language to promote and describe the effects of yoga and meditation and speaks of an underlying unity to all religious traditions. The temple's advocacy of self-realization through union with the divine principle also coincides with Vedāntic teachings. But when Aiya uses scientific language to explain how temple deities and rituals generate and perpetuate sacred power—that far from being symbols, the stone forms are "fully alive"—he begins to defy typical expectation.[12] This mix of traditional temple and Vedāntic philosophies is consistent with Śrīvidyā's emphasis on both external rituals and internal yogic meditation. Contrary to perspectives gaining momentum in India and the United States, Śrīvidyā not only proclaims the importance of rituals but also views them as necessary supplements to meditational practices (Brooks 1992: 171).

In traditional Hindu temples, one of the most basic understandings of ritual power—underlying the idea that a temple *mūrti* or deity image can be considered fully alive—has to do with the tangible form of the *yantra*, a geometrical shape carved onto a metal plate, positioned beneath the temple image.

Ideally, the *yantra* will have been "charged" with sacred energy through the repetition of mantras performed by a priest before the installation of the temple deity. After the deity is installed, daily temple rituals maintain this charge and keep the *yantra* "motor" running. The *yantra* releases the sacred vibrations into the *mūrti* form of the deity that, in turn, emits these vibrations into the temple.[13] The *yantra* that keeps Rush's Rājarājeśwarī *mūrti* charged is the *śrīcakra yantra*, composed of forty-four triangles. The five triangles pointing down represent the female principle of the universe, and the four triangles pointing up represent the male principle. According to Aiya and other goddess devotees, the *śrīcakra yantra* is the most powerful of all, "the Mother of all *yantras*."[14]

Although the *yantra* is key to the *mūrti*'s power, the physical composition of the image itself is not irrelevant. Aiya asserts that marble and metal *mūrtis* quickly soak in the *yantra*'s vibrations; their subsequent quick release into the temple minimizes their effectiveness. Granite, he asserts, is perfectly constituted for slowly soaking in and emitting sacred vibrations. This allows sacred energy to flow into the temple at a steady rate, sustained until the next ritual "charging."[15] The Rush temple's main deities are therefore, of course, granite. But there is more. In the following excerpt from one of Aiya's Saturday temple talks after morning *abhiṣekam*, he uses geological terms to describe variations between granite temple images. He talks into his microphone headset while standing beside a maroon curtain that shields the three main, granite deities, Ganeś, Rājarājeśwarī, and the Śiva lingam. They have just received their weekend *abhiṣekam* milk bath and cleaning. Behind the curtain, devotees busily dry, dress, and decorate the deities.

> The *Śilpa Śāstra*, if you check with it, will tell you that whatever *mūrti* is to be made, to be erected in a temple, it has to come from the bowels of the earth. That means it has to be primary rock, or what geologists refer to as igneous rock. Igneous rock also falls into two categories according to the *Śāstras*. One is male rock and the other is female rock. If you are going to carve a Dattātreya you will use a male rock—a male stone. If you are going to make a devī like a Rājarājeśwarī, female stone. If you're going to make an Ardhanārīśwara [a half male, half female deity], you use neither male nor female, you will use a neutral rock.[16]
>
> How is this determined? Simply, the sculptor will reverse the chisel and tap the stone. You should hear. . . . [*Aiya turns on the electric drone*] See, the music scale in India is [*Aiya sings up the scale using tones C, C#, E, F, G, G#, B, C*]. . . .[17] [*Sings C, C#, E*] Male stone. [*Sings F, G*] Neutral stone. [*Sings G#, B, C*] Female stone. [*Repeats sequence*] So they tap it off and if there is a pitch in any of these things that is higher, then it is a female stone.
>
> Chemically, the female stone carries a preponderance of ferrous

> salts—iron salts. And it will be reddish brown. So that stone you find in female *mūrtis*. What's the difference in the male stone? It has a preponderance of silicon dioxide. So you'll find shiny specks. And that will, when you tap it, it will be [*sings C, C#, E*] those three. So now you know. After we finish *pūjā*, remind me to tap Ganeś and Devī [being dressed and decorated behind the curtain]. Then you will understand the sound.[18]

Aside from the composition of the *mūrti* and the physical presence of a charged *yantra*, ritual power is dependent, according to Aiya, on human composition as well. In other words, a resonating temple image will have more impact on a person who inwardly resonates from his or her practice of chanting and meditation. Aiya introduced this topic during our very first taped interview while we sipped tea outside the temple kitchen. He animatedly described a priest from Montreal who was, as he put it, "completely blown away" by the Rush temple's energy: "He went and stood in front of the Devī for a long time and quietly came out and told me [*Aiya speaks in whispered reverence*], 'My God, I have never felt so much power!' Because, you know, for them the inner clock begins to tick." When I asked what he meant by this, I received an expansive lecture that eventually wound its way back to my question. Because Aiya was talking about people and not rocks, he borrowed from physiology and physics to make his point. He began with Vedāntic ideas of self-realization infused with—for my benefit, it seems—a neo-Vedāntic leveling of interreligious distinctions. Leaning back in his white plastic lawn chair, feet crossed at the ankles, Aiya knew his explanation was going to be lengthy and began with a deep sigh.

> AIYA Okay. Whatever religion you belong to, whether you are a Catholic, Pentecostal, or Buddhist, Hindu or Native American, the realization that you are a spark of the Divine Being—that is of God—until that "realization" quote, unquote, comes in you, dawns on you, not in theory but in actual experience, everything that is written in any religion, in any scriptures is just that—it's written. It's theory, right?
>
> CORINNE Right.
>
> AIYA I can keep telling everybody, "I am God. All you see is God. God is everywhere, God is omnipotent, omnipresent." It's just theory, it's just like my teacher or my professor teaches me something and I am repeating it like a parrot. That's not realization. That's not experience. So, in the olden days, some people were troubled by the same question. "If everybody says, 'God is everywhere,' why am I not able to feel it? Why do I have to be buffeted by violence and illness and emotions, anger and lust and all these things?". . . .
>
> The yogis have found that there are two separate nervous systems in

the body. There is the sympathetic nervous system and a spinal nervous system. The spinal nervous system of course begins with the brain—with the attendant lobes and ventricles and the pineal stalk and the brainstem. And it continues down through the spinal cord and it ends there at the base of the spinal cord. And they have also found that there are places along that spinal cord where important nerves meet. For example, the brachial nerves, right? Or the femoral nerves. All these meet at various points.

They have found that continued focus by the person who is trying to discover the truth in particular religions will evoke, will create particular reactions. And they have found also that you can become a perfect instrument, perceiving the changes that are taking place in your mind, in your emotions, in your outlook, and you can correlate it with certain regions that are being activated along the spinal chord. Hence, the evolvement of the system of *cakras*.

CORINNE And the *kuṇḍalinī*.

AIYA *Kuṇḍalinī*. If we cut a segment of the spinal column you will see something like this [*makes a rounded heart shape with his hands*]. This section you will see. Where my forefingers are joined, just about a half an inch from there in the center of that area you will find a small opening. That is called the neural canal. And that is continuous from the base of the spine right into the brain, into the ventricles. It's filled with cerebral spinal fluid, neural fluid. Composition: complex proteins.

This *kuṇḍalinī* is not a tangible thing, you can't see it coming up, but something is moving inside you. When the energy begins to rise and starts to pass through each of these centers, when it is at a particular center, your perception of your environment, your relationships, they will be in a particular way. When it moves further up, they have changed, so you can sense the dynamic force it has released.

When it begins you can hardly perceive any sound inside you. When can you hear it within? When the energy has begun to move up and when it has crossed the heart, then you begin to hear it. When it starts, it's at .01 cycles a second—please remember my guru was a physicist. When it passes through the first center it is .07 cycles a second. When it is passing through the third one, it is .09. When it has come up to the heart, it is almost at .1. So, you can see, the frequency is increasing as it is moving up. So when it comes here, to the heart center, you can hear it when you are quiet. With your eyes closed, you can hear a hum inside of you.

Aiya then instructs me to clench my teeth so I can hear a simulation of the unstruck, primordial sound. He brings his explanation full circle by reiterating that the *kuṇḍalinī* can be raised and the sound made audible through practices found in any religious tradition. Still wondering what this might have to do with the priest from Montreal who stood by the main temple goddess and sensed her power, I asked about him again. From here, Aiya makes the connection between the internal reverberations of one who regularly meditates and performs rituals and the vibrations emanating from statues or *mūrti*s resulting from active *yantra*s and regularly performed mantras and *pūjā* offerings.[19]

> There is a *yantra* and into it 2.5 million iterations of the mantra have been done over three years by a gentleman who is super dedicated. . . . The moment the *yantra* goes in there—and it's enhanced by the addition of other things like the nine gem stones, fine metal, mercury, and all these things—that energy begins to escape out into the ether. To maintain that level of energy is why the ritual is done every day—the chanting, and all that is going on is being absorbed and emitted. And people will come, the devotees come, and they will experience that shower of grace.
>
> If a person has been trained, if the person has begun to look long and hard enough inside of himself, this sound will manifest. When you are aware of your sound, you walk in there and it will suddenly go bbbbbbbbbvvvvvvvvvv [*making a low to high-pitched sound*]. Immediately you will think [*in an awestruck whisper*] "Oh, they have done so much work here!"

During the winter workshop I attended in 1999, Aiya once again connected religious dedication with physiology. Here he described the special chemical composition of holy men's brains, citing postmortem examinations of ascetics who spent their lives in isolated caves or on mountaintops. "And what they found was that in some of these people, the pineal stalk [at the center of the brain, above the pituitary gland] was calcified. But in the majority of cases it was still there and they isolated three chemicals. Three substances they found. The first one was melatonin—which is now a rage. Any paper you pick up, they're selling melatonin pills. The second one is seratonin. And the third is methoxyharmalan. It's a three-ringed compound. They're all neurochemicals; they're all neuropeptides. They're all hallucinogens."

As Aiya's language became increasingly technical, Aparna, a Euro American woman in her mid-thirties, whispered something to an increasingly confused Sri Lankan–born high school student sitting next to her. She told her, for clarification, that these chemicals are like drugs but in a different form. Aiya overheard the whispered exchange and continued, "So if you just take them in the synthetic form you will see psychedelic colors in front of you. You will see Priya with 50,000 arms around her, dancing. You will see anything you want." Aiya then turned to his easel and flip chart and started drawing the outline of a human body so he could explain how the rising *kuṇḍalinī* affects the neural canal in the spinal column and, finally, the pineal stalk.

By referring to Priya's 50,000 arms, Aiya jokingly implied that depictions of gods and goddesses with multiple limbs have psychedelic rather than authentic origins. Later he dashed the faith of many in the room by debunking the idea that Lord Ganeś really has an elephant head. Yet, in spite of his occasional critique of religious credulity and his allegiance to a scientific, rationalistic worldview, Aiya does not advocate that devotees blandly rely on the laws of physics and physiology to perform their anticipated effects. Proper cultural, emotional, and intellectual packaging also plays a role. This is, in part, his concession to the importance of the symbolic in ritual, primarily in the form of applied meaning, cultural association, and emotions that arise from them. Such associations and emotions have power as well, leading practitioners to higher levels of devotion.

One of the most important human supplements to a temple's intrinsic power is, in Aiya's view, knowledge. At nearly every large gathering, he impresses upon visitors that they cannot simply sit back and reap the benefits of temple rituals. They must work to understand what is going on. This insistence is somewhat consistent with Śrīvidyā ideology that values knowledge as part of the formula that produces ritual power. Simply chanting is not sufficient; the initiate must internalize the mantra's esoteric meaning as well (Brooks 1992: 98). Not consistent with the Śrīvidyā tradition, or with normative temple practice, however, is the fact that Aiya explains Sanskrit chants and ritual mechanics not just to initiates but to the general public.

Although Aiya believes that ritual performances are more powerful when devotees understand them, cultural cues can aid effectiveness as well. One Wednesday in December 1998 I brought Rose, a friend with extensive meditation and chanting experience, to the temple. At one point, when Rose and Aiya were discussing the intrinsic power of the Sanskrit language, Aiya informed us, shaking his head in disbelief, that some North American temples had recently tried to make rituals more accessible by translating Sanskrit chants into English. Regardless of the importance of understanding for him, this defies the point of having a temple. In addition to the fact that Sanskrit, as he sees it, carries its own power, Aiya argued that it brought those familiar with it "into a state of reverence. It is part and parcel of worship, just like the incense and the music." The cultural resonances present in the temple's sounds, smells, and sights have a religious impact of their own.[20]

Another component of temple practice that, according to Aiya, expresses and evokes emotion in the performer as well as in the spectators are *mudrās*, hand and arm movements that accompany ritual chanting. Because Rush initiates often chant in unison, the incorporated *mudrās* make temple events seem a bit like a synchronized dance or a staged chorus production. At the winter workshop, Aiya offered a rather amusing analogy to illustrate the function of *mudrās*, acting out the scene as he talked:

> Let's say you are very late for work. You were supposed to have been there ten minutes ago. So you get into your car and start driving and find yourself at a stoplight behind another car. The light turns green but the car ahead of you doesn't move. The guy inside is fiddling with the radio and is distracted. So in your anxiety you honk your horn. The guy in front of you puts his hand out the window and shows you a *mudrā* which reflects all his feelings and emotions [*laughter around the room*]. *Mudrās* to the Devī are the same thing except they express much higher feelings and emotions.

On another occasion I asked Aiya more specifically about the benefits of *mudrās*. I was curious, since he speaks so regularly about the benefits of mantras and not about their accompanying gestures.

> AIYA The benefit has to do with the connection for the devotee who is watching it, the uninitiated. For the practitioner who is doing it, he is expressing certain emotions that are welling up from inside and it is directing a certain flow of energy.
>
> CORINNE So there are psychological as well as physiological benefits.
>
> AIYA [*chants in Sanskrit*] *Mudrāhā pradakśakena iti devatā prīti. Mudrāhā*—to perform a *mudrā. Devatā*—the deity is pleased by the performance. And what is deity? Is the deity from somewhere outside on another plane that has come in a spaceship and landed down? No, the deity is inside you. It's your consciousness. So, somewhere a part of your consciousness, pure consciousness, is satisfied by this performance. Pleased by it.

Note how deftly Aiya deflects my attempt to reduce religious practice to human psychological or physiological benefit. This brings us to a final point. Although a mix of intellectual, emotional, and cultural engagement—added to ritual and meditational practice—is crucial for encountering divinity, such human perceptions and practices cannot succeed on their own. Although temple theology dictates that the Goddess reside in the temple and in all creation, she can be, paradoxically, separate from the will and perception of her devotees and nonsynonymous with science. Although mantras, *mudrās*, *mūrtis*, and *yantras* express and contain divine power, she can override all such human contrivances, no matter how elaborate, old, or sophisticated. In other words, the Goddess has ideas of her own, sometimes known as grace. Aiya illustrated this point during a lunchtime conversation with Krishna, a Sri Lankan–born doctor from Los Angeles; Lily, a Hispanic American college student; Mohan; and me. Aiya was discussing the protective properties of mantras and the potential dangers of the Śrīvidyā path. He painted a rather daunting scenario that gets transcended by the particular grace and patience of the Rush temple deity.

AIYA Why does your mind need protection? Otherwise it will go off in two thousand different directions. And you will lose focus. We are all going to end up there [achieving *mokṣa*, or release from the cycle of rebirths]; the mantra just focuses the attention and speeds up the process. Instead of doing it in a million years, you do it in three score and ten years. Now, both systems, both pathways, both time spans, have their advantages and disadvantages. The million years' route, you are walking. If you trip and fall, at the most you might scratch your knees. If you're doing it in seventy years, you're flying faster than the speed of light through the cosmos. If you fall over then. . . . [*Aiya pauses and people around the room grimace.*] So you have to watch your mind all the time. Watch what it's doing.[21]

KRISHNA That's very difficult.

AIYA It is, it is. That is why it's called *sādhana*. Achievement.

KRISHNA I think I'll try it in a thousand years.

CORINNE [*as we're all laughing*] Yeah. The middle plan.

AIYA It's almost too late now. She's caught you. She won't let you go like that. If you think that you're going to get away from the Mother you have something else coming. She won't let you go. No way.

MOHAN Or else she'll let you go and bring you back.

AIYA This particular form of the Mother, if you stand there and tell Her [*Aiya cocks his head and wrings his hands*], "There are beautiful flowers, Mom. I want to pick some." She will let you go pick them. Then She will take you firmly by the hand and lead you. She will wait for you. Ones like Kāī won't have the patience. They will say, "Uh uh! No such thing!" [*Aiya mimes chopping off someone's head.*] Klunk! That's it. You're done!

According to Aiya and Śrīvidyā theology, the ever-patient Śrī Rājarājeśwarī, manifestation of the great triple goddess Tripurasundarī, is kindly present to and in her devotees.[22] Her granite statue, perhaps simply a beautifully carved, well-dressed symbol to outsiders, is experienced by insiders to be much more, thanks to the temple's elaborate rituals, enhanced by meditative practices, cultural resonances, and scientific explanations. As Aiya sees it, none of this—not her representations, devotional expressions, nor her presence—would be possible, however, without her overriding compassionate grace, enmeshed within yet transcending all human effort and understanding.

A Leap of Faith: From the Scientific to the Divine Realm

Experiences of the goddess's presence in temple rituals and images is, for very few, consistent and palpable. For most, an assurance of divinity requires, at various junctures and to varying degrees, a leap of faith. According to Aiya, this admittedly difficult leap can make all the difference in a devotee's experience. If mantras and temple representations are treated as symbols, they may just function like symbols, inspiring, at best, positive thoughts and emotions. If faithfully approached with the intensity and awe of bodily approaching the goddess herself, devotees are more likely to receive attendant, tangible blessings.

One midweek morning in August, I arrived at the temple to find a young woman in her early twenties, her brother around twelve years of age, their parents, grandmother, and two other women who appeared to be aunts, all present for *pūjā*. They were, I later learned, originally from Sri Lanka and currently living in Toronto. As they sat in the temple, Ammamma, a woman in her seventies, Aiya's kindergarten through second-grade teacher in Sri Lanka, skillfully performed *pūjā* offerings to the temple deities. About ten minutes into the ritual, Aiya made his entrance, freshly showered, and asked the young woman and the boy to stand in front of the nine planet *mūrtis*. As the two stood side by side, the woman in an elegant black salwar kameez and the boy in khakis and T-shirt, Aiya began a *sarpa doṣa* ritual. As he chanted, he spooned water into two *kālasam* pots filled with milk and sprinkled with cloves, turmeric, *kuś* grass, and flowers. After about twenty minutes, he walked up to each of them and, still chanting, pointed to different parts of their bodies with a foot-long stick woven from *darbha* grass.[23] The young woman, clearly unsettled, flinched as Aiya moved the stick near her head. Amused, he laughed and said, "I'm not going to hurt you, Amma." He then turned to me and said "I'll explain all this to you later."

Once this segment of the ritual was finished, Aiya announced cheerfully, "Now we're going to have a bath!" He asked the young woman to take one of the heavy *kālasam* pots outside while Kumaran, a devotee in his early twenties, carried the boy's *kālasam*. The group of us walked from the temple down a grassy slope to "Kāśī," a shrine that sits by a stream, dedicated to Śiva. As we walked, Aiya told me that if I would walk slowly, he would explain the ritual to me. Making sure that the young woman, shouldering her *kālasam* pot and walking slowly, was in earshot but directing his comments to me, Aiya explained that some people's planets are arranged in such a way that they block certain life events. In many cases, it becomes difficult for these people to get married or bear children. Typically a person's six main *cakras*, lined from the base of the spine to the top of the head, are bound by a criss-crossing of energy from particular planetary stations, with the energy from Uranus and Neptune going straight from top to bottom without crossing. Those people whose astrologers tell them that Uranus and Neptune are intersecting through the middle of their line of *cakras* are advised to have a *sarpa doṣa* ritual done to straighten out the abnormality and the potential problems that arise from them.

After Aiya carefully explained the mechanics, he added, still within earshot of the young woman, "None of these rituals works, of course, unless a person has faith. Otherwise it's just hocus-pocus mumbo jumbo." Down at the Kāśī shrine, the young woman and boy were given *abhiṣekam*, the contents of their *kālasam* pots poured over them by Aiya and Kumaran. Heading back up the hill to the temple, Aiya again reminded me that rituals such as these cannot work without faith. I nodded my head and noted his persistence. He then mentioned that out of the eighteen people who had this ritual done at the temple because of difficulties conceiving, twelve—of whom he is aware—were successful. In some cases, they had been trying for over a decade. At Guruji's temple, moreover, all rituals have been successful. He added for emphasis, "Whatever this is about, those are pretty good odds." In the case of those who were hoping to get married, he was not as aware of the outcome. Once inside the temple, after the young woman had showered and changed into jeans, Aiya brought out a pad of paper and a pen. Bringing her into the discussion by asking her to name the various planets and zodiac signs, he drew a diagram of the *cakras* and planetary stations and explained again how the system worked.

After the family left, a small group of us ate lunch around the *homam* pit behind the temple. Aiya assessed the morning's events, commenting that the young woman was not at all interested in doing the ritual. It was clear to him that she only came at the insistence of her parents. As he put it, she resisted because "she's too cool for all this stuff." I told him I felt his explanation and comments about faith seemingly directed at me were really for her benefit. Admitting this was true, he added that he could not blame her entirely. This attitude among young people, he believes, is molded by the prevalent temple culture. Many priests perpetuate the idea—perhaps unwittingly—that rituals are "mumbo jumbo" because they do not explain them. It is no wonder, he shrugged, that people, particularly the youth, are turned off. Those who eagerly participate in ritual transactions, on the other hand, often treat them as utilitarian at best. "They get their horoscopes done and come running to the temple. They just want things fixed, that's all. That is all the temple means to them."

Faith, a favorite subject of Aiya's and in many ways central to the workings of the temple, cuts across multiple levels of practice and perception. It also comes in different forms and can be arranged hierarchically. While for some faith is fundamentally utilitarian, and they bank on external rituals to do their "work," other purportedly higher kinds of faith encourage the realization of divinity within. When I first started discussing these matters with Aiya, I often found my understanding of faith—loaded with North American Christian associations, referring to belief in an intangible, transcendent, abstraction—inadequate. In applying the concept to the Rush temple—or any temple context that relies upon bodily practices and experiences and invokes divine power through material substances—"faith" must break out of narrow Christian confines.

The summer after the *sarpa doṣa* ritual, I revisited the subject of the doubting Sri Lankan woman with Aiya. I had just finished helping Ammamma clean the kitchen after lunch and joined a group of young regulars—Kumaran, Vijitha, and Devi—who sat on the floor outside the kitchen, talking and joking with Aiya. Aiya was describing the positive effect of temple *homams* on those living in the nearby neighborhood, even on those unaware of the ritual. I interjected that this seemed to undercut the role of faith he argues is so central to ritual power. Surprised that his explanation triggered yet another adventure in temple physics, I learned I was under the mistaken impression that faith was somehow disengaged from the "science" of ritual power.

CORINNE If you say that faith is important, then if someone just stands there and goes "bleah" the ritual won't work. Right?

AIYA No, Amma, not if you just stand there and tune out. Let me see. Now this calls for physics. Here is the spectrum. Okay? Visible spectrum is here, then there's alpha, beta, delta, gamma, all those things. Okay?

CORINNE [*not fully understanding but not wanting to deter him*] Okay, yup.

AIYA If you focus from the brain stem and from the pineal and what is connected down to the pituitary, immediately there will be emissions from the delta frequency, if you focus. If you don't it will drop below. If you just focus and listen to what this fellow is saying and look at the *homam* fire, y'know, blocking out everything else—blocking out Vijitha, Kumaran, the green sari Devi's wearing—you will get something. It will stay there. But if you look at that and keep thinking, hmm . . . [*Aiya distractedly looks around and mumbles to himself*] already it's come down. They have actually measured this, Amma, the response. Not that the benefits will be completely denied you. But it will not have the same intensity.

CORINNE So that's the explanation for why things can happen anyway [referring to the *homam* benefits for community members who are not only unfocused but unaware of the ritual in their midst].

> AIYA So I say what use is it if you're only going to get 10 percent? Let somebody else do the ritual and stand there and breathe the damn air and go home. There's a difference.

At this point, the office phone started ringing. As Aiya got up to answer it, he announced over his shoulder, responding to my comment about the benefits of ritual for the unaware, "There was one lady who came here during the consecration ceremony who had *no* idea. . . ." I rightly assumed he was referring to a woman whom I interviewed the previous spring. She lives at a nearby dairy farm and was asked to bring one of her cows and a calf to the opening *pratiṣṭhā* festival. Soon after the event she discovered she was pregnant, and attributes her ability to conceive with her presence at the festival. Since her doctors had given up on this possibility after many years of treatment, she considers her baby boy a temple miracle.[24]

The term "focus" as described above is clearly not the same as my Christian term "faith," although it becomes related when understood as the absence of doubt and questioning. I wondered if perhaps the dairy farmer, although she had no idea what was going on, was somehow well focused on the *pratiṣṭhā* rituals, or if Linda, my friend from Massachusetts who is a very focused person to begin with, is temperamentally suited for rituals to "work" even if she does not understand them.[25] The importance of a disciplined, unwavering mind and its connection to external ritual was put another way during an extended conversation I had with two brahman Śrīvidyā adepts, a father and son pair who visited the Rush temple from Chennai (Madras). Yegnarathnam, the sixty-something father with an easy laugh and distinguished gray topknot, explained this relationship to Vijitha and me:

> If you do *pūjā*, and the daily things that are prescribed, after that time you will have self-realization that will lead you to *mokṣa* [release from the cycle of birth and death]. Afterwards you do not have to do any *pūjā* at all. By just sitting, this *pūjā* can be done inside yourself. You just call the goddess into your mind. But that will come only by practicing this outside *pūjā* first. The reason is that [at an advanced state] you are thinking you are God. But at first God is not coming to your mind, your neighbor is coming. Or your teaching is coming or some dog which is whining. So many other things are crossing your mind. You won't be able to concentrate. To be able to concentrate you must do the outside activities first. We seek only to focus.

Focus, normally illusive and fickle, can, with proper training, rein in and transcend exterior variables like stray thoughts or whining dogs. Below, Aiya describes faith in a similar manner. Whereas average faith is fickle and fair-weather, extraordinary faith is unconditional and, like well-developed focus, unwavering. The subject came up during a conversation several of us were having in the little house by the temple. The following is a response to a question Dipi asked about people who seem to have total faith in the Devī but become doubtful when bad things happen:

> AIYA Let me tell you something. Just because you chant Her name and think of Her twenty-four hours in the day does not mean that your life is going to be trouble free. Whatever debts that you have accrued [in your past lives], somehow or other you're going to have to pay for them. Right? If you expect that your life is going to be trouble free, that expectation becomes *kāmya pūjā*. It's like a business contract. I do this and you do that for me. Understand? [*Dipi is nodding.*] You are not "in love" with the Mother, quote unquote.
>
> CORINNE It's unconditional then.
>
> AIYA Unconditional. It has to be totally and completely unconditional. Then these doubts won't arise in your mind.

True love, out of which emerges full faith and focus, does not seek the Other for its own purposes. From Aiya's Śrīvidyā perspective, a person with fully developed faith in and focus on the Mother cannot approach her in a utilitarian manner by seeking favors, since devotee and object of devotion have become one and the same. Since an abyss naturally looms between most people and this realization, the temple aims to bridge this gap through its rituals. In other words, temple practices accommodate a person's transformation from fickle to true—from a desire for material benefits, to a yearning for union with the divine, to the realization of that union.

Within Śrīvidyā temple tradition, the building of faith and focus through ritual is dependent on the goddess's three forms. In ascending order of power they are the *mūrti* image of the deity, the *śrīvidyā* mantra, and the *śrīcakra yantra*.[26] These three forms—gross, subtle, and supreme, respectively—correspond to three ways of worshiping: through the body in ritual activity, through speech while chanting, and through the mind in meditation. When I spoke to Aiya about this traditional triadic source of temple power, he added to the middle category the goddess's presence in subtle form during fire rituals. He explained that the *homam* fire ritual is a stronger source of divine energy than her gross or *mūrti* form because its offerings are permanent. There are no leftovers, or *prasādam*, collected for one's material satisfaction. The exquisite sari offered to and worn by the *mūrti* is eventually given to a flesh-and-blood woman as *prasādam* blessings. Fruit and flower *pūjā* offerings are also returned to devotees as *prasādam*. When these same items are thrown into the fire, offerings are total and irretrievable.

Although the gross, subtle, and supreme forms and their respective approaches are in many ways interrelated and interdependent, Śrīvidyā initiates, or *upāsakas*, consider the *yantra*'s emanations to offer the most powerful and direct access to divinity. Although the *yantra* is most commonly and tangibly understood as a geometrical shape carved onto a square metal plate, physically present in the temple beneath the *mūrti*, the body of the person who is fully focused and attuned to the Devī can act as a *yantra* as well. In such cases, as described above by Yegnarathnam, the devotee no longer needs to perform external temple rituals. Internal, meditational practices are enough.

Aiya's role, as he understands it, is to cultivate the interlinking qualities of faith, focus, unconditional love, and receptivity that eventually and ideally free devotees from dependence on exterior forms of worship. Extravagant rituals and meticulously orchestrated surroundings—ensuring that the temple *yantra* is functioning at its peak and that devotees are aesthetically engaged—are vital to this end. Aiya's diagrams and explanations loaded with scientific jargon also prepare the ground from which faith and focus can grow. Whether or not his audience truly understands the technical language he uses (my guess is that few people do), the suggestion that temple practices are generating something real, not just fabrications or priestly obfuscations, helps inspire commitment to the religious path. When viewing Rush temple traditions as a whole, typical distinctions such as ritual activity/meditation, materiality/divinity, science/faith are not in opposition, since they work in service to and support of one another.

Because of the great emphasis Aiya places on scientific explanation, it has occurred to me from time to time that one could view the temple as one big science experiment. When everything can be explained, little room is left for awe and wonder, qualities that, Aiya would agree, are foundational to individual faith, commitment, and transformation. In some instances, I have heard Aiya describe mystery as existing in the breach between cause and effect—in the gap between Devī's temple forms and in her manifestations tangibly experienced by devotees. In other words, although much can be said to explain the interconnections between mantras, *yantra*s, and *mūrti*s, on one hand, and although scientific language can be used to describe the workings of the *kuṇḍalinī* and *cakra*s, on the other, the point of contact between these two sets of phenomena seems to be beyond explanation. The moment in which form becomes perception and ritual becomes experience contains, for Aiya, the mystery in which divinity most starkly reveals herself.

Given the importance of mystery for the religiously inclined, this chapter's final exchange reflects not upon the power of faith, science, and understanding, but upon the power of nonunderstanding, of mystery that in turn builds faith. It was a Friday evening and Aiya, Amma, Vijitha, and I were sitting outside the kitchen after the others had gone home. I normally did not linger after hours, since Aiya and Amma rarely get a break, but this evening I forged on with one final question, since Aiya seemed in a particularly talkative mood. During our exchange, Amma sat on the floor beside her husband and leaned against the wall. As she listened to the conversation, a wry smile spread across her face.

CORINNE What I was thinking about is the mystery of the unknown. . . .

AIYA Mmm hmm.

CORINNE . . . things that you can't understand, that have power. In the Catholic Church, before the Vatican II Council, the priest wouldn't face the people; he'd be speaking Latin. People had no idea what was going on. And when that changed, some people felt, "Gosh, now I understand everything. This isn't as powerful anymore." Do you know what I mean?

AIYA Mmm hmm.

CORINNE Could it happen, just hypothetically, that people here know what's going on. They can come right on in and touch the Devī. They understand the rituals. It's so easy to touch and to interact. Maybe, in people's heads, some of the power's lost. What do you say to that?

AIYA Every Saturday when I speak about it, I tell them that the temple is being continuously charged. The charging process is going on three times a day when we sit down and do the *pūjā*. And we don't stop short of anything, we don't take short cuts, we just continue to do what we have to do. And it keeps it charged. I tell them, if you want to feel the power, sit down for about an hour or two hours after the services here, then go inside yourself. And you come back and tell me if it's powerful or not. I don't need to keep telling you that it's a powerful place. And so . . .

CORINNE So mystery is not required.

AIYA It's not required. What is mystery? The entire world is Her. What you see, what you can't see, what you feel, what you don't feel—it's all Her. So what is mysterious about it? The intellectual understanding that everything is the Mother is already there. The only thing lacking is the experience of it. And I'm trying to bring people to that experience.

CORINNE And the little girl on the bike? [Referring to what many devotees consider a particularly miraculous and mysterious manifestation of the goddess, described in the next chapter.]

AIYA That's probably an act of kindness by the Mother. Just so my faith would be strengthened.

CORINNE So you need a bit of mystery for faith. I mean, there is that. . . .

AIYA Of course. And She supplies it. We don't.

CORINNE [Aha!] *There's* the condition. . . .

AIYA If your faith is proper and is in the correct place. If your heart and mind are in the correct place, then She will take care of the rest. Otherwise, it's just a stone. And the entire temple is just a building. What's the use? It's got no use.

Allergic to what he considers the smoke-and-mirrors effect of some other temples, owing to an inability or unwillingness to help participants understand, Aiya adamantly insists that mystery is not his job; it is Hers. His job is to work with gusto within his bounds: to perform rituals with unbridled extravagance, explain the apparently inexplicable with scientific largesse—to weave together the realms of materiality and spirituality, science and devotion, moving devotees' faith, hearts, and minds to the "correct place." The area that slips between the cracks, outside the domain of relative control and comprehension, is the goddess's domain. It is not his job to fill this fissure; it is hers. Even those attuned to the fact that she permeates everything, like Aiya, are surprised when they find her here, beyond their grip or understanding. It seems that one can always find more room for faith.

3

Visions and Versions of the Miraculous

One of Aiya's favorite stories relates an event that, existing outside the bounds of scientific explanation, opened for him a world of faith. The incident took place in 1965, when he was a university student studying architecture in Sri Lanka. Over tea and crackers in the little house by the temple, Aiya described himself at the time as torn between deep religious yearning and tenacious skepticism. He attributed his basic distrust of religion, in part, to his political views:

> I had just come out of a circle of people who were ardent theoreticians of Communism. I used to think that Communism was the end to all problems on earth: if there was communal property, communal living, communal work, no distinction between high class, low class, nothing, all problems would be solved. I used to believe that. But pretty soon it seemed good as a theory, but almost impossible to achieve as a practice. So my first guru used to tell me that if you're not a Communist before you are twenty-one, you have no heart. If you're still a Communist after you're twenty-one you have no head. And so I was probably in the transition stage.

The guru to whom Aiya refers is Mataji, someone from whom he had recently received initiation. Although Aiya took every opportunity to sit at Mataji's feet at her ashram, whenever he was on break from college, he constantly argued religious issues with her, to the point of exhaustion. The topic that most bothered Aiya was that of karma and reincarnation. Although he had heard all his life that souls were born into countless bodily forms, he wanted proof. He argued that the concept of karma—that people are rightly rewarded or punished for proper or improper actions in their past lives—was invented merely to keep people in their place. It seemed to him that a belief with such serious implications required supporting evidence.

Aiya laughed as he recalled Mataji's reaction to his relentless demands for proof, "She would always say, 'My God! What a sense of humor Swami [her guru] has! He sends me all these idiots. They're always arguing with me. All this wasting my time.' And I used to say, 'Amma, you can't get away with saying things like that and laying a guilt trip on me, making me think that I'm wasting your time. You know very well that I'm trying to find out the truth.' " Reminding Mataji that most of his schooling was in Christian institutions, Aiya reasoned that if he believed everything people told him, he would have converted to Christianity long ago. Mataji deflected Aiya's demands for proof, telling him that looking into past lives was like digging up old, useless news. Aiya relentlessly persisted, believing she had the capacity to reveal these lives to him. This tug-of-war lasted for many months.

Eventually Mataji succumbed to Aiya's pestering, figuring he needed something to extract him from his rut. Aiya related the sequence of events that followed, laughing at his own expense, at his childlike anticipation and frustration:

> This happened one afternoon after lunch. She was sitting in the easy chair, I was sitting down nearby. She said, "Come! Sit! No sound!" I said [*in a small voice*], "Okay." I was really afraid. So she closed her eyes and went into meditation—maybe forty-five minutes, maybe one hour, maybe one-and-a-half hours. I didn't check my watch and I was too afraid to move or to do anything. She was in deep meditation. She came out. She said, "Come closer to me." Her right thumb went to my forehead and scratched that place. [*He put his thumb between his eyes and then quickly moved it to the top of his forehead.*] Nothing happened. *Nothing* happened. So she said, "I'm going to rest now." Because after about three o'clock or so, three thirty or so, she usually goes and takes a nap for about forty-five minutes.
>
> I did *namaskāram* to her [touching her feet to honor her and receive her blessings]. I asked her, "What should happen?" and she said, "Just be as you are during *japam* [chanting one's mantra] or during meditation session. You will see something." I couldn't *wait*, I was so excited. So I *ran* to the temple, shut the doors, sat inside. [*Aiya mimes frantically doing yogic breathing by blocking one nostril and then the other.*] I'm doing all that and doing *japam*. *Nothing* happened! [*We both laugh.*] I was bloody annoyed! I thought, "My god,

this old lady has pulled the wool over your eyes and like an idiot you're doing this!! What's the matter with you!! Forget it. It's bloody nonsense."

So she came in the evening and I was so irritated inside that I didn't even want to look into her face. No. Because this thought that she was pulling the wool over my eyes was beginning to take hold and I did not *like* that.

For the rest of the afternoon and evening, Aiya was uncharacteristically quiet, stewing in his feelings of anger and betrayal. Mataji did not call attention to his silence. At the end of the day, Aiya trudged back to the small ashram temple to sleep, as usual, on newspapers spread on the floor. Still sorely disappointed, he fell asleep around nine thirty. Aiya described being awakened in the middle of the night by the sound of a harmonium:

And I see Swamiji, that is, Mataji's guru. I'm awake now. That means I'm not dreaming. I'm awake. He's bathed in an eerie light and seated there, covered over with a nice orange robe with a yellow border, smiling. And he's playing the harmonium and he's singing. [*Aiya rubs his eyes then bugs them out.*] And I looked—still there! I said, "What the heck is this?" Then I said, "Maybe I'm dreaming." I did this [*he rubs his eyes again*] and looked. Gone. So, okay, for a total of maybe ten to fifteen seconds it was there. Enough to make a lasting impression, it was there. I saw it. After the first few fleeting seconds, I was wide awake, I know that. I was very convinced that I'd seen a nice beautiful smile on his face.

Now I was wide awake. About two o'clock in the morning. I thought I would get up and sit. I have seen Swamiji come. He's obviously come to bless me and go. I shouldn't waste this time sleeping. Let me do mantra *japam*. Y'know in your vision, when your eyes are closed, you see a haze. That haze became whiter like someone was whitewashing the thing or painting it. Slowly, I saw this eerie looking screenlike thing, with no defined borders or anything. And I saw the temple where I worshiped, how I did *pūjā*, the two daughters, the son, the wife, the village. I could, from every fiber of me, I could tell that every inch of that village was familiar. And I didn't know where the village was.

And then I could see these two girls [as they are now]; they're in their thirties or forties. *Abject* poverty, prostitution, and all that. And I could tell that these two were my children. And I came out of it and I was unbelievably depressed. I could see that sometimes they would have nothing to eat. They would have a plain cup of tea or they would share a cup of tea and they would go to sleep. Because there's no money to do anything. No proper shelter, no proper cloth-

> ing. And here I was eating three meals a day, properly, and here these people were my children and they have nothing? What could I do to help? Couldn't I even . . . I didn't sleep at all that night I was so depressed.
>
> Anyway, around three thirty, four o'clock, I got up as usual and went and had a bath and was getting ready for *pūjā* and saw that Mataji was coming. She turned and looked at me and said, "This is why I told you not to dig up your past!" And she said, "You wanted it, now live with it."

Convinced that two of his grown children from his past life were currently alive and destitute, Aiya described feeling "excruciatingly guilty" for weeks afterward whenever he sat down for a meal. He tried finding out the name of their village from Mataji, but she argued that if God had wanted him to know, He would have supplied the information. She insisted that his children must live out their karma just as he must live out his. In the end, while this experience caused Aiya emotional upheaval it also transformed his faith. He stopped badgering Mataji, to her relief, and became a quieter, more dutiful student.

Three to four days after his temple visions, Aiya experienced yet another unnerving event. It was afternoon at the ashram, and Mataji was once again getting ready for her nap.

> I did a *namaskāram* to her. I got up, and from her hut there are about six or seven steps to go down, so I climbed down and was walking towards the temple. I had to pass this banyan tree on my left. As I was passing this tree I looked at it—and I could see the roots! And I looked up and could see the tree, and I looked down and I could still see the roots! And I could see behind me Mataji's hut and she's standing there like this [*he puts his hands on his hips*] and laughing out loud, "Ha ha ha ha!" So I ran back to her.
>
> And on the way, between that twenty yards going back to her I was thinking, okay, now what is my mother doing? And my mother's eighty miles away. I could see what she's doing. She's lying on one of those easy chairs and she's reading the paper and it's afternoon. I came back inside and I couldn't say anything. I was frightened out of my skull.

Aiya recalls Mataji calming his fears, telling him that his experiences occurred only because he had asked for them. She assured him that the newly opened faculties would mostly dissipate until he was able to maintain them himself. Walking back to the temple the second time, his perception returned to normal.

Miraculous Worldviews

In the context of the Rush temple where ritual powers and effects are often explained through scientific language, miracles, the topic of this chapter, are difficult entities to pin down. If an event is an anticipated by-product of ritual and/or meditative practices, in what way can it still be a miracle? The highly charged adjective, miraculous, is moreover problematic because it is so subjective. For Aiya, the above experience was, at the time, nothing short of miraculous whereas similar, more recent, visions he describes as simply providing welcome confirmation of his beliefs and practices.

In an effort to pin down the unwieldy category "miracle," I expand on William James's classification by identifying two broad, somewhat overlapping, categories.[1] The first category I term "everyday miracles," referring to events that cooperate with the natural, everyday order, understood by believers as part of divine providence. Nonbelievers, on the other hand, view these same events as insignificant or plain good luck. Rush devotees, through their understanding that life contains no accidents, often frame positive life events (and sometimes superficially negative ones), whether having to do with finding a job, a spouse, a parking spot, or the Rush temple, as part of Devī's grand design. Armed with the conviction that the goddess's blessings permeate life's entirety, everyday miracles are an important means for sustaining a reassuring sense of Motherly presence.

The second category and focus of much of this chapter is more elusive, particularly in the context of the Rush temple. This type of miracle, termed here "temple miracle," involves events understood as directly triggered by temple rituals, gurus, or deities. Although temple miracles can include an array of events and experiences, they distinguish themselves from everyday miracles by confounding mainstream understandings of the natural order. Belief in their existence presupposes a view of time, space, and relationships that defy secular configurations. The impact of temple miracles, like everyday miracles, however, ultimately rests in the eyes of the beholder. Although an event can definitively, sometimes radically, challenge and expand a person's understanding of the natural world and of divine activity, the same occurrence might, for another person, have limited impact.

Although temple miracles include a range of experiences only explicable in supernatural terms, some with potentially earth-shattering implications are couched in everyday events. A good example of this is Margaret Case's description of the profound impact made by a large black bee at the Rādhāramaṇa temple in Vrindaban.[2] Landing at the feet of a famous woman devotee at the end of a day-long invocation preceding a Krishna lila performance, the insect mimicked Lord Krishna's visitation to his devotees in the form of a black bee, as described by the *Bhāgavata Purāṇa*. The bee's timely appearance during a major festival created a stir among the crowd, prompting the ashram's guru to arrange the consecration of a shrine the following evening in the same location. Case describes how, during the precise moment of the next night's consecration when an image was required, a black bee flew into the tent and landed next to the place of consecration, opposite the priest. When the bee was transported, with the help of a leaf, onto the platform being consecrated, "it walked directly to the central lotus, and installed itself underneath the flower. There it stayed quietly throughout the rest of the ceremony" (2000: 20). The bee's impeccable sense of timing and direction, combined with the devotees' frame of reference, created a miracle in which the bee became a manifestation of Krishna. In her prologue and epilogue, Case writes that when people asked if she believed the bee was Krishna, she responded, "within the context, yes—and context is everything" (151, see also vii).

Although shared frameworks of meaning play a crucial role in lending temple events their significance, an individual's experiential framework further determines their impact. For some at Rush, Devī's presence is so palpable and anticipated that supernatural events appear somewhat unremarkable. For others, vibrating feet and hands can be profoundly and miraculously perception-altering. People, of course, change over time; events that once seemed extraordinary can become routine. In Aiya's case, his visions prompted by Mataji's touch catapulted him from godless Communist to godfearing disciple. Since then, supernatural visions and events have increasingly become such an expected part of his ritual and everyday life that today he uses the word "miracle" selectively. Only twice in my six years of temple exposure have I heard him specifically label an event as such.

Many North Americans and South Asians alike presume secular constructions of the natural order that resist the possibility of "temple miracles." Milton Singer (1972) interviewed modern industrialists in the south Indian city of Chennai to find out how Indian businessmen reconciled the disjunction between their secular, British-influenced lifestyles and what Max Weber has coined the Hindu "enchanted" worldview.[3] In spite of apparent contradictions between Hindu ritualistic and industrial rationalistic worldviews, Singer found it rare for people to abandon their religious tradition for the sake of secular endeavors, or vice versa. Instead, most businessmen he spoke with compartmentalized their seemingly incompatible worlds; the domestic/ritualistic sphere and the work/rationalistic domain, with their different sets of rules and expectations, remained largely separate and uncontaminated.

Over a decade later, Lawrence Babb explored similar issues in the lives of Indian devotees of Satya Sai Baba, a well-known guru/godman from south India. Although many Sai Baba followers are among the educated elite, similar to the Chennai industrialists, they seem to use a different strategy for accommodating otherwise contradictory worldviews.[4] Babb felt that urban elite Indians, generally speaking, did not live with one foot in an enchanted Hindu world. Instead, like rationalist-minded Euro Protestants, many have "stripped the world of magic, and have done so with impressive thoroughness" (1986: 200). Sai Baba devotees, by contrast, have performed a kind of Weberian reversal, a "re-enchantment" of the world that fills both the secular and the sacred spheres with divine influences. They have, according to Babb, made daily life "a place of wonders to be constantly scrutinized for ever-newer marvels. These are people for whom the miraculous has somehow become part of the very furniture of normal existence" (199).[5]

Although the Rush temple probably has as many strategies as there are individuals for integrating the multivalent miraculous into various North American contexts, there are identifiable trends that reflect the temple's character and theology. Similar to Sai Baba devotees and unlike the Chennai businessmen Singer describes, Rush devotees often speak of their lives as permeated by divine grace and seem to have no need for compartmentalizing secular and sacred frameworks. Yet Babb's description of Sai Baba devotees' "re-enchantment" of the world—requiring a suspension, or minimally a deemphasis, of rationalistic, scientific beliefs—does not apply so clearly to Rush devotees. Rather than simply downplaying science in order to reframe the natural world as miraculous, many Rush devotees—and Aiya most explicitly—reframe the miraculous in order to accommodate the natural world, as well. By perceiving everyday events as supernaturally charged and supernatural power as scientifically explainable, devotees disperse the supernatural into the mundane, and vice versa.

This grand weaving act is not without its snags, its product not entirely seamless. The warp of the tapestry, abidingly consistent and flawless, however, is the sense that the goddess permeates everything in both the natural scientific and supernatural worlds. As such, she helps bind these worlds together. The weaving of the transcendent into the earthly immanent and vice versa is consistent with Śrīvidyā theology and, moreover, so is the fact that the tapestry is not perfect. The remaining irregularities in Śīvidyā are, according to Brooks, "not a problem to be explained away, but rather the key to understanding life's most difficult problems. By taking up the Tantric life, one learns to use, and indeed revel in, the incongruity between esoteric and exoteric realities as part of the divine's playful and deliberate plan for creation" (1992: 186).

At the Rush temple, Sudharshan described to me how this meshing of otherwise incompatible frameworks works for him. Gladly putting aside old views established by his mainline Protestant schooling and his modern, rationalistic upbringing in Sri Lanka, he revels in the noncompartmentalized world supported by the Rush temple:

> Aiya is sort of academically inclined; he's also mystically inclined. Not inclined, he *is* academic; he *is* mystical. He believes in the para-

> normal; he believes in magic; he believes in wonder. He still believes in logic. And growing up [in Sri Lanka], for me at least, it was not taught in my school or in my socialization that this could all exist harmoniously as a whole. I was socialized to believe that these ideologies are compartmentalized and all of them are at odds. You can't be mystical and also scientific at the same time. Classical thinking is not in accordance with passion. Or reason is not in accordance with passion. And that's how I was socialized. But innately I knew they were not in dissonance—they were in total harmony. Even though viscerally I felt that this makes sense, I was socialized to believe that it didn't. And that was why there was a conflict.
>
> And now, at this stage in my life, I'm thirty-four years old and I feel I'm beginning to make it whole again, and that feels good. This place is teaching me to do that. And Aiya and Guruji and my teachers have given me the grace to know it's working, to know that this is what's happening, and to enjoy to process. I mean when it's working it's one thing, but to know it's working is a whole 'nother high trip. So for me it's a great trip.

The difference between a worldview that allows for magic and wonder and one devoid of miracles typically marks the debate between religious and secular-scientific realms. Yet similar disagreements can form intrareligious debates, as well. During the late eighteenth and nineteenth centuries, Hindu reformers responded to British claims that Indian religious practices were idolatrous and superstitious by adopting one side of the debate. They encouraged Indians to abandon ritual and temple worship and focus instead on philosophical teachings from the *Upaniṣads* and the *Bhagavad Gītā*. Ram Mohan Roy, founder of the Brahmo Samāj reform movement in Calcutta in 1828, argued that God, present in all of nature, must be known through reason and observation, not manipulated through ritual. Reformer Dayānanda Sarasvatī, disdainful of what he referred to as religious "superstition," continued the work of his predecessors by founding the Ārya Samāj in Bombay in 1875. Sarasvatī advocated a return to an ancient, Vedic Hinduism that had little concern for temple devotion or for tales about the deities. Sounding much like David Hume, the famous English rationalist who lived over a century earlier, Sarasvatī spent much of his life systematically debunking miraculous worldviews (Davis 1998: 15–16).[6]

Within Christianity, the miracle debate among English-speaking Christians was the issue that drove the greatest wedge between Protestants and Catholics from the time of the Reformation up until the 1850s. Protestants, who tended to limit miracles to biblical times and to divine providence working within, not against, the natural order, rejected as "tom foolery" Catholic claims to contemporary miracles associated with saints, pilgrimage sites, and sacraments. Particularly problematic was the Catholic doctrine of transubstantiation of the Eucharist (Mullin 1996: 12–13). In an effort to distinguish between Protestant and Catholic worldviews, Puritan John Mather in the seventeenth century, sounding much like Hindu reformers of the following two centuries, argued that while Catholics used vain rituals and sacred objects, Protestants used abstract, godly prayer.[7] Whereas the former relied on miracle workers (the priests) and worked against the natural order, the latter relied on God's special providence, performing a seamless integration with the natural order (16).[8] A common, equally parochial, Catholic rejoinder to such accusations was that supernatural miracles in their midst proved they were the One True Church.

By the mid-nineteenth century, the divide became more complicated and the debate less contentious. Catholic miracles, rather than being labeled diabolical, became, in the eyes of Protestant leaders, mere superstition of the "folk." Catholics leaders during this era often viewed the Catholic-Protestant rift as having not to do with right or wrong, true or false, but with a difference in perception and receptivity (Mullin 1996: 115). After World War II, the English-speaking Catholic-Protestant gap caved in almost entirely due to the growth of Protestant Pentecostalism and its fascination with charismatic gifts. Similar themes emerged in the Catholic Charismatic movement beginning in the 1960s. Since then, during the last four decades, the fascination with miracles has only grown. A 1995 *Time* magazine poll states that 69 percent of all Americans believe in miracles (cited ibid.: 260–262).

This current trend is often disconcerting to mainstream Christian theologians, both Protestant and Catholic. Ironically, while many theologians are busy rethinking biblical miracles, medical journals are publishing studies on the effects of prayer on healing. New Age enthusiasts, although typically critical of evangelical religious ideology, often share with conservative Christians their view of the miraculous. Mullin suggests that this trend emerges from a loss of confidence in the scientific model that is "rhetorically connected to an assault upon the Enlightenment. The often-voiced late-twentieth-century attack on the Enlightenment—to which such diverse groups as Postmodernists and Neo-Evangelicals have contributed—has perhaps provided an acceptable atmosphere for raising anew questions regarding miracles and healing" (1996: 264).[9]

With this in mind, it seems that devotees at the Rush temple—and of Sai Baba—are ahead of the curve. What could be construed as old-fashioned, simple-minded "superstition" or a retrieval of an outmoded, old-world perspective may actually, in its current guise, be its opposite. Given this scenario, Rush temple devotees might justifiably maintain that those who do not allow for miracles in their lives are today's spiritual fuddy-duddies.[10]

Gurus and Their Miracles

Miracles emerge at the Rush temple in countless ways. The remainder of this chapter divides them, for simplicity's sake, into two broad categories. The first includes miracles attributed to and experienced by gurus. The second more directly involves particular temple deities. This distinction is by no means watertight, since all miracles are ultimately attributable to divinity, made manifest through her various forms.

While the term "miracle" is fluid, contextual, and subjective, the category "guru miracle" only becomes more unwieldy.[11] Not only do miracles owe much of their existence to the beholder but so also does the authenticity of the guru. The term "guru" most basically refers to someone who teaches and has disciples; many gurus (or so-called gurus) have reputations for performing (or faking) miracles, as well. From the disciple's perspective, a guru is often someone who has reaped the benefits of extensive religious practices along with good karma over many lifetimes, acquiring *siddhis*, or supernatural powers. *Siddhis* typically include—but are not limited to—one, several, or all of the following abilities: reading minds, reading future and past lives, bilocation, levitation, and the manipulation of matter.[12] To the skeptic, a "guru" can merely be an accomplished magician or con artist for whom seemingly miraculous events are sleight-of-hand magic tricks or emotional manipulations. Indian skeptics are not in short supply, and neither are guru charlatans.[13]

The manifestation of materials out of thin air is a practice for which Satya Sai Baba is particularly famous and is one of the many ways gurus or godmen and women regularly demonstrate to followers their access to the supernatural realm. Another method, made famous by Siddha Yoga's Swami Muktananda and his successor, Gurumayi, is *śaktipat*, the descent of a guru's sacred power into an initiate. The Siddha Yoga tradition is unique in its aim to administer *śaktipat* to anyone desiring initiation. In 1970, during Muktananda's world tour, he started performing mass initiations, making *śaktipat*, in his words, "the centerpiece of a worldwide spiritual awakening" thus creating a "meditation revolution" sustained today by Gurumayi (Mueller-Ortega 1997: 112). Accounts of Aiya and Mataji's bestowal of *śaktipat*, reflected in Linda's story in the first chapter and Aiya's at the start of this chapter, demonstrate the more typical tendency for gurus to reserve this power for special cases or for the relentlessly persistent. Although the ability to give *śaktipat* and to read minds and futures may seem miraculous to some devotees, others see it simply as part of a guru's *siddhi*, power expected to arise from intense, prolonged religious dedication.

Since moving the temple from the garage to its current barn location, Aiya has given less energy to his capacity as guru than as a temple priest and ritual specialist. Aiya's current focus tends to be on building a grand temple, to performing and teaching rituals, and to passing on the Śrīvidyā tradition. Nevertheless, he receives a steady stream of phone calls from people, sometimes total strangers, who want him to fill the guru-soothsayer-counselor role, to advise them about their present and future, and to fix what ails them. As a result, Aiya has multiple cell phones that seem to ring constantly. Few face-to-face conversations with Aiya run their natural course without interruption, prompting regular devotees half-jokingly to devise plans to hide or throw his phones far from the temple. Aiya claims he wants to be available to those who need him, but in the mix are plenty who want answers to less pressing questions or quick fixes to intractable problems.[14]

One of the ways Aiya deflects the guru-wonderworker limelight is to extol the powerful capabilities of his own guru, Guruji. I have heard Aiya on a number occasions remark that Guruji, who appears to have accumulated extraordinary *siddhis* through his extensive Śrīvidyā practice, has no need for the elaborate rituals Aiya promotes and performs. Guruji's powers are such, according to Aiya, that "all he has to do is touch you" for your desires to be realized. The only time Aiya asked me to turn off the tape recorder during an interview session was when he described in detail one of the more spectacular feats he witnessed Guruji perform. Guruji himself does not want people to know the extent of his abilities, and Aiya is trying to be a good disciple. Spending most of his time and energy developing programs for women and low-income housing in Andhra Pradesh, south India, Guruji, like Aiya, downplays his role as a guru-wonderworker.

But people, Aiya included, do talk freely about the "lesser" miracles Guruji performs. Barbara, a devotee in her late thirties with wavy graying hair and vivid green eyes told me of such an instance. During the 1999 Gurupūrṇimā in late July, an annual festival for honoring one's guru and guru lineage, Guruji and his wife were in the United States and came to Rush for the festivities. They arrived ceremoniously in a devotee's van, and were greeted by a large group who waited, barefoot, on the parking lot in front of the temple. Barbara was among them: "So I was out here with this whole crowd of people and standing on this pavement, lifting one foot at a time, trying to cool them off because it was terribly hot. And he comes up in the van and gets out, and it feels like the pavement got cold, or like it cooled down and was tolerable. And I turned to the lady next to me and—she said it first, she said, 'Is it my imagination, or did the ground just cool?' I said, 'It's not your imagination, because I was about to ask you.' " Barbara then described how she met Guruji face to face that evening. He had just finished a talk and was handing out CDs of his temple in Andhra Pradesh. Devotees lined up to receive the CD and to receive his blessings by touching his feet.

BARBARA That's the time when my eyes were getting bad, really bad. And my doctor told me he couldn't operate on them. I had had both reti-

Aiya and Amma with Guruji and his wife, garlanded by their students, during the 1999 Gurupūrṇimā. Photo by author.

nas reattached, then slowly got cataracts over the years. And then they accelerated within a six-month period. It just got worse and worse. I went up [to Guruji] and thought, "Somebody who could step on that hot pavement and make it cool has got to have something. Something different." Like I told you before, I just wanted one of those kind of miracle things.

And I touched his feet and felt this kind of energy going through them and I looked up at his face and his eyes were blue. I mean blue, blue like yours are. But I knew they weren't. There was this kind of glow to them. And I said, "Could you heal me?" And he put his thumbs over my eyes. I didn't even tell him what was wrong, he just put his thumbs on my eyelids and said something, I don't know what it was . . . and he touched my head and then he said, "You're cured."

And I thought, "Oh cool." [*Barbara chuckles.*] And he gave me a CD and I almost said, "I don't have a computer" and handed it back to give to someone else, but I still have it. And then I went outside and said, "Hey, I got cured!"

CORINNE And could you see as soon as he'd done that?

BARBARA No, I couldn't. But the thing was, a couple days later I went to see my doctor and he said, "I don't see the uveitis. It's not active. I

> asked if I could have the operation, and he said, "Yes as long as the disease remains inactive." So I told him about the guru. And Dr. Chawla usually laughs at whatever I come up with, but he sat and intently listened.

Barbara explained that after the disease was in remission long enough, she was able to have surgery that completely restored her sight. She owes her ability to see to Guruji's touch.

Although Aiya's promotion of Guruji's power may function somewhat to deflect attention from himself, it also arises from a genuine sense of awe and appreciation. If anyone's life is steeped in the miraculous or, more accurately, in appreciation for the omnipresence of divine power, it is Aiya. Although he occasionally chastises devotees for overcredulity, for reading too much into life's small details, Aiya's overarching conviction is that all the Mother's children, including himself, are lead by her grace to their present situation. Seemingly negative events are, when viewed from the proper perspective, divinely ordained. The fact that Aiya and Amma managed to recover from extreme financial difficulties after moving to the United States, for instance, verifies for him that the Mother will always provide. Amma, the practical one of the pair, does not embrace Aiya's ideology of divine surrender with the same enthusiasm. Although she fully supports and participates in the ritual life of the temple, she, unlike Aiya, worries about making ends meet.

A "miracle" story illustrating the clashing of Aiya and Amma's worldviews involves a sequel to Aiya's past-life vision described at the beginning of the chapter. It took place in 1981 soon after Aiya, Amma, and their young daughter, Sarumathi, arrived in North America. They were, at the time, living temporarily with Amma's sister and her family in Sodus, New York, where their bedroom doubled as a shrine room: "My wife and I were sleeping in the middle of the night. I woke up and I was doing *japam*, with beads. I was doing a repetition of the mantra and I suddenly saw, like a television in front of me, a screenlike thing, and I saw a funeral procession. I saw a fifty-five-year-old woman being carried to the ghats to be burned. And her right leg was smaller and I knew that that was my daughter. Immediately." Aiya explained that his elder daughter from his previous life had suffered from polio. She was, he surmised, in her late teens when Aiya, in his previous life, died around the age of forty. He had another daughter in her early teens when he died, and a young son who died within the year. He had been a poor temple priest, and his family had to vacate the temple after his death since they had no means of support. An old shopkeeper took the girls in, but they were forced to become prostitutes to earn their keep. Aiya continued with the scenario as it played out that night in 1981: "So I woke my wife up. . . . No I didn't wake my wife up. I sat there crying. And she was sleeping next to me and she woke up. She asked [*Aiya whispers with great concern in his voice*], 'What happened? What is this? Why are you crying?' She thought I was sobbing because I didn't have a job at that time or anything like that [*Aiya bursts out laughing*]." While Amma began to comfort Aiya, attempting to allay the fears she projected onto him, he explained to her a very different kind of grief, having to do with dire poverty and desperation beyond their imagining and beyond their present family configuration. Aiya believes Amma and he have been together as husband and wife for six lifetimes; his late-night experience and conversation thus engaged for them a sense of "extended family." The vision of his daughter was not particularly miraculous for Aiya at that point in his life. It simply validated his already expanded sense of time, space, and relationships—a sensibility at odds with secular understandings. So also did it confirm his relationship with a goddess who allows him to see beyond the immediately apparent.

Another series of visions that extend conventional constructions of time, space, and relationships occurred to Aiya in his Park Circle home during the days when the temple was in his garage. I heard about these supernatural visitations during my first winter at the temple, when a group of us were eating lunch outside the temple kitchen area. During a lull in our conversation, Amrit, the woman who brings flowers to the temple, asked Aiya, "Does that woman still come? Do you still get visions of her?" Aiya answered, "Yes," and explained to the rest of us that a Native American woman regularly appeared to him at Park Circle when he was doing *pūjā* there. "She'd stand there right next to the Devī with a very kind, motherly look on her face." Judging from the clothing she wore, Aiya figured she was Native American. Wanting to get information about her tribe, he called a museum in Rochester where a curator told him to talk to Sheldon Fisher, a local authority and advocate for Native American causes.

Aiya spoke with Fisher on the phone and asked about the tribes who lived in what is now his neighborhood. Fisher named a number of tribes, though he felt the most likely was Iroquois. When Aiya questioned him about burial sites, Fisher asked why he wanted to know. Aiya responded, "Promise you won't laugh at me?" The man assured him, as Aiya put it, that he had been laughed at so many times while advocating for Native Americans that he need not worry. So Aiya described the old woman he saw, her clothing, and, at Fisher's request, the beadwork she wore. Fisher identified her as an Iroquois medicine woman. Aiya explained to the group of us eating lunch that he knew she was buried right below where they installed the Devī in his garage. She had, according to tradition, been rolled in mud and dried and then stood straight up below the ground.

After Aiya finished describing the burial procedure, I wanted to return to the subject of Sheldon Fisher. I asked how he responded to Aiya, expecting to hear reports of his astonishment or perhaps, more dramatically, that he began attending *pūjā* at his garage temple. Aiya simply recalled that they both agreed

Aiya should not do anything with the body. Just let her be. I then wondered if the woman in his visions had any messages for him, thinking perhaps this would be a good opportunity to promote the universal value of all religions, one of Aiya's favorite themes. Aiya said, no, she never said anything. She just seemed very happy, very content. Maybe, he surmised, she liked what she saw.

I guess I was a little disappointed that Aiya did not include an overt "moral" to his vision account. I was ready to hear a larger message, that the miracle increased someone's faith or explicitly validated Aiya's work. Instead, the vision stands on its own, subtly commenting on the fact that the goddess was installed on sacred land and that a holy woman from earlier times is pleased with the connection. Although the visions Aiya describes usually portray expanded notions of time, space, and relationships, not all accounts are meant to embellish or broadcast profundity. Particularly for those whose ideas of time and space already extend beyond conventional parameters, some "miracles" speak in measured, softer tones.

Deity Miracles

Other miracles, however, announce volumes. The two instances labeled explicitly by Aiya as "miracles" since the building of the temple, of which I am aware, were brimming with significance for him and for the Rush community. In both instances the miracle's larger meaning had to do with divine validation of the temple itself, and in both instances Aiya experienced the event secondhand. I begin this section with the first of the two miracles, that of the little girl on a bike.

The little-girl-on-a-bike episode occurred on a Wednesday evening, mid-March, in 1999. I arrived for morning *pūjā* the week after it happened. When *pūjā* was over, Aiya, bursting with enthusiasm, clapped his hands together and announced to me, "Amma! There's been a major miracle! Wait till you hear!" All anticipation, I stood by while Dipi gave him a message about a phone call that Aiya quickly returned. Once he hung up he proceeded with the story, reveling in its details, building to the end. He began by describing his usual evening routine in which he picks Amma up from work and the two of them return to their home, where she fixes him a cup of tea. Afterward, they drive to the temple. That Wednesday evening, as they neared the temple, Aiya noticed a green Dodge Caravan a number of yards ahead of them, with three Euro American adults in it. It turned left at the stoplight, as did Aiya. He then saw it slowly approach and then enter the temple driveway. As Aiya and Amma turned into the driveway, they saw the van stop at an angle in the parking lot and then drive back out again, passing them on the way. He and Amma figured they had made a wrong turn and simply needed to turn around. Amma and Aiya performed the usual nightly *pūjā* and afterward headed home.

Thursday morning, as Aiya was back on the road to the temple, he stopped just opposite the driveway, his left blinker on, waiting for a clump of morning traffic to clear. As he sat waiting he saw, once again, the green Dodge Caravan heading his direction, this time with one middle-aged gentleman inside. He turned into the temple, and Aiya followed. Once in the parking lot, the man got out of the van, approached Aiya, and asked if he had a little girl. Not one for giving straight answers, Aiya said he did have a little girl, but if the man saw her he wouldn't think she was little at all. To him, however, she would always be his little girl. The man asked who lived in the house and Aiya said that he occupied it off and on during the days and evenings. The man then told Aiya that the previous night—it was around seven and almost completely dark—he and two family members saw a little girl who appeared to be from India riding her bike on the side of the road. When they saw her turn into the driveway they wanted to warn her parents that, as Aiya put it, "this is a beautiful village and everything, but it isn't perfectly safe. They should be a bit more careful about having her out at that hour." The man explained that by the time they drove down the driveway they lost sight of her and figured she had entered the house.

Aiya explained that, at this point, his heart was pounding and his mind was racing. He knew there were no Indian families living anywhere nearby and he also knew whom this man had seen. He felt he could not tell him who She was, as he would have no way of understanding. Instead, he thanked him for his concern and they said goodbye. As Aiya put it, "As soon as the guy drove off, I marched straight into the temple and yelled at Her! 'How dare you show yourself to this American and not to me!!!' " After we had a good laugh at his expense, I asked Aiya if the man had any idea how his story had affected him. He said, still laughing, that he tried to keep his shock to himself, but he may have noticed his eyes bugging out as he told his story.

On the basis of accounts from temples in India as well as stories from various devotees at Rush, I was aware that a common type of miracle at Indian goddess temples is that She appears as a little girl to bless those with eyes of faith. Aiya's consternation over this particular sighting of the little girl on the bike, who he was certain was the goddess, is twofold. One, she showed herself to people who were totally unaware of her existence and two, it seems she blocked two of her most ardent devotees from view. Although they were driving only about forty yards behind the green van, neither he nor his wife saw any little girl riding a bike. Furthermore, Aiya had recently been hearing that some neighbor girls occasionally saw a little Indian girl playing on the temple property when no one else was around. Before this incident he figured they were imagining things, but now he considered that perhaps Devī was appearing to them as well.

Once the story had spun to its conclusion, we walked from the temple to the little house where Dipi, on spring break from college, Aiya, and I spent the remainder of the morning analyzing the event. Aiya sat holding a huge box of Saltine crackers into which he regularly dipped, ate a few, and briskly brushed the crumbs from his hands. In the midst of our speculations, I wanted to know more about the little-girl-as-goddess phenomena. Knowing that age plays a role in the Rush goddess tradition, I rattled off the chronology of the Great Goddess of Śrīvidyā, Tripurasundarī, who comes in three forms: Lalitā is sixteen, Kāmākṣī is twenty, and Rājarājeśwarī, installed at Rush in *mūrti* form, is twenty-eight.[15] I asked Aiya why he thought sightings of the goddess at this temple and at others are in the form of a much younger girl.

> AIYA Now. There is a little nine-year-old girl. She's running around. She's kind of cute. So I say [*whispering*], "C'mere, c'mere, c'mere," and she comes. And you want to touch her and you say [*whispering*], "What is your name?" Now, you're just asking the question so you can enjoy her company. Can you do that to a twenty-eight-year-old woman? She'll whack you!! [*We all laugh.*] Can you say [*Aiya squinches up his face*], "C'mere, c'mere"? She would say "No!!" and reply in kind. So . . .

> DIPI When you talk about, okay, Rājarājeśwarī as Mother. Are you supposed to see Kāmākṣī or Lalitā more as your wife?

> AIYA They're all the same forms of the Mother, you have to recognize that. She is just coming down and playing around just to show that She is present.

Divine *līlā*, or play, is a pervasive theme in Hindu traditions, used to explain the behavior of the gods, particularly when a deity's antics are beyond human understanding. Aiya refers to the goddess's playfulness partly in response to her confusing jumble of forms. In the context of the temple miracle, where she appears as a little girl to the threesome in the van, *līlā* takes on added appropriateness. *Līlā* not only helps explain why the goddess would bother showing herself to outsiders, but her childlike form, riding a bike no less, drives the point home. As Aiya explains it, the goddess's playfulness is also part of her strategy for being accessible to the earthly realm. Not only does she make herself visible to humanity but she also does so as a little girl, a form infinitely more approachable than that of a young woman. Although she typically only shows herself to a chosen few as a reward for their devotion, her appearance in this instance—forever a puzzle in some ways—seems designed to increase the faith of those who did not see her. Believing this to be the case, Aiya recognizes that faith can only grow if the news gets out, and considers the fact that the goddess could not have chosen a better publicist:

> AIYA They say there are several forms of communication. Telecommunication, television, right? There is telephone, and then there is tele-Haran. [*Aiya laughs.*] You tell something to him and then everybody will know.

[*After a few seconds' delay Dipi and Corinne get it and laugh. Haran is Aiya's given name.*]

CORINNE So *that* was what She was using.

AIYA So that was what She was doing. She was using this. And She knows I am an O.M.I., so . . . [*Aiya waits for us to catch the bait.*]

CORINNE [*Catches it.*] O.M.I. What's that?

AIYA Opened mouth idiot. [*We all laugh.*]

Still pondering the fact that the goddess showed herself to outsiders, Dipi suggests to Aiya that an outsider's perspective is in some ways more credible than an insider's:

DIPI It kind of makes sense that an outsider saw Her. Because what if you saw Her, right? And you told everyone. And then everyone would say, "Well, he's a priest . . ."

AIYA Yeah, "He's probably imagining this . . ."

DIPI Right. And if an outsider sees it, it might be a little more convincing to other people. Like you said, it builds their faith that way.

AIYA But then a counterpoint is also there. Okay, fine. She shows herself to a stranger. Why didn't those strangers come on a Saturday afternoon when the temple was crowded, and ask us their questions?

CORINNE [*Chuckling*] Into a microphone.

AIYA "Who's little girl is this? Are you guys crazy?! Why the hell do you let her ride out on the bicycle alone on the streets at night? This is wintertime!"

Reflecting on the fact that the miracle is not foolproof to skeptics, Aiya added that although miracles are often meant to increase faith, there is almost always space for doubt that must be filled in by faith. The miracle is dependent not just on a shared frame of reference that understands that the goddess can appear as a little girl but also on individual faith that we bring to the event.

Three months after the little-girl-on-the-bike incident, a group of five of us sat in the hall outside the temple kitchen. Jean, new to the Rush temple, had not yet heard the story, and Aiya asked me to tell it to her. After I finished, Aiya, on a roll, started relating more little-girl anecdotes. The following took place during a trip he had recently made to southern California to perform his friend's son's engagement ceremony. On the days subsequent to the event, he performed *pūjā*s at all of his friend's sisters' homes. During the final sister's *pūjā*, while chanting the *Lalitāsahasranāmam*, "The Thousand Names of the Goddess Lalitā," one of the most important devotional chants within the Śrīvidyā tradition, a little girl made an appearance that was both routine and surprising, depending on the seer:

AIYA And while I was doing the *pūjā* and was chanting the thousand names, I saw a little girl in a yellow skirt with a green border seated on my lap. Right? And playing with flowers. This happens to me very often when I get into a particular state—I see Her.

CORINNE Is She always wearing the same thing?

AIYA No. Different colors. But, y'know, you don't go and tell everybody, "Aha!"

CORINNE "There she is!!"

AIYA [*Making moronic sounds, giggling, and pointing to his lap*] "Look! Look!" They would think, "He's gone!" They already think I'm nuts anyway. Half of them think I'm nuts anyway.

Anyway. After the *pūjā* was over, the sister who invited me to do the *pūjā*, she was here [*pointing to his left side*], right here next to me. And this [sister of hers] saw Her get up and walk to her. One second She was there and the other second She turned around and [*Aiya claps*] She was gone. But the same dress—yellow dress with a green border.

CORINNE How did this come out?

AIYA At the end of the *pūjā*, they asked me to tell this story about the little girl. The lady of the house asked me to tell the story. So I was telling the story when she [her sister] saw Her. See, all of them were still seated. I was telling the story when she saw Her. To me, She was still seated on my lap but she had seen Her get up and come near her sister and go away.

CORINNE So at the same time you see Her seated, she sees Her do something else?

AIYA Mmm hmm. Same clothes though. Green border, yellow skirt. And as soon as I finished, y'know from the corner of my eye, I can see her moving and getting excited and once I finished the story she said, "Haran, I saw Her. I saw Her, I saw the little girl now!"

Amazing. This happened in California.

Aiya's main motivation for telling this kind of story, aside from providing entertainment, is to increase the faith of the listener. When I first met Aiya, I asked if there were any aspects of North American religions that he consciously blended into his practices, and he identified the Christian testimonial, a personal story geared to empower and increase the faith of the listener. Tales from his own past, a regular part of his repertoire, indeed tend to reflect the theme of growing faith, particularly his own. Many of the "testimonials" Aiya relates about miraculous events, however, involve other people's experiences. This seems to reflect his concern that others might assume he is religiously extreme, gullible or, as he joked in the above account, psychologically "gone." Accounts of other, less extreme, people's supernatural experiences give the temple extra validity and further increase the faith of the listener. This strategy is effective for the most part, yet there are exceptions.

The little-girl-on-the-bike incident had a tremendous impact on nearly all temple devotees. People were abuzz with the story for weeks, even months, afterward. During this time I had a series of interesting exchanges with Aparna, a Euro American devotee in her mid-thirties with whom I regularly exchange e-mail. An ardent disciple of Aiya's, Aparna has had decades of experience with Hindu traditions, with gurus, and consequently has her own history of encounters with the "miraculous." Because of this, events that seem earth-shattering to others tend to be commonplace for Aparna. Although aware of this, I did not anticipate her response to the excitement generated by the little girl on the bike. In an e-mail she sent soon after the event, Aparna expressed her confusion over the prevalent interpretation the sighting. She did not agree that the Mother appeared in order to strengthen the faith of those who did not see her. She felt the three Americans in the van were not pawns in a larger game meant to increase devotees' faith, but were led to the temple for their own reasons. In any case, Aparna felt she had had enough experiences of her own, had heard enough of Aiya's, that she was having difficulty understanding peoples' strong reactions to this secondhand account. As she put it, "I believe in miracles, and I believe this incident is true. I just don't get why it is so significant."

After our e-mail exchange and subsequent related conversations, I decided that very little surprises Aparna. Her faith is such that she is hard-pressed to label anything explicitly a miracle, at least the kind that would make her faith stronger. I was therefore quite interested in an anecdote Aparna told me one summer morning when we met at a restaurant in California while we were both visiting our families. This was the summer I started writing about the temple, and Aparna was interested in hearing how I would organize things. When I explained how the first part was going to be tricky, how miracles and ritual power so fundamental to the temple are difficult to present in an academic work, she perked up, her brown eyes gleaming, and said, "I have a miracle story!"

The event took place during the 2001 *pratiṣṭhā* festival in late spring. Aparna was seated in the festival tent by the *homam* fire, sitting in one of eight small groups offering *tarpaṇam* to (pouring milk over) one of eight Ganeś *mūrtis* stationed around the fire. When the *homam* was over, devotees rounded the fire, as usual, offering worship to the flames. As Aparna made her way around the fire, Vijitha motioned to her from across the tent and whispered, "Aparna, come here! Ganeś is drinking milk!" Aparna nodded at her, not wanting to be distracted during her final act of worship. Vijitha persisted, saying, "Come *on* Aparna, he's drinking milk!" Aparna went over to sit next to Vijitha and watched as devotees excitedly placed spoons full of milk under Ganeś's tusk, watching as the milk slowly disappeared. She could not believe her eyes at first—he actually *was* taking in the milk. Aparna watched the miraculous offerings about ten to fifteen times before trying it herself. When she later told other devotees about her experience, she learned that several of the Ganeś *mūrtis* who received *tarpaṇam* that day were drinking milk. Aiya was also aware of the various instances, and asked Aparna and the others not to tell too many people. As he put it, "I wouldn't want to do that to Ganeś."

When I reminded Aparna of her reaction to the little girl on the bike several years earlier, she remembered and laughed. She admitted that this experience with Ganeś, unlike secondhand visions of the Devī—which she nonetheless believed wholeheartedly—took her completely by surprise. Although she mostly anticipated Devī's sometimes sudden presence around the temple, her experience of Ganeś physically consuming something before her eyes was startling. This more concrete miracle, involving the transformation of a physical substance, was, for her, tangible evidence that divinity can flow through our reality. She had to admit that the world itself was different from what she had earlier believed. Also dramatically distinguishing these two miracle events is the fact that Aiya did not feel Ganeś's milk drinking, unlike a little girl riding

Granite temple Ganeś dressed in festival finery. Photo by Pathmanathan.

a bike, was an appropriate opportunity for increasing the faith of the masses. His response to Aparna presupposes that Ganeś enjoyed blessing and receiving heartfelt offerings from a few slightly stunned devotees. Staging a sideshow was not Aiya's, or Ganeś's, intention.

As I discuss in detail in Part II, the group of people whose horizons of faith Aiya seems most interested in expanding are the religious elite, orthodox Hindus whose beliefs are challenged by the Rush temple's unconventional practices. In most cases, Aiya hopes to broaden this type of mindset through the power of reason or the strength of the temple's elaborate rituals. On some occasions, however, it seems the deities themselves help argue his case. Aiya related one such incident, prompted by Mohan, who enjoys hearing this story. The event took place in Miami, where Aiya was invited to perform a home *pūjā* for two brahman devotees. The couple invited some of their friends, many who were very traditional and apparently skeptical of Aiya's nonbrahmanical status. Mimicking, in exaggerated style, their sidelong, suspicious looks, Aiya described himself as an oddity among them, dressed and acting like a ritual specialist *pūjāri* yet without the requisite sacred thread across his left shoulder to mark his upper-caste status.

After *pūjā*, as is his custom, Aiya offered a short discourse to what he felt was a half-attentive audience. The topic was Dattātreya, the god with the faces of Viṣṇu, Śiva, and Brahmā, considered to be founder of his guru lineage. He explained to the group that Dattātreya is often depicted surrounded by four dogs representing the four Vedas that are, like dogs, perpetually loyal and true. On a lighter note, Aiya added that, after all, D-O-G backwards spells God. At that moment, a strange dog meandered into the shrine room and proceeded to lick the food offerings in front of the deities to whom Aiya had just performed *pūjā*. When finished, the dog wandered out of the room, never to be seen again. Laughing, Mohan interjected, "Right on cue!" and the rest of us in the room laughed with him. Believing the canine visit was not a coincidence, the *pūjā* participants suddenly became serious and attentive. As Aiya put it, "They stopped their chattering and really sat up to listen." He surmised that the disdainful among them had perhaps begun to suspect that the production of viable rituals and their attendant miracles could extend beyond their own, elite, domain.

A final miracle account again involves a challenge to a group of religious elite. This incident also offers a means for increasing the Rush community's faith, validating not only the presence of the Mother in their midst but also the unusual style in which their temple is run. It is the second of the two events that Aiya, in my presence, expressly and enthusiastically labeled a "miracle."

During the summer of 2002, I attended an afternoon *pūjā*, accompanied by my friend Harvey from Syracuse. Abhi, Amma's niece, home from college for the summer, performed the ritual while Ammamma chanted in the background. I had not seen much of Aiya that day; he had been meeting with community members and contractors regarding the soon-to-be-built temple extension. About three-quarters of the way through the ritual, Aiya arrived, cranked up the piped-in music, and added his own impressive voice to the chanting. I felt satisfied that Harvey, a musician, could now enjoy the *pūjā* even more fully. After the ritual was over, Aiya warmly welcomed Harvey and then turned to me. Clapping his hands together, he quietly announced, "Amma, there's been a little miracle."

Early that morning Aiya found someone waiting to chat with him on the temple's internet chat line. It was a Smārta brahman, a Śrīvidyā initiate from the Ujjain region, writing from his workplace in north India. He described himself as part of a group of around twenty Smārta Śrīvidyā *upāsakas* who gathered regularly to study scripture. They were studying the Sanskrit hymn *Lalitāsahasranāmam*, "The Thousand Names of Lalitā," and a few days earlier they had been discussing one of the hymn's names for the goddess, *Suvāsinī Ārcana Prīta*. Taken separately, the three words roughly mean "married woman," "worship," and "pleased." Most of the group agreed that, when combined, the words meant, "She who is pleased by the worship of a married woman," reflecting a ritual where temple priests give offerings to a married woman as a form of the Devī. The elder of the group, however, challenged them to consider a different interpretation: "She who is pleased by married women who worship." Although most of the men felt this was incorrect since it was not their custom, a bit of a debate ensued.

The next night, four of the group members had a dream, exactly the same dream, in which Devī appeared to them like a mother figure. She led two devotee-children by the hand, one of whom was the dreamer himself. She brought them to a place where they read a sign marked, "Sri Vidya Temple Society," and together they walked down a narrow road and into a temple. Inside, rows of women were standing and doing *pūjā* to the Devī. The goddess then announced to her companions, "You have kept me locked up in your shrine rooms. Here I am free to roam among the people." When they asked her where the temple was, she said in Sanskrit, *Krauṁca Dwīpam*. Because they were surrounded by gold *mūrtis*, the dreamers figured the temple must exist on another plane.

When the group reconvened, four of them discovered they had had the same dream. *Krauṁca Dwīpam*, they learned from the elder, is Sanskrit for the North American continent. Wanting to know if the temple actually existed, one of the men who had the dream decided to check the Web while he was at work. Using a search engine, he typed in "Lalita" and found nothing. "Rajarajeshwari" also brought up nothing. When he tried "Srividya," the Rush temple appeared on his screen. He could see from the Web site that it looked like the golden temple in his dream. Once he found Aiya on the chat line, he asked, for verification, if women performed rituals at the temple. When Aiya affirmed this, the man told him about the dream. Aiya, understandably floored and interested in what the Ujjain group planned to do next, asked if they would start letting women perform rituals. The man, according to Aiya, waffled by saying that it is probably easier for people to get away with such things in the United States.

Aiya did not make much of this response from the Smārta brahman—he is used to people disagreeing with his style. The only true validation he feels he needs at this point in his career is from the Mother, and this "little miracle" was just that. That evening a temple member brought Amma from work to Rush, so Aiya's first chance to tell her about his morning e-mail exchange was while she was in the kitchen, cooking. She stopped chopping vegetables, put down her knife, and leaned against the counter while Aiya related the story to her in Tamil. A smile spread over her face as he animatedly described the sequence of events. A few other Tamil speakers gathered around to hear, as well. By describing how divinity trespasses human dreams, how dream realities meld with waking realities, and—Aiya's favorite theme—how unconventional Rush practices impinge upon orthodox sensibilities, this miracle story, like others, challenges and expands established boundaries. The point of telling this and other miracle stories—aside from the fact that they are simply good stories to tell—is to expand, as well, the faith of those who hear it. TeleHaran, O.M.I., was at it once again.

PART II

The Work of a Guru

Bridge Building and Boundary Breaking

4

Maverick Guru with a Cause

Amid Aiya's seemingly endless repertoire of stories, the one I have heard more than any other, told slightly differently depending on the occasion and the audience, is his initial conversion account, involving a vision of the goddess herself.[1] It represents the dramatic moment in which Aiya is transformed from relatively aimless renegade to religiously adept renegade. For our purposes, it also offers an appropriate introduction to this section's discussion of the joys and challenges of selectively breaking with yet adhering to religious convention. The life-challenging and -changing event related below, incidentally, is what prompted Aiya to seek out Mataji as his guru, leading to further life-altering experiences at her ashram, recounted at the beginning of the last chapter.[2]

In 1964, when Aiya was twenty years old, he was, as he describes it, an arrogant, rambunctious young man who sang in nightclubs. His mother worried about him, his choice of music, and his choice of friends. When she challenged him on his preference for singing film songs rather than devotional hymns, he would tout his Marxist philosophy, insisting she first bring God to sit in front of him so he could get answers about the world's injustices. Then he would sing His praises.

During a period when the glamor of singing at nightclubs was beginning to wear thin, Aiya, then an associate editor for the school magazine *Young Idea,* started composing poetry. One evening he rode his bike to a nearby village called Araly in search of a quiet spot to write. He found a secluded paddy field about a quarter of a mile from an old Devī temple and quickly lost himself in his composi-

Śiva Nāṭarāja with photo of Aiya's first guru, Mataji. Photo by author.

tions. As dusk descended, he happened to look up from his notepad in the direction of the temple and saw a small group of people inside, preparing for an evening festival. From where he sat, he could also see the *mūrti* of the goddess, tall as a full-grown woman, standing in all her festival finery.

Without thinking, Aiya walked his bike over to the temple and entered. As a matter of childhood reflex, he started walking clockwise around the sanctum in the temple's inner courtyard. As he reached the back of the sanctum it suddenly struck him that this temple had a reputation for being powerful and dangerous; rumor had it that young people between the ages of seventeen and twenty-four never set foot in it after dusk. Suddenly bursting with fear, he scrambled toward the main entrance, surprised to find an untouchable woman with a basket on her head standing near the ceremonial flagstaff. She asked him in colloquial Tamil, "Why are you afraid and where are you running?" Still intent upon getting out of the temple, Aiya managed to mumble a quick nonsensical response and flee.

As he reached his bicycle parked a few yards from the temple, he saw the temple *pūjāri* walking toward him from across the road, holding a tray of *prasādam*. Aiya hurriedly told him about his unusual encounter in the temple to which the priest responded with surprise, "You have seen Her too?" He then nudged Aiya and said, "Come, let's go in and see." Inside the temple the woman was nowhere to be found. Left where she had been standing, however, were two flat mounds of sacred ash (*vibhuti*) in the shape of footprints. As the priest carefully covered the spot with his shawl, meaning to keep the ash for himself and his temple, Aiya pleaded for some of the *vibhuti* to take home, reasoning that he was the one who saw her, after all. When the priest finally relented, Aiya claimed the left footprint. The priest swept the ash onto a piece of paper, folded it up, and inserted it into Aiya's shirt pocket.

During his bike ride home, Aiya felt himself being transformed, distanced from the person he was before the vision. Once home, he recounted the story to his mother and, overcome by his tremendous love for her yet not wanting to make a spectacle, he went to his room, layed on his bed, and let his tears flow. Once he calmed down, he took a bath, applied some of the *vibhuti* ash to his forehead, and went to the family shrine room to pray, sing, and cry some more.

After that, Aiya spent most of his spare time in the family's *pūjā* room meditating and loudly singing devotional songs. Because this was an interim period in his life, while he was waiting to hear the results of his college entrance exams, Aiya had plenty of time to dive fully into a new mode of being. He promptly stopped singing in nightclubs, he no longer joined his friends to play cricket, and he quickly gained a reputation for devotional singing at nearby temples. This one-hundred-and-eighty-degree shift in behavior understandably alarmed his mother. She worried that, at this rate, her son would soon become a *sannyāsi* renunciate, lost forever to ascetic wanderings. When Aiya did not heed her pleas to lighten up on his devotions, she wrote to his oldest sister and brother, who had moved away, and asked them to come talk sense into their brother. When they arrived with their litany of concerns, Aiya managed to stand his ground. He argued that all his life the family had preached the importance of devotion and godly behavior. Now that he was following their advice, how could they ask him to stop? In an unprecedented challenge to family authority, he threatened to leave if they forced him to change.

When his mother nonetheless continued to fret about his devotional excesses, Aiya decided the only way to stop her pestering would be to obtain *mantra dīkṣā*, or initiation, from a guru. He would thus be bound to continue his practice and, he figured, his mother would have to leave him alone. After a brief search, he learned about Mataji from one of her disciples, a boarder at his mother's house (who, years later, became Aiya's wife). Soon afterward, Aiya made the four-hour bus journey to Mataji's ashram and received *dīkṣā*. He in turn, as we know, became the troublesome disciple with endless questions. When Aiya broke the news to his mother that he had taken *dīkṣā* from a guru and therefore could not let up on his worship, she was so upset she stopped speaking to him for several days. For some time afterward, she tried her best to keep his devotion from getting out of hand, such as keeping the *pūjā* room key under her pillow at night. Over time, however, she came to appreciate the depth of her son's devotion, even defending him from the criticism of his older siblings.

Aiya often tells one of several variations of this story to first-time visitors at the temple. As such, it functions as a testimonial to one of the ways the Mother has propelled him on his religious path and eventually the temple into existence. Aside from the overarching theme of conversion, this story features a number of other issues foundational to Aiya's religious progress and character. Family disapproval, for instance, is only the beginning of a long line of human obstacles and misunderstandings Aiya has had to confront once on the religious track. The fact that he had to plead with the priest for some ash left by the apparition, something to which he felt entitled not through birthright but through experience, reflects a resonant theme in these future struggles. His early Marxist views, although fairly swept away once he was firmly ensconced as Mataji's disciple, remain influential, albeit in a different form. His early focus on economic justice and equality shifts toward the concern—strengthened with each obstacle he encounters—that ritual practice and divinity be fully accessible to everyone without discrimination.

Finally, the particular manifestation of the goddess who catapulted Aiya into the religious realm and into a new self happened to be a woman from the scheduled classes, an "untouchable" who would have been, in those days, barred from the temple premises. An untouchable divinity whose startling temple presence represents a type of divine transgression offers benediction for Aiya's subsequent transgressive and startling road to temple priesthood.

A Very Brief Spiritual Biography: Obstacles and Openings

Aiya is quick to tell anyone who will listen that the single most important force in his life has been his mother. Perched inside the temple shrine dedicated to Dattātreya, the god considered to be head guru of Aiya's lineage, is his mother's framed black-and-white photo. Her presence in this shrine signifies not only her role as mother but as spiritual teacher or guru for Aiya. Aiya commonly asserts that a nurturing, motherly divinity makes perfect sense to him because of his own mother's constant and unconditional love for her children. Aiya's father, who worked as a railway engineer, died when Aiya was twelve, giving his mother's role added importance.

According to Aiya, his mother strictly enforced her children's religious observances for as long as she was able. An unbending rule, as he describes it, was that all her children pray with her in the family's shrine room at six every evening—or else: "And you had to sing *Tēvāram* or a hymn or something like that.[3] If you came out of the shrine room without *vibhuti* smeared on your forehead, Mom would whack you. She'd say, 'What is this??!!' So you had to do it. There was no question. At that time, she was trying to instill discipline. Y'know, that habit-forming discipline."

As a young boy, Aiya would dutifully accompany his mother on her visits to the local temple, although he admits his primary attraction was not to the resident deity but to the sweet *prasādam* distributed by the priests. Furthermore, even as a little boy he nagged his mother about the aspects of temple worship he considered bothersome. Aiya described his boyhood skepticism to Anusha and Ravi, Sri Lankan-American siblings on spring break from graduate school, and me as we sat in the small temple house eating lunch:

> The temple was just about fifty yards from my house, from where I was born. And [my mother] would hold me by the hand and take me to the temple. And I used to go and walk around with her and do all the things she was doing, y'know like children do. And then I would ask her, "Amma, why is there a priest inside there?" Because, y'know how the Hindu temples are over there, you are perhaps twenty-five, thirty yards away from the sanctum. You can't go anywhere near [the deity]. So I used to say, "You always tell me that God is everywhere. Do you mean to tell me that He won't listen to me if I say things to Him? Why does he [the *pūjāri*] have to be there?"
>
> And Amma used to, in the old tradition, do *arcana*s in the temple. And she would tell the priest what he should pray. [*Aiya makes a confused kidlike face.*] "Why is she telling him? Why can't she tell God straight?" So I used to ask this kind of thing. And she used to tell me, "This is the way it has been done for thousands of years." And I would say, "That's not right. If you say that God is everywhere and knows everything, that means He must know what I am thinking. Why do I need somebody else to interpret? Does God speak a different language?"

Although Aiya may have besieged his mother with questions when he was little, he did not protest his trips to the temple until he was a teenager. Aiya continues: "At that [earlier] time I took things for granted. Whatever my Mum told me was like God's word. She was such a nice woman. Anyway, by the time I reached thirteen, fourteen years old I lost interest in all these . . . all that nonsense. I was more interested in cricket and the things going on around me. Every time she would pray I would tell her, 'Bring God here. Let me ask Him a few questions!' [*Aiya laughs.*] But I guess the training, once it has been given to you, basic as it was with my Mum, it never dies."

Aiya had no direct exposure to the Śrīvidyā tradition while growing up, yet he learned when he was ten years old that it had been in his family for generations, let go by his father's father after the loss of his daughter. Aiya described the scenario one August afternoon to Yegnarathnam and Raghu, father and son brahman Śrīvidyā *upāsakas* visiting from Chennai. These two men, Aiya, Vijitha, and I sat in a circle in the hallway outside the temple kitchen while Aiya explained how his aunt's death from double pneumonia triggered further losses:

> My grandfather was so upset he said [to the goddess], "You have taken the one lamp which was burning in my house. I will never do *pūjā* to you again." And he didn't. My father told me that the family fortune started a slow nosedive after that. By the time I heard this story it was 1954. I was ten years old. Appa [Father] was talking like this and saying he gave this up. My brother and I never took the trouble to learn the *pūjā* or learn the ritual or anything like that. We had wasted our time. As a ten-year-old boy I remember thinking very clearly, "*Pūjā* is a good thing. Why did they stop this? When I am older and have the capability, I will start."
>
> [*To Yegnarathnam*] Appa, from that time, I think the Mother slowly started planning. The desire was there. In '54 I heard, in '74 I got the first Devī in my house. In '76 I started chanting.

The religious ennui of Aiya's teenage years was broken by his dramatic spiritual awakening in 1964, yet the following decade was one in which obstructions were thrown, one after another, in Aiya's path toward goddess worship and Śrīvidyā practice. The following story, related to Ravi and me over tea, recounts the winding and slightly muddled path leading to a particularly significant break for Aiya in 1974: his access to and mastery of the Sanskrit hymn *Lalitāsahasranāmam*, "The Thousand Names of Lalitā," central to goddess worship. Aiya's narration begins in 1970, in a temple in the Sri Lankan capital of Colombo where Aiya heard a particularly heartfelt rendition of the *Sahasranāmam* chanted by a temple priest. Ever since hearing the hymn at Mataji's ashram in 1968, Aiya—who was not yet a devotee of the Devī—had been looking for someone to teach it to him. He thought perhaps this priest would be a good candidate.

> So I waited until the *pūjā* was over and went and told him, "I heard you chanting the *Sahasranāmam* and I enjoyed it; it's great. Not many people can chant like this. Will you teach me?" And he looked at me like this [*Aiya skeptically sizes up Ravi sitting next to him from head to toe*] and said, "Are you brahman?" And I said, "What has that got to do with it?" And he said, "It has everything to do with it. If you're not a brahman then you're not eligible to be taught. [*Aiya makes a shooing motion with the back of his hand.*] *Po, po*" [Go, go]. "You stick with the *Tēvāram* [devotional poetry composed by Tamil *bhakti* poet-saints]. That's in Tamil. That's good enough for you." I

said "okay." [*Aiya shrugs sheepishly.*] I didn't say anything else. So I left.

I didn't think much of this incident because it happened many times before. I was probably around twenty-five, twenty-six at that time, and from the age of about nineteen any Tom, Dick, or Harry who chanted anything and created the same kind of feeling inside me, I'd go and ask him. And on many an occasion, unfortunately or fortunately, the person was of brahman persuasion and he said, "This is not for you." So, I didn't think too much of it. So I went off and went to Zambia.

Aiya moved to Zambia in 1971 with his wife to work as an architect, and quickly became known by members of the Indian community as someone who led devotional *bhajan* singing and performed basic home *pūjās* to Subramaniam, elephant-headed Ganeś's brother. Since Zambia had no established temples at the time, Aiya's house quickly became a place for south Indians to gather. Among the regular visitors was a man named Balasubramanian, known as Balu, a high-ranking electrical engineer about twenty years Aiya's senior. Balu, a soft-spoken, gentle man, impressed Aiya on a number of accounts. He taught Aiya to perform simple home *pūjās* and, over time, became a kind of religious confidante.

AIYA So one day I was talking to him about Mataji. And I told him that when I first heard this *Lalitāsahasranām* being chanted in this ashram, without knowing what it was, my hair stood on end and I had goose pimples all over my body. The sound did something to me. Believe me, I didn't understand a single word. But the way it was being chanted and the sound did something to me.

[When I asked Mataji if she could teach it to me] she asked, "How old are you?" I told her I was nineteen or twenty and she said, "You're too young. Finish your studies, get a job, get married, have a few children and then come back to me and I'll teach you the . . ."

CORINNE [*Laughing*] And she's eighty-what?

AIYA No, she was about sixty-eight, and I was thinking, "This old one will be gone by the time. . . ." [*We all laugh.*] She looks at me and says, "Bloody rascal, I know what you're thinking!" [*We laugh again.*] She was very friendly that way. Mataji was an *awesome* person that way. Anyway she says, "Now that you have the desire, believe me, someday somebody will appear and teach it to you. Even if you're in the middle of a deserted island."

And I told this guy [*Aiya hunches up his shoulders, his voice very quiet*], "Now I've left Sri Lanka, I've come all this way. Now who's going to

> teach me? Where am I going to learn this?" And he said, "Haran, I'll teach it to you." And I said, "No, not just me, teach it to all the devotees who come!" That was always the . . . I would never take anything like this just for myself.
>
> So, on a Śivarātri night, Balu came over for the *pūjā*. Since we were going to stay awake all night anyway, we thought this would be a great way to start. And there were people leaning against the walls and going "Aaaahh." [*Aiya sits up at angle, head back, mimicking a person sleeping with his or her mouth hanging open. Ravi and I laugh.*] Fast asleep. But anyway, we were chanting. And that first day I thought, "O my God, why the hell did I even have this desire?" Because I couldn't pronounce even one word. I thought, "How am I ever going to get out of this?" I wanted to get up and run away from it. It was like I had about ten marbles in my mouth and I was trying to chant.
>
> Balu sensed it. He said, "Haran, it's all right. Everybody goes through this. Don't worry, it will come." He said, "You have the desire, keep at it. It will come. We'll read again. I'm ready for it." I thought, "My God, if this guy, with all this knowledge and all this experience is willing to go through with this, teaching a dud case like me three, four times, why not? The least I could do is make the effort."

Thanks to Balu's kind persistence and with the help of tapes to which Aiya incessantly listened through earplugs—even at his drafting table during his workday—he was able to commit the *Sahasranāmam* to memory within one week. After mastering the hymn, Aiya's house regularly filled with even more people wanting to hear and/or to learn it. In some cases, according to Aiya, people who were initially curiosity seekers returned to listen and learn. There were also some who disapproved of a nonbrahman chanting and teaching Sanskrit, but Aiya noted that many of them eventually came around, as well.

The story's next scene, taking place back in Sri Lanka, relates a similar change of heart. Aiya was on mandatory extended leave from his job and found himself back at the goddess temple where earlier the priest had denied him access to the *Sahasranāmam*. He arrived well before the scheduled *pūjā* to a nearly empty temple and, without considering the implications, sat in front of the goddess and softly chanted the hymn:

> And this same priest, he had been doing something, he was preparing the deity for the *pūjā*. And he had gone to the kitchen to fetch something and he was coming back. He saw this young person seated there and chanting and he didn't make a sound. He came and stood behind me and listened. So I finished chanting and I did *namaskāram* [prostration before the deity]. And he came around and he said [*Aiya rears back with surprise*], "Oh! It's you!" Who taught you this? I said [elusively], "Somebody." [*Aiya mimics the priest's pensive*

> *faraway look.*] "Mmmmm. Could you chant this line again?" There was one particular line and so I chanted. And he said, "Oh, that is the way it is to be chanted." I said, "Yeah. How else is it to be chanted?" So he chanted it and it was wrong. And he said, "This is the way, are you sure?" And I said, "Yeah, look at the words." "Hmmm. Okay. Who taught it to you?" he asked. I said, "Some gentleman in Africa." "You learned this in Africa?" I said, "Yes."
>
> I felt very strange. I felt no animosity or anger toward the guy or anything like that. I still remember thinking, "I should be angry with this guy." Right? Because he chased me out of the temple and told me I had no right to learn this. It was as though I was looking at myself from the outside and saying, "So what? That's his point of view." Maybe I thought, "You don't have to hold that against him."

After the priest asked Aiya a number of questions about his worship in Zambia, he encouraged him to come again to the temple. Aiya returned a few times but did not have any further conversations with the priest. Aiya finished his narration by noting the importance of the *Lalitāsahasranāmam* to his practice: "So anyway, that is the way I learned it and from that time, up to today, every time I chant it, new experiences are there. It still is the cornerstone and foundation of my practice. Up to today. So naturally, all the people who come into contact with me, I tell them the same: 'This has given so much happiness and pleasure and things like that to me. You should learn it too.' And so slowly people have learned it."

Once Aiya started chanting the *Sahasranāmam*, his focus began shifting away from Subramaniam and toward the Devī. Aiya wrote to Mataji to tell her that he found someone to teach him the *Lalitāsahsranāmam*, as she predicted, and expressed his desire to learn *śrīcakra pūjā*. She approved of his progress but warned him not to launch into *śrīcakra pūjā* too hastily. This powerful ritual, she felt, was not to be taken lightly.

Through no restraint of his own, Aiya did not learn *śrīcakra pūjā* right away. The pathway leading to the ritual was even more congested than the one leading to the *Sahasranāmam*, since it is primarily the domain of Śrīvidyā initiates. Finding people who openly admit to being *upāsakas* can be difficult at best and, furthermore, caste restrictions for those desiring initiation are typically insurmountable. After several years searching for Śrīvidyā *upāsakas* and asking for initiation, Aiya finally found Guruji. A professor of nuclear physics at the time, Guruji had a reputation for both spiritual precocity and unconventional thinking. Intending to ask him for initiation and afraid he would be turned down once again, Aiya asked Balu to accompany him to Guruji's house for moral support.

Guruji answered the door when they arrived and led them directly to his shrine room. He seemed to know, according to Aiya, why they had come. Once in the shrine room, Aiya asked Guruji if he would initiate him into Śrīvidyā, and Guruji, without skipping a beat, said, "Of course." Immediately feeling guilty, thinking Guruji must have assumed he was a brahman, Aiya blurted out, "But I'm not a brahman!" Aiya recalls Guruji adamantly responding, "What difference does that make?" Guruji asked his wife to bring him the *pañcankam*, a book he consulted to determine auspicious times and dates for events such as initiation. On second thought, Guruji said he would just go and ask Her. As Aiya was thinking to himself, "Ask her? Who is he talking about?" Guruji went into meditation. During his two- to three-minute silence, Aiya remembers thinking, "Oh God, I've come this far and now I'm going to be refused by the Devī herself!" When Guruji emerged from his meditation, he told Aiya that he would come to his house in two weeks to initiate both him and Amma into Śrīvidyā. When the time came, Guruji initiated the two of them with the entire gamut—all sixteen mantras.

One of the most enduring effects of Aiya's initiation experience, aside from his long-awaited access to Śrīvidyā's "secrets," is a product of his guru *dīkṣā*. Normally guru *dīkṣā* involves a tangible gift given to the guru by the new initiate—an article of clothing, a fruit, a flower, or some other token of appreciation—in exchange for the guru's care and guidance. Instead, Aiya recalls Guruji explicitly instructing him, "I want you to promise me something. Whatever knowledge I give you, whatever experiences you get, whatever happiness or joy you get out of it, share it with everyone." Just six months after initiation, Aiya, his wife, and their young daughter emigrated to the United States, commissioned with blessings from Guruji to spread the secret teachings of Śrīvidyā. Aiya, conveniently armed with the personality of a maverick, one for whom elitism is particularly irksome, began teaching students from all walks of life. His eventual establishment of an elaborate, ritual-centered temple emerged as part of a natural progression. From this point in Aiya's life, obstacles were less daunting and openings plentiful.

Revealing Secrets and Sharing Power

Aiya's difficult path to initiation becomes a bit more comprehensible when we look at Śrīvidyā *upāsaka*s' multifaceted motivations for guarding the secrecy of their tradition. From a theological perspective, the protection of Śrīvidyā knowledge has to do with its potency. Many adepts object to public mention of the main fifteen-syllable *śrīvidyā* mantra, be it written or spoken, since its power is such that to utter it is to "enunciate the source of power that creates, maintains, and destroys the universe" (Brooks 1992: 112). Practitioners rightfully fear that misuse by the uninitiated could be particularly dangerous. When considering the issue of initiation, however, it seems that secrecy may have as much to do with caste as with theology. Although it is understandable that powerful, potentially dangerous, religious knowledge be handled by those with proper training, why is it so difficult—under traditional circumstances—to receive this training in the first place?

A partial response to this question can be found in Hugh Urban's work on tantric secrecy in Bengal, where he demonstrates that as knowledge becomes scarce its value increases, as does the perceived power of those possessing this knowledge. Secrecy, value, and power are thus intricately connected. Urban compares this to a kind of market value boosted by scarcity (2001: 21–22). Brooks fleshes out this argument by noting that the Smārta brahman community, the segment of society typically associated with Śrīvidyā, carefully guards the tradition as a means for maintaining the privilege of their own community. He traces Śrīvidyā itself as coming into prominence during the seventh century as a means to reassert the importance of ritual expertise during a time when it was being questioned both inside and outside the brahman community (1992: 163). The Smārta community's assumed exclusive access to specialized Śrīvidyā knowledge helps them continue to claim ritual virtuosity during modern times, as well, and furthermore supports conservative understandings of caste and gender roles.[4] Naturally there are Śrīvidyā *upāsakas* who defy caste values and gender distinctions, depending on lineage and individual inclination, but Brooks maintains that few in south India dare to do so (1992: 183).

Although some members of the Śrīvidyā community in Tamil Nadu disagree with Aiya's guru-endorsed defiance of gender and caste restrictions, resistance to his style arises in other arenas, as well. Stirring criticism within ritually conservative segments of the south Indian and Sri Lankan diaspora communities is the fact that Aiya, a nonbrahman, is a head temple priest who furthermore encourages his students, regardless of caste, gender, or ethnicity, to assume roles normally reserved for male brahmans. Rush temple rituals that invite group participation in practices normally reserved for priests, facilitated by a floor plan that, against south Indian tradition, does not enclose the main temple *mūrtis* for exclusive priestly access, further unsettles the status quo. As Aiya expressed it to me one late morning while we prepared incense and fruit offerings for the midday *pūjā*, "[Some priests] come and see that what I'm doing is not what they're doing. They're struggling to keep that separation between the common folk and the mystical. They're trying to maintain the unknown quality so that they can exert control over them, over their behavior. When they find that I am breaking that, they get a little disturbed."

Undeterred (and sometimes inspired) by opposition, Aiya forges ahead, determined to make temple worship, Śrīvidyā, and the divine Mother accessible to the widest possible audience. One of the earliest and boldest examples of such efforts is his production and dispersal of books and tapes containing highly secret Śrīvidyā mantras and rituals. By transliterating Sanskrit liturgies into Tamil and Roman scripts, he has ensured the books' accessibility to nonbrahmans. Beginning in 1976, Aiya produced a new book and tape every year and distributed them for free to people who came to the Navarātri festival held at his garage shrine. He produced from two hundred to three hundred copies of each and handed them out until they were gone. This pattern continued until 1998, when the temple moved from his home garage to Rush.

In 1984, Aiya took on a more ambitious project, transliterating by hand the *śrīcakra pūjā* from Sanskrit script to Tamil. The book took him a year to transcribe, but because of the difficulty of the transliteration and his inexperience with Sanskrit he was unhappy with the final product. Aiya describes how, amid his disappointment, he had a meditational experience in which Devī revealed to him a female nuclear physicist, Gnanapurani from Tamil Nadu, the mother of one of his students, who possessed high proficiency in Tamil, Sanskrit, and English. She was the perfect candidate for helping him with a new edition. Gnanapurani and her husband, Madhvanath, subsequently came to Buffalo to live with their son for a year and a half. Aiya recounted how he leapt at this divinely sent opportunity:

> One look at her confirmed what I had experienced in my meditation. And I also found out that her grandfather was one of the greatest Tamil scholars that ever lived. So naturally, this is flowing through the family. So I told her, "I have a big job for you. A great task."
>
> I gave the book to her and said, "Please make the important diacritical marks, make sure that the Tamils who don't have any idea of Sanskrit can pronounce the words correctly, and you devise the method where we can prescribe numbers." Because there are four ta's in Sanskrit, you know the labials, palatals, dentals, and gutturals. So we ascribed 1, 2, 3, 4 for them.[5] It took her one year to transcribe the book and rewrite it in Tamil.
>
> As I said, the Mother sent her purely for this purpose. My guru happened to be visiting at this time, and when we were checking some pronunciation for a hymn, he turned around to me and asked, "Where did you find this lady?" I said, "I didn't. The Mother found her." Then he said, "Very good. This is exactly what needs to be done." And then she took the text back with her to India.

When Aiya looked into publishing the book, he discovered that in the United States one thousand copies would cost about fifty-two thousand dollars. In India he found a publisher who would do the same for five thousand dollars. With the help of donations from his students in North America and from Gnanapurani and Madhvanath themselves, the Indian publisher produced one thousand books. The couple also agreed to help distribute the book from their home in Chennai. Aiya instructed them to give away the book for free to anyone sincere in their wish to learn Śrīvidyā and to keep records of those who received one. In Aiya's words, he furthermore asked Madhvanath to

> find out what lineage they belong to, whether than have been initiated into Śrīvidyā, whether they do *śrīcakra pūjā*, what [*mūrti*] is in their house, if they feel like diverging, what mantras have been given to them. This identified for me the people who do *śrīcakra pūjā* and Śrīvidyā in Madras because it has been held super secret. They won't talk about it because of the obvious power that comes with it. People are afraid of it. So I told him not to publicize it. "Send [the book] to the Theosophical Society, to their library. Send one to the Ramakrishna Mission. If anyone comes and asks about it, find out these details. . . ."
>
> So actually the deluge started with a person who is a good friend of mine now called Ramesh. So this guy and another lady [called Delhimammi] who is an ordinary housewife—she is about sixty-eight now—had been interested in Śrīvidyā for about twenty to thirty years. They get together and go scouting to find out whether there are any new publications. So, in their usual rounds at libraries, they went to the Ramakrishna Mission and there, sitting on the shelf, is this book, *Śrī Vidyā*. It's this thick. [*Aiya shows me two and a half inches with his thumb and forefinger.*]
>
> So they got totally excited and went to the librarian and said [*Aiya lowers his voice*], "We have to take this book." It turned out that the material in there blew their minds away.

After making several phone calls, Ramesh and Delhimammi eventually located Madhvanath, who informed them that the books were not for sale, but if they were practicing *śrīcakra pūjā* or had been initiated into Śrīvidyā they could come to his house, write down their names, answer some questions, and he would give them the book for free. Aiya continues, "Now the elderly lady is saying things like, 'Aiyo! At least you know a lot of things that are in Śrīvidyā. They will never give me a book. I'll never get one.' Ramesh said, 'Let's just go.' So they both showed up and [Madhvanath] talked to them for about ten minutes and then he knew how interested and involved they both were, so he gave them the books. [*Aiya pauses.*] *That* is how it started."

Apparently Delhimammi showed her copy of *Śrī Vidyā: Śrī Cakra Pūjā Vidhiḥ* to her guru, also a woman, who was impressed by its comprehensiveness. Not only did the book contain an elegant and complete Tamil transliteration of the *śrīcakra pūjā* but it also included step-by-step instructions for preparing for and performing the ritual. Also included were descriptions of the nine planets as well as Sanskrit verses Aiya and Guruji were inspired to compose.[6] Delhimammi's guru told all her disciples to get one for themselves;

within three weeks, sixty books were gone as word spread further throughout the community. Aiya describes the process of Śrīvidyā coming out of the closet: "Now, in Madras, there are thirty-five different groups practicing Śrīvidyā. One group would not talk to the other group because of their secrets. Then each one individually found out when they all came to Madhvanath's house and met there. And they started thinking [*Aiya sneaks a sly look at me*], 'Corinne comes from Syracuse and I have come from . . . [*under his breath*] so you know Śrīvidyā and you practice it?' So now you would have to say, 'Yes, I do *pūjā*.' So, like that, they began to talk among themselves for the first time."

When I asked Aiya if any of these people were upset at him for printing Śrīvidyā rituals in Tamil script, he insisted that they were not at all. The one exception was an ochre-robed *sannyāsi* whom he met later in Madras. Aiya recalls their conversation:

> AIYA He said to me, "You should never have written this book in Tamil." I asked him, "Sir, with all due respect, why not?" He said, "If people are interested in it they must study Sanskrit." Then I told him, "Sir, with all due respect again, you know that Sanskrit is usually only taught to the brahman children. And the brahman children who grow up will not teach Sanskrit to anybody else. Are you telling me that the Mother is not to be accessible to other people, but exclusively to the brahman community?" He looked at me and wouldn't answer yes or no. Then I knew that he was still holding onto the notion that the brahmans were superior and that it should not go to anybody else. He said, "I don't care about this, but you should not have written it in Tamil." I said, "I beg to differ with you. Because I have written the book, and the reason I have written is that at least five hundred people, to my knowledge, have now been given access to this and are doing the *pūjā* in their house." [He responded,] "How do you know they are doing it right?" Then I said, "Can I ask you a question? How do I know that you are doing the *pūjā* right?"
>
> CORINNE That was very brazen of you.
>
> AIYA Right. But my Guruji, he was sitting right next to me. And he always told me, "If you find that somebody is denying knowledge to really interested seekers, you have to stand up." Because for too long this has been going on."

Aiya went on to assert to the *sannyāsi* that only the Mother can determine whether or not someone is doing *pūjā* correctly; it is not for us to judge. Aiya also told him about the promise he gave his guru upon initiation—that he share the *vidyā* with anyone who wanted to learn. He reasoned, "I don't think you or anybody else, even the Śaṇkarācārya, has any right to deny me that."[7] Apparently the *sannyāsi* was unmoved, not persuaded by Aiya's appeal to his guru, or even the goddess herself. The fact that Aiya ultimately did not have to heed the *sannyāsi*'s opinion is, as he sees it, the marvel of his tradition: "And thank God Hinduism is not organized. If there were a head or any such thing I'd have to listen to him. There's no such thing. So I told [the *sannyāsi*], 'With all due respect, you do what is right and I will do what I think is right. And I will leave everything to my guru. If there is any mistake, let him tell me to stop and I will stop.' And Guruji looked at me and sweetly smiled and said, 'You carry on' [*Aiya laughs heartily*]."

Aiya's positive reception from a segment of the Śrīvidyā community, the *sannyāsi* being an exception, reflects a certain receptivity to innovation among today's Smārta Śrīvidyā *upāsakas*. Although it is likely that some brahman *upāsakas* had no interest in a book of Tamil transliteration compiled by a non-brahman and perhaps steered clear of Madhvanath's house, about forty to fifty people who received the book were so impressed with the publication they gathered to meet Aiya when he visited Chennai several months later. Aiya describes this occasion as a humbling and pivotal event for him, forging relationships that continue to be important to this day.

Although Aiya admittedly delights in challenging convention, he cannot act alone. A theme running throughout the above commentary is his consistent appeal to various authorities, particularly to his guru and to the Devī herself.[8] He figures that, with this kind of endorsement, he need let nothing stand in his way. On one occasion Aiya referred to his divine support system by cheerfully pointing out, "The Mother loves a maverick. That's why She's using me!!"

In the final analysis, Aiya does not see himself as breaking rules at all. Rather, he understands his work as doing quite the opposite. From his perspective, backed by his guru, his goddess, and selected scripture passages, he is returning the tradition to its pristine form, before it was corrupted by human restrictions. In his public address after the Dattātreya *homam* during the 1999 *pratiṣṭhā* festival, he speaks passionately to this point:

> This is the secret behind the temple. You will notice that all the *pūjās* are being done by men, women, children, old people, young people—there are no exceptions. If you were here last night for the *sappara tiruviḷā* [festival procession] you would have noticed how everybody enjoyed themselves. There is no difference between us. And that is the way it was in the old days. Unfortunately it has changed. We must change it back—otherwise we will not deserve the little bit of knowledge that has been given to us. Change it back we will, or die trying![9]

The Public Service of Breaking Rules

Religious reform and concern for equal access within Hindu traditions are nothing new. One of the most notable periods of reform in South Asian history, posing serious challenges to conventional gender and caste restrictions, is the *bhakti* movement.[10] This egalitarian movement flourished in south India in the seventh through ninth centuries, swept northward and eventually established itself in north India by the twelfth century. It featured *bhakti* poet-saints who preached, sang, and displayed through their lifestyles the conviction that religious fulfillment and union with divinity can be achieved through intense devotion, or *bhakti*, a sentiment available to the masses, not just an elite few. In its heyday, the *bhatki* ethos consciously downplayed brahmanical values of caste and priestly ritual as well as the physically demanding path of asceticism.

The *bhakti* saints' words of devotion and social critique—expressed through poetry and song composed in the vernacular, not in Sanskrit—can be heard today throughout India and Sri Lanka. The tradition has lost some of its radical edge, however, as the saints' songs are often incorporated into traditional temple settings. In fact, after Aiya's conversion as a young man in Sri Lanka he became locally known as a temple singer for his renditions of the deeply devotional songs of the Nāyaṉārs, the Tamil Śaiva saints. Today he integrates these same songs into ritual performances at the Rush temple. Incorporating Tamil *bhakti* hymns during, not after, the Sanskrit liturgy is yet another item on his long list of ritual innovations.

While the *bhakti* ethos of religious reform continues to have a limited effect on today's Hindu traditions, the strongest contemporary force for change and innovation is the individual *sādhu* or guru—a category into which Aiya fits, though with a difference. Although guru innovations are particularly noticeable today, the fact that Hinduism is not centralized, as Aiya appreciatively stated, means that guru-disciple relationships, unhindered by brahmanical ritual prescription, have been a consistent and potent source of regional transformation and innovation throughout Indian history (Narayan 1989: 85). Part of the guru tradition's contemporary appeal has to do with its streamlined nature, adaptable to the busy schedules of middle-class Hindus, both in India and abroad, who have little time for complex temple rituals. Furthermore, the guru's authority is not dependent on accepting verbatim a range of Hindu traditions and mythologies and thus more comfortably conforms to today's scientific worldview held by many Hindus (Gold 1995: 231; Coward and Goa 1987: 79).

Guru-disciple traditions also appeal to contemporary Hindus who find temple practices lacking in democratic or ethical concerns (Clothey 1992: 136). Whereas traditional temple worship tends to focus on particular deities and insular human communities, guru ashrams, by contrast, tend toward more universalistic neo-Vedāntic philosophies. Working from nondualistic teachings that all life forms are indistinguishable through identification with an all-encompassing Absolute, or *Brahman*, neo-Vedānta typically espoused at today's guru ashrams impels individuals to live this philosophy by promoting the well-being of all of creation. Ashrams thus have become a common source for outreach activities, appealing to a modern sense of religious ethics. This trend, beginning in the mid-twentieth century and currently gaining in popularity, is changing the course of the larger tradition, constituting a modern redefinition of Hinduism itself (Narayan 1989: 72, 165; Miller 1976: 86). While outreach activities of most socially aware gurus operate on a local level, megagurus such as Ammachi and Sai Baba have the financial backing of tens or hundreds of thousands of devotees, which permits social projects such as hospitals or schools for the poor to take on grand, even international proportions.

Passionately egalitarian if not radically antiestablishment in his views, Aiya nevertheless understands his guru role differently from many socially aware gurus working in present-day India and, most especially, in North America. As described in the first part of this book, Aiya's emphasis on Śrīvidyā practice and ritual power is foundational to this difference. Not a typical neo-Vedāntic guru, Śrīvidyā guru, or temple priest, Aiya carves his own atypical niche—particularly in North America, where the individual authority of ashram gurus and the traditional orthodoxy of temple priests seem to be more strictly separated than in India.

Aiya's nonconformity to commonly anticipated categories emerged in an interesting way during a colloquium in Rochester that celebrated Nazareth College's one hundredth year. Colloquium organizers invited Aiya and several other local religious leader-activists to speak at a session that focused on connections between religious ideology and activism. Aiya's talk demonstrated how the framework of the colloquium, perfectly suitable for the Jewish and Christian speakers—and probably appropriate for a more conventional modern guru—fit him awkwardly.

Leading up to the colloquium, Aiya and I had several conversations about what he might say that evening. We thought together about how his efforts do and do not constitute social outreach or activism. The one aspect of his work that he felt fit loosely within the category of community outreach had to do with Sri Lankan Tamils in Sri Lanka and in North America. Aiya is deeply concerned about the repercussions of the communal riots and civil war that have ravaged his country since 1958. When he was fifteen, he and his family were left destitute due to the riots and spent three months living in various refugee camps before resettling. As a young man he witnessed the regular fits of violence that continue to devastate his country to this day. To help victims of violence in Sri Lanka, Aiya stations a donation box outside the temple. On the front of the box are photographs and a brief description of the recipients: an orphanage founded by Aiya's first guru, Mataji. Caught in the crossfire, Mataji's original orphanage and ashram were destroyed by the Sri Lankan armed forces in 1987 and have since been rebuilt. Most recently run by Mataji's senior disciple Kalyanasundaram until her death in 2002, the orphanage is currently run by Kalyanasundaram's son.[11]

Aside from offering direct assistance to the victims of the Sri Lankan war, Aiya also hopes his temple can provide spiritual uplift for local members of the Sri Lankan Tamil community, some of whom have refugee status in Canada, and most of whom are in North America not by choice. Of particular concern to him are the displaced youth, some of whom are troubled and without parental guidance or, worse, involved in gangs. Aiya feels the temple could foster a sense of purpose and focus to help save these young people from negative influences. Although Aiya understands that his support of the Sri Lankan community is a kind of outreach, he knows that it is different from running an orphanage like Mataji's and from Guruji's schools and low-income housing for underprivileged women. Although Aiya holds the efforts of his gurus and others like them in high regard, he does not apologize for his difference in style. The ritual life of the temple is what sustains him and, he firmly believes, sustains on many levels those who participate with him.

In spite of these differences, Aiya espouses neo-Vedāntic philosophies virtually identical to those of the more conventional modern guru. Because he feels these views provide important inspiration for social outreach, Aiya told me he might make mention of them during the Nazareth colloquium. He added to this the fact that his Śrīvidyā tradition trains people to focus, giving them the means to recognize that the Mother encompasses all, thus supporting the practical execution of neo-Vedāntic philosophies. During our mid-morning tea break before the evening colloquium he proposed the following analogy to animate his point:

> God is like gold. Now gold exists everywhere in the world in the form of beautiful pieces of jewelry, *gorgeous* pieces of art. People look at the gold but they don't realize they're looking at gold. They think they're looking at a beautiful piece of art. The substance that is behind this thing, the substance that completely encompasses all these pieces of jewelry and nice things that you see, it's just a lump of gold and it's not going to be attractive to you. But the moment somebody kneads it and hammers it and does all those things and puts it out, you go, "Ooooh! Aaaaa!! Mmmmm!!" not realizing that it is the same metal.
>
> To me God is like that. If you are aware that He is around everywhere, present everywhere, if you're aware, God is what you are going to see.[12] But if you let your focus drift away and see only the surface and the art, you're lost. You will eventually come back to it but it's going to take you a long time. That is the scenic route.
>
> Gold is gold, whatever you do to it. It won't change. God's like

> that. He may be in Corinne, he may be in my little pussy cat that died. He could be in that flower. He could be in the little girl on the bike—who cares? If you're able to latch onto that immediately and say, "Oh!" and see it for what it is . . . You have to be able to recognize God in everything. I may be talking to you or I might be talking to two others at the same time, or somebody might be on the telephone with me, but the awareness that I'm talking to God, it's got to be there.
>
> It is *that* which impels us to act and do things. It comes back to the original point I made of being aware, observant of everything. You must be observant and slowly the power of observing becomes second nature, so you don't have to consciously involve your mind. You look at it and think, "That is God. This is God's work here. This is the way it is." It doesn't have to be something alive; it could be the stream rushing past you. You'll still see it there. That's how it is. So God is like gold. Precious.

In the wake of our discussions connecting social activism with neo-Vedāntic philosophies, the colloquium session was very interesting. Bill Shannon, an eighty-one-year-old Thomas Merton scholar and Catholic priest, started off the evening with a keynote address. As he spoke, I was surprised to hear a Christian rendition of Vedānta that could as well have been Aiya talking. Describing something he referred to as "communion spirituality," Shannon discussed the need to be vigilant to the divine within us and in others. The next logical step, he argued, was to recognize that through divinity humanity is united. Other people's concerns are therefore not separate from our own and we must carefully tend to them as if they were our own. After Shannon's address, we heard from Catholic and Jewish activists, two women who easily and gracefully wove their theologies into their commitment to social action. Invited leaders from the Muslim and Native American communities unfortunately were not able to attend, so Aiya was the next to take the podium.

Aiya began by acknowledging the striking similarity between his views and those of the prior speakers, especially Bill Shannon's. Then, after brief reference to his belief in a divine Mother who pervades all of creation, he launched into an emotional appeal describing the plight of his homeland, the violence and oppression of which North Americans are largely unaware, and his efforts to help the most helpless: the widows and orphans of war. Midway through his talk he returned briefly to his Śrīvidyā tradition and a tribute to Mataji, then back to the plight of Sri Lanka. Aiya's concern for the innocent victims of war was palpable to the audience in the small auditorium. You could have heard a pin drop. It occurred to me, as I listened, that the pain he feels for Sri Lanka is truly a core part of who he is; it runs almost as deeply as does his passion for his divine Mother. When Aiya's talk did not ultimately succeed in weaving his concerns for human rights into his dedication to his religious tradition, it seemed to me that a connection was nonetheless tenuously made by virtue of the depth of importance both issues held for him.

Before I hastily paste together for Aiya these two spheres of concern, it is important to note the significance of the disjunction itself. Rooted in earlier Marxist convictions, Aiya's activism is still a part of him, even beyond his concerns for Sri Lanka. He speaks eloquently against human rights abuses throughout history and across the globe. He boycotts Shell gasoline and Nestlé's chocolate in response to their history of corporate and international racism. In spite of his activist impulses, however, Aiya chooses to channel nearly all of his eloquence and energy into the temple and its rituals. While he hopes the power of his rituals can make a difference to the wider world, he understands their effect to be indirect if not incidental. His priorities are aligned in this way in part because Śrīvidyā theology traditionally has little interest in instructing *upāsakas* to change their behavior or critique global power structures. There is no precedent within Śrīvidyā to help Aiya link ritual practice with activist concerns. I nevertheless would argue that, contrary to this disconnect and the resulting disjointed colloquium talk, Aiya's tendency toward social activism *does* grow out of and inform his religious practice—just not in the ways anticipated by conventional twentieth-century Christian or Jewish formulae.

During my next meeting with Aiya we discussed over tea and crackers the colloquium and the fact that his religious and activist views had trouble flowing together. Aiya mentioned that when he heard Bill Shannon echoing his initial thoughts, he felt free to talk about other issues. After hearing the women activists speak about human rights concerns, he felt invited to educate the (mostly Euro American) audience about the plight of his people. He greatly appreciated the attentiveness of the crowd and their outpouring of support once the formal event ended. When I suggested that perhaps the theme of the colloquium was not something that "worked" for him, that his concern for justice in Sri Lanka was in many ways separate from his religious practice, he agreed. I proposed that the colloquium in some ways assumed a Christian framework, and he agreed with this as well. After a moment's thought, Aiya suggested that the assumed interrelationship between religion and social concerns stems from the Christian impulse to convert others. Although he did not elaborate, the statement made sense to me. Aiya's exposure to socially conscious Christianity has mostly been through missionaries working in Sri Lanka, often among the poor. In many cases, these people wove into their work subtle or not-so-subtle invitations to join the faith. For him, Christian outreach and missionary work were inextricably enmeshed.

I was not entirely comfortable with this conclusion but was unable to deny Aiya's position; so we ended the conversation in agreement. Yet by our next meeting, I had spent some time thinking about instances in which Christian social action had nothing to do with mission and how, when viewing religion through this lens, Aiya's activism and religious practices are inextricably bound. Our conversation took place in the little office just off the temple hallway. We had finished working on a lecture Aiya was preparing to deliver at an upcoming conference and continued to chat as the computer screen blinked off. I suggested that Christianity's concern for social justice historically comes not from missionary efforts, but from internal reform that critiques abuses of power by religious leaders. I described Jesus' critique of the material excesses and hypocrisy of the religious elite, Francis of Assisi's resistance to the entanglement of the Church with the state and its conspicuous display of wealth and power, and Latin American liberation theology's more recent critique of the Church's complicity with governmental oppression of the poor. Leaders of these movements promote earthly justice not in order to convert outsiders; they do so to reform their own traditions from within for the sake of their own people.

I suggested to Aiya that when activism is construed in this way, it looks a lot like what he is trying to do at Rush. By reconfiguring Śrīvidyā and temple traditions, encouraging nonbrahmans and women to become initiates and perform rituals, he enacts a critique of what he considers the injustices and abuses of power within his tradition. In accord with like-minded Christian reformers as well as Hindu reform movements such as the *bhakti* movement, he aims not simply to shake up the religious status quo but also to press for structural change. As Aiya agreed heartily with my assessment, Priya's smirking face appeared in the window that connects the office to the hallway. Aiya added jokingly, "Yes! Look how I'm trying to reform this one!" Priya, seemingly anticipating a joke delivered at her expense, rolled her eyes.

Religiously sponsored outreach programs—Christian, neo-Vedāntic, or otherwise—may indeed be effective tools for relieving the effects of poverty and for challenging corrupt power structures worldwide, sometimes without conversion strings attached. Yet there is something to be said for internal critique—for getting one's own house in order. This issue was poignantly raised during the Nazareth colloquium when an eighteen-year-old college student stood up at the end of the question-and-answer period and posed one final question for the evening. After apologizing for her boldness, she pointed out that although the two Catholic panelists' presentations about bringing justice to the world were inspirational, they were of little help to her. As a churchgoing Catholic, it seemed that everywhere she turned men were in positions of authority as priests, bishops, and popes. Yet she regularly was assured that all are equal in God's eyes. Her question for the panel, the quaver in her voice reinforcing its urgency, was how such words can console her when reality so contradicts them. The Catholic panelists responded with great sympathy, agreeing with her, encouraging her to keep asking questions and to be a leader for change.

When they had finished, Aiya raised his hand and asked if he could add a few words. He began by assuring the young woman that his tradition was no different from hers. He described his feminist sentiments and his sense from a very young age that something was terribly wrong with women's exclusion from temple rituals. He went on to explain that he tries to do his small part to correct this problem through his work at the Rush temple. This work, he explained, he does with the blessings of his current guru:

> So in our temple, in spite of all the opposition from the established clergy, and in spite of very orthodox people coming and looking sideways at me like that [*Aiya stiffly turns with an astonished look on his face, drawing chuckles from the audience*], I make sure that if a lady knows the service and wants to lead it, she performs the service. We have to start somewhere. I'm glad you ask that question because it encourages me that I'm on the right track.
>
> It's okay for me to chant something but it's not okay for the mother who carried me for nine months to chant? That to me is the worst injustice. And I think of God as the universal Mother, the loving Mother who gathers all Her children to Her bosom. That was one of the teachings that [my guru] gave me, "Think that they are representatives of the Divine Mother. Touch their feet with your mind."
>
> I'm very glad you're thinking like that. I wish I was that smart when I was eighteen.

At eighteen Aiya was a proper Marxist, more concerned with eradicating religion than righting religious injustices. But this does not mean that his postconversion self, emerging two years later, is entirely unfamiliar. Social critique lives on in Aiya in complicated and innovative ways. There is no known precedent for the tangible challenges Aiya levels at Śrīvidyā's elitism and very little precedent for his type of challenge to south Indian temple traditions. Confident that he is on the right track, Aiya is convinced and encouraged that opening up an exclusive tradition makes the Devī happy. The manifestation of the goddess who first appeared to Aiya the young hooligan indeed might not only be pleased, but could also claim a particular stake in his progress. The underclass form of the Mother who blessed Aiya with the ash from her left foot would have been, if she stayed long enough, unwelcome in the Sri Lankan goddess temple. If she were to show up at the Rush temple, however, keeping her inner identity to herself, she would not only be invited in but, if so inclined, trained to perform her very own rituals.

5

The Changing Faces of Temple Worship

The Young, the Women, and the Rest

I feel Aiya is making things very comfortable for the younger generation. Because usually the younger generation is simply told to go to the temple, give seven bucks, do the *arcana*, and they have no idea what is going on.[1] So Aiya is explaining what it means. This I feel the younger generation is very much attracted to—to know what it means. Because we all have a brain, obviously. And we can think clearly. I think this is how he is drawing the younger people. Whereas the older people are more old-fashioned. So they may disagree.

—Devi, first-generation temple devotee from Chennai

First-time visitors to the Rush temple are often struck by its unusual demographics. The average age of those gathered at any given ritual or large festival will probably be younger than at other North American Hindu temples. Inner-core devotees who busily work behind the scenes and perform elaborate rituals will, on average, be even younger. On the basis of conversations with dozens of visitors and regular devotees, I have found the Rush temple's ability to attract disproportionately large numbers of teenagers and young adults to be mainly associated with its invitation—or more accurately its mandate—to learn about and participate in ritual activities.

The Young

Devi's quote, cited above, reflects a religious divide commonly found between first-generation Indians or Sri Lankans and their young adult children. While many perceive this divide to be absolute—with young adult South Asians having little or no interest in the religious traditions of their immigrant parents—Rush temple demographics reflect a slightly more nuanced picture. Although second-generation South Asians may reject their parents' *style* of religious commitment, this does not necessarily mean a rejection of South Asian traditions altogether. Ironically, in spite of their apparent disinterest, it seems many North American Hindu youth want to know more, not less, about their religious heritage.[2]

In her study of South Asian communities in the United States, Karen Leonard notes that when parents struggle to pass on their cultural and religious heritage to their children, something often gets tangled in the translation. Leonard describes a skit written and performed by second-generation Californian Sikhs that humorously portrayed parents setting unrealistic curfews, monitoring friendships, violating privacy, nagging about eating habits, and bragging in public about their child's academic and career successes. Although the skit evoked laughter from an audience composed mostly of parents, the truth of the portrayal seemingly hit a nerve. During the conversation following the skit, teens complained that parental expectations were too high and teaching inadequate. Particularly troublesome were their explanations of their religious tradition. When young adults asked about religious practices, parents, rather than explaining them, merely insisted that they be accepted and followed. Young people argued that they not only wished to understand the tradition for themselves but also wanted to be able to explain it to their non-Sikh friends (Leonard 1997: 157–158).[3]

Reflecting a similar divide between generations, the Washington, D.C., Shiva-Vishnu temple literally operates on two levels. Upstairs, the priest performs rituals largely meaningful to the older generations, while the lower-level community hall, more appealing to the youth, holds philosophical lectures and discussions of religious texts as well as Indian music and dance performances (Waghorne 1999: 121–122). At the First National Indian-American Students Conference at the University of North Carolina, Chapel Hill, second-generation Hindus moreover expressed their disdain for temple rituals, describing them skeptically as "a show." Like the Sikh youth about whom Leonard writes, they discussed their alienation from practices they are neither able nor asked to understand (Waghorne 1999: 123).[4]

Generational differences in religious styles can be traced partly to disparities in lifestyle patterns across the globe. Coward and Goa note that first-generation immigrants often learned sacred chants and texts in India as a matter of routine, through a process resembling cultural "osmosis" nearly impossible to duplicate in North America today. For instance, it would not have been unusual for children in upper-caste families to rise early with parents or grandparents and daily hear chanting and passages from texts such as the *Rāmāyaṇa*, the *Vedas*, or the *Upaniṣads*. Regular trips to local temples further reinforced these chants and texts. Coward and Goa surmise that such opportunities are lost to children of immigrants once they enter the busy pace of North American life. The absence of grandparents further weakens their link to tradition (1987: 82).

Yet even if religion-by-osmosis were possible in North America, it seems that first-generation Hindu parents would still be faced with their children's seemingly impossible questions. In other words, whereas the transmission of chants and texts from family elder to child may be part of an ongoing, culturally embedded process in some parts of India, explanations of these chants and texts typically are not. As a first-generation Canadian man who learned to chant in India put it, "I never asked my father any questions as to why I should learn, or of what benefit it is going to be for me. He simply said, 'Repeat what I told you yesterday' " (Coward and Goa 1987: 81). Steven Vertovec notes that the challenges and questions posed by North American Hindu youth are part of a self-questioning intrinsic to North America's brand of religious pluralism. "Under such conditions, believers are often compelled to realize that the routine habitual practice, rote learning and 'blind faith' underpinning previous contexts (where their faith may have been homogenous or hegemonic) are no longer optional" (2000: 149).[5]

Jeya, a computer programmer from Canada in his mid-thirties and core Rush devotee who plays *miruthangam* drums at temple functions, understands the generational conundrum in a similar way.[6] Because he left Sri Lanka in his early twenties, he has sympathy for both first- and second-generation perspectives. As he sees it, young people ask parents questions that their elders were never in a position to ask, and the resulting impasse creates a kind of double bind: "Kids these days are very smart because they see many cultures. There's Muslim, Hindu, white, brown—all cultures. And they go out and have to explain [their tradition] to others. If they don't explain they'll look stupid. Back home [in Sri Lanka] you do things because you're *supposed* to. Back home you can't ask these questions. If you ask, you're stupid—so you don't want to ask. Here, if you do it [without understanding], you look stupid."

Religion scholar Vasudha Narayanan expresses similar sentiments from her own first-generation perspective:

> It is always difficult to perceive oneself clearly and to articulate one's faith and tradition to oneself, the community, and to one's children, especially if one has had no formal training or education in the field. But such is the predicament of a Hindu here; having grown

> up in India, soaking up the Hindu religious experience, does not make one a specialist in it. And yet, we are forced to articulate over and over again what it means to be a Hindu and an Indian to our friends and to our children, and one feels ill-equipped for the task. Frequently, all that one remembers of a festival in India is the food that was prepared for it; one was never called upon to explain Deepavali or Sankaranti and, least of all, "Hinduism." (1992: 172)[7]

While many first-generation immigrants work hard to transmit their tradition to children who perceive them as overbearing and underinformed, younger members of the first generation, sandwiched in between, may approach things slightly differently. Although raised in a South Asian context, traditional practices once familiar can become, for some, embarrassing and eventually obsolete. The root cause of their disenchantment, as Jeya sees it, is lack of information. He illustrates his point by discussing the practice of placing ritual markings of red *kumkum* powder and *vibhuti* ash on one's forehead, commonplace in Sri Lanka but not typically done in North America:

> People from our culture, they come here and in ten or twenty years, they forget about it. They're ashamed to say that they are Hindu. When I go to work, I apply *vibhuti* and *kumkumam* on my forehead always. I don't care what other people think of me. Without that I cannot look at my face. So I go. And some of the Sri Lankans, people in our own community, don't talk to me because of that. They feel ashamed.
>
> I think the problem is that people put *kumkumam* on and don't know the reason they're putting it on. Even our own people used to say to me, "Only girls can do this. Why do you?" They don't know the value of the *kumkumam*. They don't really know why they are wearing it. They have no idea because no one teaches it. So when other people ask, like you, if you come and ask, "What is the red spot on your forehead?" What can they say? Nothing. So they feel embarrassed. That is the embarrassment. The reason why they don't wear it is because they can't explain.[8]

Among the young adult devotees who were either born in North America or whose memories of Sri Lanka or India are dim at best, many described being brought, as children, to traditional North American temples by their parents. By their teen years, many had developed noncommittal or negative views of temple traditions until they discovered Aiya and the Rush temple. Kumaran, a nursing student from Toronto who came to Canada from Sri Lanka with his family when he was five, described to me a fairly typical view of traditional south Indian temple activities:

> [The priests] just chant whatever they chant. And then they come out with the camphor, and they just show it to you and you just walk around and then that's basically it. You're not taught anything. You don't learn anything. All you do is go, and you pay five dollars for *arcana* to get something done under your name. And so, okay, fine. It's just twenty minutes, one-half hour. And if it's a festival you stay there for like half a day and that's it. And it's like I'd be there thinking, "I don't care. Whatever." It was like going to a show or a movie. You just come back and that's it.

Kumaran's older brother, Muralee, a technical system analyst in Toronto, was much less inclined to take temple events in stride during his teen years. He recounted what he perceived to be the irreverence, disengagement, and neglect of details that made temple visits, particularly during festival occasions, extremely negative experiences for him:

> I hated it. I really hated going to the temples in Toronto because it was just like a big gathering, pretty much like a big party. At least that's what it seemed to me. Because people just come, stand there and chat, look at the *pūjā*. So it's like a gathering where you meet people. I would've liked to have had stricter rules. I would've liked it if they had kept it clean. And if people were nicer. People were pretty stiff-handed, like if you did something wrong it's okay to say something, or whatever, but they went overboard.
>
> It's not like it is here. You don't get to do *abhiṣekam*; it's all done by the priest. So you just stand there and watch. So there's no involvement. You stand, watch, and leave. So it's okay, but I really hated it when the big functions came along. At temples there it's just really crowded. And all the people, what they do is they don't wait for things to come to them, like the camphor. They want to push and shove with an "I want it first!" sort of attitude. I hate that.
>
> And once when my sister and I had questions about certain things, when we asked the priest there why you do this and why you do that, he said [*in a gruff voice*], "Go read a book!" So there's no communication there. They don't explain or anything. So you're like, "okay, gee, thanks." How much help is that? Anyone can read a book. But they just say, "Go read a book!" They don't even tell you which book to read.

It is important to note that, among Rush devotees, South Asians were not the only ones who expressed a desire for stronger religious guidance when they were younger. Barbara, a Euro American devotee in her late thirties, described to me her disappointment at not being able to understand the Catholic

Mass: "When I was a kid Vatican II came in. Things changed. Priests didn't face away and speak in Latin. They faced forward and [spoke] in English. But you still couldn't understand them. So you sat still and listened because you knew that someone would whack you in the head if you didn't." Lily, a Puerto Rican American devotee in her mid twenties, raised primarily in a nondenominational Pentecostal church, expressed similar sentiments: "When I became really involved in Christianity I had certain questions that weren't being answered. And the church was focusing on certain, you know, morals and things that were basic. But I had other questions. People would say to me either 'Oh, this is just the way it is,' or 'Don't question,' and that kind of thing."

In spite of similar frustrations experienced by young adult North Americans—probably reflecting intergenerational conflicts across cultures and religious traditions—tensions experienced within the more recently established South Asian communities are understandably more complicated. In an essay published in a collection of writings by diaspora South Asians, Sucheta Doshi, a graduate student in the United States, describes a seemingly impossible balancing act for young South Asian Americans:

> We have to be "Americanized," or else we are not cool enough for other members of our generation who are always out at bars and clubs and refuse to learn their South Asian languages because it "just isn't cool." We have to be "proper South Asian" for our parents. (1996: 210)
>
> . . . I'm tired of being told what I have to be, and I am tired of defending who I am. If I choose to be "Western," I shouldn't be told by some politically correct advocate to claim my culture. If I choose to be interested in Indian history and politics and learn classical Indian dance, I shouldn't be told by an Indian American that I am allowing my parents to lead my life or be patronized by other Americans as being "so in touch with my culture." No one has the right or authority to judge how "South Asian" someone is; after all, what is an authentic South Asian? Who defines what is authentic and what is not? (211)

In our discussion of this conundrum, Muralee depicts the two main forces with which young Sri Lankan Canadians must contend—traditional culture as presented by parents and mainstream culture prevalent in Canada—as necessary parts of an admittedly difficult whole: "It's like your right side and your left side, right? People are realizing that you need both." This realization, as Muralee sees it, has prompted recent efforts in the Toronto Tamil community to round out their young people's largely mainstream Canadian worldview by establishing Tamil-sponsored schools. While these schools typically focus on the arts, teaching south Indian dance and Karnatic music, formal education in religious philosophy and ritual has also become available within the past decade.

Devi Parvati, a Euro American devotee at Rush and pioneer in Hindu youth education, knows well the complicated expectations lived out by South Asian youth.[9] After studying and practicing yoga and meditation for several years at an ashram in Pennsylvania's Pocono Mountains, Devi Parvati helped her guru and fellow disciples, all of whom were Euro American, establish the Hindu Heritage Summer Camp in 1976. The camp taught Hindu philosophy and religious practices to the teenage children of the first significant wave of U.S. Indian immigrants. Devi Parvati described how ashram members seemed well equipped to run the camp in spite of (or perhaps because of) their ethnicity. Not only had they received years of instruction from Hindu religious teachers brought from India, they asked the kinds of questions North American converts—and second-generation youth—are inclined to ask. "So we were Americans teaching this culture because we were the ones learning about this culture. This is because we asked why and we found answers, whereas nobody else knew the answers anyway. So, through all of our studies with the pundits and priests who started coming from India we learned about the tradition. And so whatever we knew, we'd share with the kids and the kids just loved it. So the camp was growing and that was another issue. The camp was taking over the ashram."

The Hindu summer camp indeed became an overwhelming success as word caught on in the Indian community.[10] Although the ashram in the Poconos has since closed down, Devi Parvati continues to direct Hindu summer camps in the Rochester area. Reflecting on the ethnic divide between herself and her students, Devi Parvati elaborates, "I'm a bridge. I'm a bridge between East and West who is able to translate into the Western, modern world, for the kids, their tradition. So what happens over and over again is they go back and tell their parents how great it was. And their parents tell me how surprised at how receptive they've become: 'I said the same exact words to them and they didn't listen to me!' The fact that it's a white woman who's instructing them, just like the teachers in school, they're able to accept it."

The fact that Devi Parvati's bridgework is so successful in spite of its ironies is testimony to the divided allegiances often felt by many Indian youth. Feeling the sway of their parents' deep desires that they act in particularly successful and traditionally "Indian" ways and feeling the pull of North American culture as something quite different, young South Asians sometimes have difficulty piecing together—as Muralee put it—their "right side and their left side."

In many ways like Devi Parvati, Aiya also works at mending seemingly contradictory components of his young students' lives by offering them a chance to learn about and participate in religious practices on their own terms, not necessarily their parents'. Traditional temple rites packaged in a democratic and seemingly North American way—completing both sides of the equation, so to speak—appear to be the secret behind the Rush temple's success. I describe Aiya's style advisedly as "seemingly North American" since North American Christian traditions can be just as undemocratic and/or noninclusive as their Hindu counterparts. Also, youthful critique of traditional religion is not unique to North America, as Aiya, a rebellious teenager in Sri Lanka nearly half a century ago, knows only too well.

Because Aiya's mixing of priestly ritual with ideas of democratic inclusivity is so unusual, particularly within the traditional south Indian temple context, people are often taken aback when they first encounter his style. Muralee describes his first rather stunned impressions of one of Aiya's *pūjās*, performed at a local school facility in Toronto: "It was amazing. It was like, wow! He was so enthusiastic, he was just up front, and he was talking and telling stories and giving explanations and everything. That caught me the most. It was so interesting, listening to stories and explanations about why a person should do this or shouldn't do that when doing the *pūjā*. It was amazing how everyone was involved in it." Sudharshan describes his first encounter with Aiya's style during a wedding engagement ceremony:

> Aiya was doing the ritual. As usual he was explaining everything and I thought, "Oh my God, nobody has ever explained this to me!" And I pride myself—this might be a slight character flaw—but I pride myself on being very academic and everything has to be explained. Articulated for me. Verbalized. No innuendoes, no subtleties. And he verbalized everything, the ritual, everything. And I thought, "Oh my God, this is a brilliant man! He is so articulate, making *me* understand." So after the ritual I went and said, "I am Sudharshan, Jeya's friend, and I really appreciated you explaining this to me. Nobody has ever explained this to me."
>
> Normally, if you ever want to ask anything in our cultural paradigm, when you ask things, they'll just say, "Oh no, no, you don't need to know this," or "Who are you to ask?" You just do it. It's about the *gods*.

The growing popularity of the Rush temple, particularly among the youth, does not go unnoticed by other temple organizers and priests, particularly at Sri Lankan temples in Toronto. The fact that many Sri Lankans, a good number in their late teens and twenties, would simply prefer to make the three-hour drive from Toronto to Rush than go to a temple nearby is difficult to ignore. As a result, some Toronto temples have made efforts, with varying degrees of success, to involve and entice young people. Others, such as the temples dedicated to Durgā and Aiyappan, regularly draw young people by featuring rituals relevant to them.[11] Temple organizers who do not specifically reach out to the youth, who do not try to make their rituals more inclusive, understandable, or relevant, find it an uphill battle to get teenagers and young adults to attend willingly and regularly.[12]

As for first-generation parents, it seems their perceived role in their children's religious upbringing may be, in many cases, forever at odds with their offspring's expectations. Raised in different cultural contexts that formed different religious styles and expectations, the impasse between generations cannot be solved without some give on both sides. On that note, I conclude this portion of the chapter with a quote from Jeya, as someone sandwiched between generations. As we finished our interview, sitting in white plastic chairs under a maple tree near the temple, Jeya wanted to offer one last reflection on the generation gap. As he saw it, young people's commitment to the temple could not be complete unless it was brought full circle to a commitment to one's parents, no matter how "impossible" they may seem.

> I give my advice to whoever comes to this temple as Aiya's student, not as a visitor: "Your home is a temple too. Try to do the same thing you're doing here at your house. The older generation, if they have grown up back home and then come here with the same ideas, if they are fifty, sixty years old, they are not going to change their attitude or their mind. It's too late. Try to understand and support them instead of saying, 'Oh no, we are so Westernized we won't believe our parents.' Don't do that. One day you will regret that you didn't do things for them."
>
> This is what I tell everybody when they talk about their parents: "It's fine, I understand your frustration, but you're trying to make Amma, Aiya, and Devī happy. You're able to ignore people [at the temple] who are making mistakes and putting garbage everywhere. You're cleaning up after them. Why don't you try that at your house? What about your parents? They're the ones who love you no matter what you do in life. Accept them as they are. They're not stupid just because you know things they don't, just because you are growing up in this world and you're seeing different kinds of people. That facility, that advantage, they didn't have."

Women Who Lead Rituals

The Śrī Rājarājeśwarī Pīṭham is fairly unremarkable when it comes to gender distribution. Women are slightly in the majority, and men who are present, although sometimes devout and highly committed, include a good many husbands who tag along after their much more enthusiastic wives. What sets the Rush temple apart, of course, is the fact that some of these women—South

Asian, Euro, and Latina American alike—lead rituals normally designated for male brahman priests. Inner-core devotees, those most likely to lead rituals, are also fairly evenly divided between males and females yet, during crowded festivals, Aiya makes it a point to assign women positions of ritual leadership to give visitors a stark visual cue into how his temple is not like others.[13]

Part of the reason the Rush temple gets away with such admittedly orchestrated displays has something to do with its North America location. As the Ujjain brahman rationalized to Aiya on the internet (recounted at the end of chapter 3), women are free to do the otherwise impossible in Aiya's temple because it not in India. As such, there are signs of similar, although less dramatic, innovations at other North American temples. In many cases, women's roles fill the breaches created by the shift from one cultural context to another. For instance, Karen Leonard describes the Malibu temple's tradition of stationing several women at the temple door to hand out pamphlets and explain temple beliefs and rituals to newcomers. Although there is no analogous task in Indian temples, some feel that temple priests would be better suited for the job. But their limited English skills force them to pass the task on to volunteers—who happen to be women (Leonard 1997: 113).[14]

In spite of increased opportunities for women at North American temples, in some cases it seems they are ready for more responsibility than is given. For instance, at the Sri Siva-Vishnu temple in Washington, D.C., women expressed discontent over their lack of serious decision-making roles at the temple. Their aspirations for a larger ritual role were also communicated, as Waghorne interpreted it, through their actions. For instance, during rituals in which women purportedly sat "listening," they often quietly chanted Sanskrit along with the priests. On another occasion women hijacked a festival palanquin holding the god Murugan, held traditionally by male devotees. Waghorne asked one of the women if this is something they would try in India and she replied, "In India they are male chauvinists, but this is America" (Waghorne 1999: 124).

The attitude that more is possible for women in America is also provoking more dramatic shifts in temple practices throughout the continent. Women palanquin bearers are becoming more commonplace, as are women's helping roles inside temples.[15] The significant line yet to be crossed, however, is that of women performing the public, central role of *pūjāri* during traditional, Sanskritic temple rituals. The image of a woman confidently leading a formal south Indian temple ritual indeed speaks volumes, yet the frequency with which it is practiced at the Rush temple causes regulars, myself included, to grow used to it. One Wednesday in October, after I had been attending the temple for about one and a half years, I was struck anew by the radicalness of this everyday occurrence. I was standing at the sink in the temple's right front corner, washing some bowls and trays used during ritual. From this spot I had a good view of the faces of some first-time visitors as they watched Priya, then in her late teens, perform the priestly role for the afternoon. The following is an excerpt from my field notes:

> At some point in the middle of Priya's *pūjā* today, a group of young professional-looking South Asian men arrived, probably on lunch break. They didn't look at all familiar to me and they weren't chanting along so I figured they were new. I tried to imagine what a sight it must have been for them to sit and watch this slender young woman bounding confidently around the temple, honoring the deities with bells and camphor and graceful *mudrās*. They watched respectfully and intently, following Priya's every move as she went about her work. The looks on their faces gave me a renewed sense of the potency of Aiya's agenda.

Although women middle-aged and older can be as willing to lead rituals as their younger cohorts, some are a little reticent. One morning in August while Jambu, an unassuming woman in her early fifties, Vijitha in her early twenties, and I chatted at the front of the temple while preparing for the midday *pūjā*, Jambu mentioned that she was scheduled to lead the following night's Lakṣmī *pūjā*. The event was expected to be well attended and Jambu, who had never performed *pūjā* in front of such a large crowd before, was feeling tentative. Vijitha warmly and thoughtfully responded to Jambu's concerns, answering her questions about procedure and encouraging her. She assured her that whatever she did would be absolutely fine, stating emphatically, "Just do it with confidence! Don't worry." The next night Jambu rose to the occasion in spite of her jitters, gracefully conducting Lakṣmī *pūjā* with Rupa, an elegant woman in her late thirties, standing by her side, chanting into a microphone headset. The crowd in attendance was nearly one hundred.

Among those who perform rituals at the temple, one of the least timid is a woman in her seventies who devotees refer to as Ammamma, Tamil for Grandmother. One of Ammamma's greatest claims to fame is that she was Aiya's school teacher in Sri Lanka for kindergarten through second grade. Another is that she leads chanting and *pūjā* with great confidence and finesse. Demonstrating the disconnect between traditional expectations and the altered Rush temple reality is an incident that occurred during one of Ammamma's weekday *pūjās*. Midway through the ritual, a group of first-time visitors arrived from Toronto, one of whom was an elderly woman about Ammamma's age. Apparently stunned at the sight of one of her peers performing *pūjā*, she pulled Priya aside and demanded to know why she was doing the ritual. When Priya blandly responded, "Because she knows how," the elderly woman snorted in disgust, walked out of the temple, and spent the rest of the ritual in the hallway, noisily shuffling through a Tamil newspaper. Although not surprising, this kind of reaction is not common at Rush, since most people who visit, particularly those making the three-hour drive from Toronto, know in advance that a woman could very well be performing *pūjā* when they arrive. I suspect this elderly woman's family brought her along hoping she would react differently.

Always looking for ways to communicate to visitors that the Rush temple supports women's ritual participation, Aiya added a new innovation during the summer of 2001 to the midday Saturday ritual. Just before the weekly procession led by the ritually charged *kālasam* pot, carried on the shoulder of the ritual's sponsor, Aiya asked for first-time female visitors to step forward.[16] He then removed the temple's ten large, rare right-spiraled conch shells from around the base of the *kālasam* pot. He handed these shells, representative of the ten directional deities and containing ritually charged liquid, to ten women.[17] He instructed the women to lead the procession, winding first around the inside of the temple and then around the outside, stopping at various stations along the way. Conventionally, the ten shells are an optional and exceptional processional feature and are, along with the *kālasam*, solely the domain of brahman priests.[18] This is something of which newcomers are typically quite aware. Sudharshan describes their reaction:

> The reason [the shells are given to] the women who are there for the first time at the temple is just to make them feel welcome. And once they get it in their hands, you should see their eyes! They well up, they can't believe they've been given this honor. Because everybody who gets it is coming to the temple for the first time and they understand the gravity of holding onto ritual objects which are usually a privilege not afforded to the lay person. Because the priests get to carry all this. And here you're a woman being called forward to touch it. And the husbands are like [*Sudharshan makes a surprised face*] "Hmm! This is interesting!"

Aiya regularly underlines the gist of such practices by publicly espousing his feminist views whenever he gets the chance—during festivals or on weekends after Saturday *abhiṣekam*. Wedding ceremonies offer special teaching opportunities, since the gatherings often include people who otherwise would not enter a temple. In the fall of 2002, Lily, a Puerto Rican American devotee, married Tim, raised a Jehovah's Witness but no longer affiliated with the tradition. A number of inner-core devotees attended the ceremony along with select members from the bride and groom's families who dared venture into a Hindu temple. Aiya began the ritual with feminist verve, proclaiming that Lily was an honored temple member, having full privileges as a "priestess." Recalling the traditional Christian wedding enjoinder to "obey," doubtless familiar to many of his listeners, Aiya took the opportunity to offer commentary on a contrasting Sankrit phrase traditionally recited while the couple walks around the marriage fire together: "Here there are no sentiments like obedience—like *obey*. The ancients say, '*Sakā saptapadī bhāva*.' *Sakā* means friend. You and I will be friends for life, let us walk through this planet and our life

Lily and Tim's wedding ceremony. Photo by Pathmanathan.

span as friends. Friends don't expect anything from each other. There is only love there. And they do for each other what they think is correct. So friendship is what is emphasized."

The effect of spoken and unspoken support for women's participation and gender equality at the Rush temple, helping to build self-respect and confidence in the women themselves, makes its mark on male temple devotees, as well. Although the effect can be felt across the generations, first-generation immigrants who have come to North America as adults report the most dramatic impact. Charu, a quick-witted Maharashtrian who grew up in Tamil Nadu and moved to Syracuse from Hyderabad with her husband in 1974, talked to me from the Syracuse University Library where she works. In her experience, practices and insights learned at the temple are particularly eye-opening for men:

> The men especially, they learn to see women differently. Because in all women, or anyone you see, you see the Devī in them. And all are like a mother to us. And you can see her in any way. You can see her as a mother or see her as a girlfriend or see her as a friend. You

> can create her in yourself, see her in that way and that changes your perspective of the whole world around you.
>
> You can talk to my husband—you can ask him about the change and he will explain. Most of [the men], their outlook has changed. They don't treat women as dirt, they are not just kitchen helpers, they are not just to entertain them or keep their kids. So the understanding between husband and wife creates a good feeling instead of fighting over silly things. You understand, so life goes kind of smoother.

Charu's older sister, Sheela, privately practiced Śrīvidyā rituals in India. She reports that once she met Aiya and Guruji in 1988, three years after arriving in the United States, she experienced a dramatic strengthening of her practice and self-esteem, enabling her to negotiate a difficult stage in her life. An extremely confident, independent, and generous woman, Sheela described to me her transformation while we sat at her kitchen table and finished a dinner she had cooked for us:

> Oh, before I got into this, I was kind of, y'know if anybody says, "You have to do this" I used to do it. Right? Like a rabbit, you're too afraid to talk, to talk back. Like that, you are afraid, "Oh, if I do this and say things like this, they might ask, 'Oh why is she doing this?' " Y'know, we are always thinking of others, what they will think. Even if we don't want to do something, we are doing it for others' sake. That is how I was.
>
> Then slowly when I started going to the *pīṭham* I started thinking, "Why should I shut up? If it is right, if it looks right to me, I will do it." So that's how, slowly, I started. But people, they started seeing these changes in me, "She was not like this before. Now she's talking back. She's doing what she wants to do, she's not listening to us." Or "Oh, she's arrogant." I didn't care.
>
> Before, if someone said something like this, I used to cry. I didn't like them being mad at me. Honestly now, I don't care. I don't care what people think. I know I'm doing the right thing.

Female devotees' increased confidence, mixed with their newly honed ritual abilities, means that temples outside Rush and, more dramatically, outside North America, must on occasion contend with them. Mohan, proud husband of Rupa, gleefully described to me one such instance. Rupa, a woman of regal stature who possesses a strong, clear voice and has mastered numerous extensive chants, decided during a recent return trip to Goa to continue her chanting practices when visiting her neighborhood temple. As she sat behind the priest and chanted in full voice along with him, he eventually turned to her and told her to be quiet. Rather than allowing him to silence her, Rupa looked at him and simply asked, "Why?" The priest apparently stopped dead in his tracks, unable to giver her an answer. When he resumed the ritual, she continued to chant along in unison.

Of the various types of temple rituals, the fire ritual, or *homam*, if practiced at all, is typically perceived as one of the most powerful and demanding and, as a result, has the greatest shock value when performed by women. Aiya naturally invites women initiates to be among the eight who sit closest to the fire to chant and give offerings, two on each edge of the square pit. Sometimes women sit as members of husband-wife pairs around the *homam*, sometimes as female duos. During the 1999 *pratiṣṭhā* festival, Aiya validated this unusual practice with a reference to scripture: "In all the Vedic rituals we find that they have quietly omitted the females. The ladies are never permitted anywhere near the *homa kundam*. Was it like that always? No. In the ancient days, a very prominent brahman and his wife will do the *homam* together. That is why they say [*Aiya chants Sanskrit*], 'In the company of his wife he must do the *homam*.' "

A particularly public reverberation of Rush women's *homam* participation occurred in India during the summer of 2001. The occasion was a Śrīvidyā conference in Chennai that Aiya attended with several of his students, including two Euro American women, Aparna and Kathy. The five-day conference consisted of early-morning *homam* rituals, afternoon presentations, evening cultural events and scripture readings, and was organized by a gentleman Aiya met as a result of his *Śrī Vidyā: Śrī Cakra Pūjā Vidhiḥ* book. The conference marked a milestone within the Śrīvidyā community, since its organizers proposed to practice and discuss openly their otherwise secret tradition.

Although the event itself represented an unprecedented unveiling of tradition, elements of it, particularly during the morning *homam* segment, demonstrated that much Śrīvidyā business was carried on as usual. The Rush contingent, representing an unconventional group of *upāsakas* and expecting a slightly less conventional gathering, were taken aback when they found full ritual participation to be limited to male brahmans. Aparna described how she and Kathy challenged conference restrictions during the eight-hour-long morning ritual segments involving five simultaneous *homams*.

> So they have their forty brahman priests, all in there chanting. And other people who were not participating were not even paying attention. It was more like a sideshow. The area was roped off—if people sat at all, they sat twenty feet back. So Kathy and I sat *at* the rope. Every time we made it perfectly clear that we were going to chant aloud. And we got there at four o'clock in the morning every day, we were never late. . . .
>
> At our [Rush] temple, everyone who is in the room, in the *yagña śālā*, would be chanting the mantra with the *swahā* ending.[19] And on

the fourth day, after I felt like I had gained a certain degree of approval, someone came up to me and told me I was not allowed to chant the *swahā* endings. The first day they said it over the loudspeaker, and on this day someone came up to me specifically and said, "Excuse me, what are you doing? You've been requested not to chant the *swahā* endings. This is only for the people who are making the actual offerings into the fire."

So that was the line they drew. Again. It pissed me off. I had been feeling so high from the *homams* . . . Kathy immediately stopped chanting the *swahā* and I just sat there for an hour and fumed. I couldn't even say the mantras without the *swahās* in them. It was interfering, the rhythm was off. What am I supposed to do? I have the intensity, I'm chanting, and now I drop that one word? [*Aparna laughs.*] I was so pissed!!

So we had been at the conference now for four days and at this point I had created a connection with Mohan [the conference organizer]. When he came out of the fire area for the break, which he did every three hours, I was standing right at the sidelines waiting for him. I snagged him—and Aiya was off to the side watching it. I could see he was laughing, like "Here's my daughter, going in for the fight!" [*We laugh.*]

So I told him, "They told me I wasn't supposed to chant *swahā*!" And he just said, "Yeah, that's right." He didn't even *see* my problem with it at first! So I said, "You already pushed us out. You won't let us into the *homam*. I'm sitting by the edge of the rope. I'm chanting every mantra. I'm [mentally] offering just as much as you are. For you to even deny the fact that I'm part of it, it's like you have no comprehension! I *am* making offerings!" And he's like "Oh." And I said, "I can't stop chanting *swahās*. It ruins the rituals for me." So he looked around at his entourage of about five people who were seeing this young girl have a tantrum in front of him, and he said, "Okay. Chant *swahā*."

A couple years before the Śrīvidyā conference, Kathy made a different kind of breakthrough involving entrance into the Kāmākṣī temple at Kāñcīpuram in Tamil Nadu that, as a policy, is denied to foreigners. While this stipulation has nothing to do with gender but rather with the problem of non-Hindus and potential pollution to the temple, Kathy's ability to "prove" herself, making temple entrance a possibility, had much to do with her impressive abilities in an almost exclusively male tradition. Kathy recounted for me the sequence of events as we sat on a grassy slope outside the small Ganeś shrine behind the temple. The story begins with temple officials denying access to a male Euro American devotee accompanied by his Indian wife and two other Indian Rush devotees. In spite of his companions' insistence that he was a Hindu, he still was barred from entering. Months later, during a visit to India, Aiya met with the Śaṇkarācārya of Kāñcīpuram, one of the most esteemed religious leaders of India, and argued his case for allowing his students of non-Indian descent into the temple.[20] The Śaṇkarācārya eventually agreed to admit foreigners who were sincere in their devotion. Kathy, the first test case from Rush, continued the story:

> KATHY So the first time we went, after Aiya had this conversation, I went with the Madhvanaths, Aiya's devotees who live in Madras.[21] Steve [another Rush devotee] came with me. This was his first time in India. The Madhvanaths had called ahead to the śāstri's house and said that Aiya's students are coming, so they were kind of anticipating us. . . .
>
> So we went straight to his house and went to his shrine room. They're all speaking in Tamil and we're having tea, and I have no idea what they're talking about. And then he turns to me and asks, "Do you know the *dasamahā mudrā*s?" And I said, "Yeah." And he said, "Can I see?" . . . So I did it up to their standards and then he turned to Steve and said, "Let's see you do it." And Steve had not been doing *dasamahā mudrā*s at all, and apparently he said that a month prior to going, he sort of got this idea that maybe he should learn them . . . So he quickly sort of tried and kind of halfway did it, but the guy said, "Okay, okay, you've got it. Enough." So that was the test. He was testing us to see if we were Devī *upāsakas*, but I didn't even realize it was a test. I thought he was just curious. And so he said, "Okay, let's go."
>
> I was scared to death. I was like shadowing his every step. And I don't want to look up because I don't want anyone to see my face. So I was just staring down. Because you kind of go down [into the temple], it's a little disorienting. I'm not looking where I'm going, I'm just staring at Kamakotri śāstri's feet who are in front of me, walking. . . .
>
> CORINNE Did you have dark hair? [Kathy's hair is naturally reddish brown.]
>
> KATHY Oh, and oh my gosh, also I had dyed my hair black! I had dyed my hair black. Yeah, just to like "pass" even more. Aiya told me, "Dye your hair black. Wear a huge *pottu*" [the red forehead mark of an auspicious woman and/or goddess devotee]. So I had a big, red *pottu* and I was wearing a sari. And I'm not much of a makeup or dye person, like I never permed my hair or dyed it or anything, and I'm like "No problem!" I dyed my hair black.
>
> And we just went in. I was totally overwhelmed. For me, of all places on the planet, other than this temple, Kāmākṣī is like the heart center of the whole universe. If I could be anywhere other than here, Kāñcīpuram is just for me the most amazing place in the world.

At the Śrīvidyā conference two years later, Kathy was offered the podium during the afternoon presentations to share her story with conference participants. She related fully her sense of nervous anticipation, relief and awe, and the devotional intensity she felt while chanting the *Lalitāsahasranāmam* in front of Kāmākṣī. While relating her experiences it seems she enlightened some audience members to the pain felt by a committed devotee who is left on the margins of an exclusive tradition:

> KATHY And then, when we went to the Śrīvidyā conference, they were very protective about the *sampradāyam* and giving *dīkṣā*, and controlling the guru lineage and controlling Śrīvidyā, and so they asked me to speak in front of the whole conference. So I told that story about getting in to see Kāmākṣī. And people were just crying, totally overwhelmed. It just struck them that they can casually stroll in and see Kāmākṣī any old day they want, and they take it for granted. And to hear that for somebody it was a miracle to go there. . . . Yeah, and I started crying when I told the story, in front of all these people. Yeah, everyone was crying. [*Kathy laughs.*] Everyone was just really touched. And I tried to give a message of equality for women, for foreigners, y'know.
>
> CORINNE And Aiya was cheering you on.
>
> KATHY Yes! And Aiya was like, "Oooh!" He was right there in the front row. Yeah. [*We laugh.*]

With Aiya paving their way or egging them on from the sidelines, women trained at the Śrī Rājarājeśwarī temple continue to make an impact on a largely male-oriented tradition. While clearly benefiting from Aiya's maverick approach, they return the favor by helping him challenge and change tradition—something he cannot do by himself. This growing cadre of self-confident female students, possessing a variety of strengths and styles, seem more than eager to help Aiya with his cause, one that is also their own.

A Community of Priests: Challenges to Outsiders and Insiders

After finishing a lunch of rice, dal, and curried vegetable one summer afternoon, five of us lingered around the temple's empty *homam* pit to hear Aiya tell his own Śrīvidyā conference story. Soon after he arrived at the meeting hall, one of the *upāsaka*s who, like nearly all other conference *upāsaka*s except for Aiya's entourage, was a brahman male, asked him if he was a brahman. Because his reputation preceded him, Aiya guessed the man probably knew the answer and so, rather than honoring the question, volleyed it back: "Are you a brahman?" When the man answered in the affirmative, Aiya then proceeded to list the qualifications for brahmans specified by the first-century

Hindu law book, the *Laws of Manu*, by asking more questions. Do you have a bank account? Do you earn a living? Do you wear shoes? Do you have a fire burning in your house to which you do rituals three times a day? The man refrained from answering these questions since his lifestyle, like that of most brahmans throughout most of history, did not fit ancient law-book specifications. Aiya finished his story by saying that after his "tirade," in which he deconstructed the category "brahman," conference participants left him and the issue of caste alone.

Aiya's determination to level caste status by critiquing assumed male brahmanical privilege and by teaching anyone interested the ritual arts of the priestly trade, aims in essence to create a community of priests, of people who gain ritual entitlement through learning rather than birthright. Although a number of Aiya's students are brahman by birth, and a good many temple priests support his style, other members of the larger South Asian community openly criticize Aiya and the Rush temple for breaking with tradition. What seems to bother some people the most is not the fact that Aiya is performing Vedic rituals as a nonbrahman, but that he is teaching others, as well. As Sudharshan describes it, "If he were a nonbrahman quietly doing [rituals] in some place, nobody would care. But this is a threat. Because he's creating monsters. That's exactly what he's doing, right? He's creating monsters." Rush temple devotees seem particularly threatening when they use their priestly knowledge to challenge the abilities of priests at other temples. Normally, temple goers do not notice the quality of ritual performance or, if they do, they feel it is not their place to say anything. Sudharshan describes the scenario:

> It happens now that people in their congregations know the litanies. And they've been telling [the priests], "Look! You're cutting short on X litany. Why don't you complete *Śrī Suktam*? By the way, how come when you say the *Durgā Suktam* you only say the first three stanzas?" Well, first of all, they might be offended and pissed off that someone would correct them. And then they think, "My God, you're right! How could I have missed seven stanzas and only said the first three? [*pause*] Because I only know the first three. So I've got to go brush up with a refresher course on the other stanzas."

Although a number of people confirmed for me that alert Rush devotees have prompted some priests at other temples to attend refresher courses, other shifts in protocol are taking place at Sri Lankan temples in Toronto as well, seemingly in indirect response to Rush temple practices. For instance, the Mīnakṣī temple in Toronto, run by one of Aiya's initiates, has started to assign women the task of carrying the processional deities. Although this already takes place at a few other temples in the United States, it is a first for Toronto. The Sri Lankan Toronto Aiyappa and Vara-Siddhi Vinayaka temples have also begun to make the *abhiṣekam* ritual available to the public. Although the *abhiṣekams* are performed on proxy *lingams* set outside the temples, the fact that they are encouraging communal participation represents a dramatic shift in style. Some priests are also beginning to adopt Aiya's unusual wedding format by prefacing the ceremony with a twenty-minute explanation of ritual mechanics and meaning.[22]

Whether priests have begun to shift their practices because they agree that ritual access and knowledge are important or whether they do so to keep up with the competition is difficult to say. In any case, mingled with explicit support and solidarity by default are highly negative reactions to Aiya and the Rush temple style. Because this criticism has little impact on the temple itself, Aiya can afford to take a rather generous perspective. As he once said to me, in passing, "[Their disapproval] doesn't bother me because I didn't build the temple for them and I didn't build the temple for those people in Toronto or anybody else. I did this because this is what I wanted to do all my life! [*Aiya chuckles.*] If others want to join and participate in the feast, good! Otherwise, let them go."

Although the process of offering the Rush temple "feast" opens up opportunities for insiders and perhaps forces what many consider to be positive challenges to surrounding institutions, it is not without its internal challenges. Although joyful and bountiful, a rich and generous feast can end in heartburn if one is not careful.

Diaspora communities, it seems, are naturally endowed with certain challenges. Studies repeatedly show how internal tensions, intrinsic to all religious organizations, can be more visible and strident among immigrants because stakes are higher. As Raymond Williams puts it, religion provides for diasporic groups a crucial "anchor for memory that relates personal and group identity with the past" for people who feel their lives are too quickly changing (1992: 229).[23] As a result, South Asian communities often find that traditional caste, regional, and sectarian identities gain renewed importance and become a considerable source of friction when building and maintaining places of worship. Disputes commonly break out over temple design and ritual format, particularly over whether they will reflect north or south Indian styles. The decision as to which family of deities to install—Vaiṣṇava, Śaiva, or Śākta—can also cause conflict. As in any organization, the question of how to spend money and with what strings attached also creates dissension (Narayanan 1992: 175; Wood 1980: 286; Bilmoria 1996: 35–39).[24]

Because the Rush temple is not a typical North American Hindu temple—established and directed primarily by an individual rather than by the local South Asian community—the fact that it is decidedly Tamil Sri Lankan in style, dedicated to the Goddess and to the Śaiva-Śākta tradition has never been under significant dispute. Lack of overt conflict over these issues is noteworthy, since a considerable minority of inner-core devotees are not Sri Lankan, nor were they originally Śaiva or Goddess worshipers.[25] Money matters sometimes raise a few hackles, but Aiya's veto power, although it sometimes creates resentment, prevents most arguments from reeling out of control. On an organizational level, the Śrī Rājarājeśwarī Pīṭham thus more closely resembles a guru-led ashram than a committee- or community-led temple.[26] Yet its ritual structure and South Asian demographic make it, on a practical level, look and act more like a temple. Defying tidy categorizations and eluding the kinds of tensions that normally break out at diaspora temples, Rush's "community of priests" nonetheless demonstrates that priests are people too and not immune from conflict.

The source for both celebration and tension at typical diaspora temples seems to be its role in galvanizing national, regional, sectarian, and/or caste identities by linking them with the sacred. Although the Rush temple celebrates a regional (Sri Lankan) and sectarian (Śaiva-Śākta) identity, its focus, particularly for inner-core devotees, is on individualized sanctity established through connections to the guru and deity. The fact that the Rush temple works to cut through hierarchy and create a community of priests makes the sacred reassuringly accessible to all but, at the same time, unnervingly up for grabs. The Rush temple's unique commitment to full participation—creating the delectable "feast" to which Aiya refers—fuels, in return, its greatest challenge.[27]

Because initiation and spiritual progress at Rush are matters largely left between guru and disciple, and because temple scheduling allows regular opportunities for those willing and able to perform rituals, the area of operations most up for grabs has to do with support tasks performed in and around the temple. Particular tasks tend to fall to those who possess appropriate skills and experience as well as preference. No task is officially assigned greater or lesser value, yet certain jobs seem more important because of their proximity to the deity. If someone has skills associated with a seemingly prestigious task and also has firm opinions about its execution, less experienced people who try to help may end up feeling slighted. Amid the tensions it is often difficult to know if inflexible bossiness or inexperience and oversensitivity are to blame. Less prestigious (although no less important) tasks like cleaning toilets are, naturally, far less likely to spark disputes.

Although such tensions may seem petty to the outsider, they can be deeply significant to those embroiled in them. For many, having or "owning" a meaningful task at the temple offers not only personal and religious affirmation but also a crucial sense of belonging. Whether preparing for or assisting rituals, dressing deities, cleaning ritual implements, making garlands, chopping vegetables, building chariots, or mowing grass, contributing in a meaningful way forges one's place not only within a community but also in an extended family. Finding a sense of belonging within a temple family for which Aiya and Amma are father and mother is understandably of great consequence since, in this context, insider status and the potential for divine intimacy are so intertwined and inextricable.

Aiya often finds devotees' disputes over task ownership and entitlement nearly impossible to resolve without upsetting one or all parties. His strategy is thus typically to tread lightly in hopes that matters will be resolved on their own. Although some people do settle their differences, intractable disputes and hurt feelings have been known to linger. On a few occasions Aiya spoke to me about his concerns. During one such conversation in the summer of 2000, I was reminded of Max Weber's "routinization of charisma," a trend in which prophetic, antiestablishment movements rigidify over time, reverting to structures similar to the institutions they rebelled against to begin with.[28] I later proposed to Sudharshan that the temple's tensions over tasks and entitlement are part of a dynamic with which any antihierarchical organization contends. The natural tendency to build hierarchy mirrors the institutional entropy characterized by Weber's theory. Following are excerpts from a lengthy midmorning conversation in the temple house, miraculously uninterrupted by the telephone. Sudharshan begins by presenting Weber's theory to Aiya who, in turn, fleshes it out by describing what seems to be his nearly impossible balancing act:

SUDHARSHAN It's a radical movement where you make some kind of reform, break away from tradition and revitalize it again. But as time goes by, that thing that is reformed and new and radical gets institutionalized and orthodox. Right? So that reform becomes an institution in itself. And becomes structure and oppressive and then. . . . So we want to know what you think of that.

AIYA I was talking about this yesterday. When there is a reform movement, one thing is that you break down barriers and you empower people. The danger in empowering people, because it is open to all and sundry, is that there are some individuals who will go with the flow in the beginning, but then their base instincts, so to speak, will start to take over. And they will start the beginnings of a hierarchy. There's a pecking order established.

Regarding this hierarchy that's beginning to form, I have to tread a very cautious path. If I come down too hard on these people, it will result in the loss of enthusiasm, loss of attendance, and spin-offs from those things. So I have to keep their sense of importance and balance it with the ideals of the institution. . . . So, the idea is not to create a pecking order, but also to keep the interest of the people who are coming here. For some of them doing certain functions in the temple gives them the required focus in their own *sādhana*. And for others, the problem is that that very focus has become a distraction. . . .

I also see sometimes that there are a group of individuals coming and they are so eager. They want to do everything. And there are certain people who know the ropes, so to speak, in that particular area. They have the expertise. And for them there is an urgency that it has to be done because there is a certain time frame. And they find there is not the time to be teaching others to do this thing, so they will just go ahead and do it.

Now this will be immediately construed [by the newcomer] as, "Oh, they won't let me do it." And they wonder, "What am I doing here? Why am I a stranger?" See, that means those people are still not broken away from the emotional thing. You should be able to function as a cog in any portion or any part of the machinery. You should be able to pitch in. If you see something going on, if you can't be part of it, or if somebody else is doing it, go and do something else.

SUDHARSHAN See, that's exactly what we were talking about. Because there are all these specialized tasks that people are doing, people have also attached value to these tasks. So being inside the temple is perceived as being higher, somehow, than being out there scrubbing the toilets for the *pratiṣṭhā*. Which is very wrong. There is no hierarchy in tasks.

AIYA The person who is doing those little tasks they have specialized in, they should not become tyrannical. If they do, we're sunk.

CORINNE And they may not perceive themselves as tyrannical. They may perceive themselves as doing things correctly, and that's important too.

AIYA That's the problem.

After talking for some time about the temple conundrum, Aiya sat silently while Sudharshan and I talked back and forth for another few minutes. Aiya reentered the conversation by interjecting an analogy for what he considers the nearly impossible task of keeping everyone happy:

> So just to answer your question, I have to have this blend. And I have to see to it that it doesn't get too much sugar, or too much milk, or too much coffee, too much water. I have to make sure that this is acceptable for somebody who drinks black Turkish coffee, the person who drinks Italian immediately after lunch and is very strong, or a Jaffna blend of coffee. I have to make sure that this blend is acceptable to everybody. Now go figure that out! How difficult is that?!

In the final analysis, it seems the job of pleasing everyone, of maintaining a well-run, efficient temple that at the same time resists hierarchies—although eternally unfinished and often frustrating—is well worth the trouble for Aiya. The difficult job of providing a setting that offers equal access to learning and ritual performance reaps tangible benefits, provoking, as many see it, positive changes in participants as well as in the wider community. Furthermore, temple teachings are reminders that a person's true status cannot be measured by human standards—humans are simply not in a position to make that kind of assessment. By removing what Aiya and temple devotees understand to be human restrictions based on age, gender, caste, or ethnicity, devotees have the opportunity to reach their potential using a different set of standards. Although not without its challenges, this seems the only logical solution.

There are moments when higher authorities seem to affirm this logic. During the summer of 2002, I arrived a few days after the conclusion of the *pratiṣṭhā* festival to find nearly everyone nursing a terrible cold. For some, the cold had even advanced to pneumonia. When I remarked to Aiya that people seemed to be quite sick, he shifted the conversation from the viral to the karmic level, explaining that many of the inner-core devotees were sick from the weekend festival due to the massive number of initiations performed. According to most guru-disciple traditions, the process of initiation entails the removal of the new *upāsaka*'s karma—their slate cleaned, so to speak, to make way for their new spiritual path. Removing a person's negative karma is not entirely trouble-free, however; someone has to take the brunt of the karmic fallout, typically the guru who performs the initiation.[29] As Aiya put it, noting the coughing and sniffling surrounding us, "The Mother has to give all the left over junk to *somebody*."

The fact that a large group of devotees developed colds in return for karmic cleansing provides, for Aiya and others, concrete evidence that he is not the only one holding down the fort at the temple. Being a dedicated member of the community—regardless of age, gender, caste, or tasks performed—puts one at risk for priestly liabilities as well as benefits. Although a cold is not something to which one usually aspires, in this case, as a sign of religious leadership bestowed by the Devī herself, it is an honor.

6

A Fine Balance

The Give and Take of Religious Discipline

Limit and innovation, formation and transformation, are complementary in human life. They constitute a polarity within which ritual practice moves. Where limit is given too great a value, there ritual becomes the servant of oppression. Where innovation is sought without regard for restraint, there ritual will lose itself in chaos and confusion.

—Tom Driver, *The Magic of Ritual*, 50–51

During one of Aiya's evening storytelling sessions, a weekly tradition originally held after Friday evening *pūjā*, the group in attendance consisted mainly of Sri Lankan Tamils who had traveled to Rush from Toronto for the evening.[1] Aiya had just finished the *pūjā* and the air was a haze of camphor and incense. As he stood at the front, to the left of the main Ganeś *mūrti*, he prefaced his evening's story by explaining that these gatherings were for the youth who, he felt, spent too much time in front of the "boob tube" rather than learning traditional songs or stories. As Aiya saw it, this was not the fault of the children but, rather, as he put it, "We are to blame." He insisted that the younger generation's ignorance about their culture was entirely the fault of their neglectful parents. Once finished with this short but sharp reprimand, Aiya explained to the small crowd, still seemingly attentive, that tonight's story was from the *Periya Purāṇam*, a collection of Tamil religious classics.

The tale is set in a hilly district in Tamil Nadu and features a hunter king's eldest son, Thinnan, adept in the arts of archery and hunting. Thinnan and two of his friends, Kadan and Madan, are on a hunting expedition and are led into a jungle while chasing a boar. They eventually shoot the boar down, and Kadan and Madan head toward a nearby river to prepare the carcass for cooking. Thinnan sights a hill nearby and proposes they climb it and receive the blessings of the god stationed at the top. Kadan and Madan opt to stay and work on the boar while Thinnan turns to explore the hill. Aiya continues:

> So Thinnan starts climbing the hill. As he starts climbing, something in him is completely being changed. He feels this irresistible pull; something is pulling him. And he goes there and sees this [Śiva *lingam*]. On top of it there are flowers, there is *vibhuti tripundaram*,[2] there is *kumkum*, and water has been poured over it [as signs of worship]. For some reason he can't pull away from there. He falls in love with the *lingam*. He is walking around, singing, and behaving in a very fine manner when he thinks, "The Lord will become hungry. Let me go and get some food for Him."
>
> When he finds that his two friends have already skinned the wild boar he says, "You stay aside," and begins to cook the meat. He takes portions of the meat, tastes it in his mouth, and the tasted portions he keeps aside. Now, this would appear completely contradictory to what we are used to. If we offer something to Devī, do we taste it first? [*A few people shake their heads.*] It becomes *ucistam* [polluted through contact with saliva]. But here he is in such a state of ecstasy, he doesn't know what he is doing. The only idea he has is, "I should feed the Lord, and I should give Him the tastiest." So he tastes it and then carries it.
>
> Next he collects some flowers. He can't hold them because he has taken quite a lot of meat in his hands. Where is he going to keep the flowers? So he takes the flowers and puts them on his hair. Then he also sees water. He has to offer water, but how will he take it? So he goes to the river, keeps the meat on leaves, and fills his mouth with water. Flowers there [*Aiya puts his hand on his head*], and he's taken the meat [*Aiya mimes holding handfuls of meat*], and he goes running up with his mouth full. And he starts making offerings and says, "Look, I have brought tasty meat for you." Like this he is talking to the Śiva *lingam*. And he's offering and he's worshiping.
>
> When the friends come and ask him to accompany them back to the village he says, "No. I don't feel I should leave the Lord alone in this jungle with all the wild animals around. I am going to stand guard and protect him." So, the two friends, after unsuccessfully trying to get him back, they go and tell the father, "He's lost his head,

he's refusing to come, and he's behaving in a funny manner." So, the parents come and they try to get him down. Mmm mmm [*shakes his head*]. Nothing doing! He refuses to come.

The whole night he's there, and in the morning he thinks he will take a bath in the river and then come. When he is gone, the brahman priest who normally looks after the Śiva *lingam* comes up to the place and he's shattered! He says, "Who would do this? Oh my God!" and he brings water and washes it all and he performs the *prāyaścittam* [rite of atonement] and then performs the *pūjā* and goes. And then Thinnan comes back. He's shot something else that he's brought to eat. He cooks it, and the same process is repeated. This goes on for a few days. And the priest is beside himself with the desecration that's going on. He's thinking, "How can I find out who is doing this?" He's very disturbed.

Then one night, in a dream, Śiva appears to him and tells him, "The person who is doing this desecration, his very nature is love. From each hair follicle in his body, devotion exudes. And his single-mindedness itself is worship. Come! Hide somewhere and watch what he's doing." The next day, Thinnan, as usual, is coming up the hill. He's hunted, he's brought the meat, and he's come with his mouth full of water and flowers stuck on his head.

There are two eyes on this Śiva lingam from the vibhuti. From the left eye, Thinnan sees that blood is pouring down. And he says [*in an incredulous voice*], "Who would do this to you in my absence?" And he wipes it away. He is very disturbed. He is feeling extreme pain. He says, "Ah ha! One eye is gone and I have two eyes. I'll give you one." He takes an arrow from his quiver and takes one eye out and places it on the left side of the *lingam*, and it stops bleeding. And he's happy. Before he turns away, the right side starts to bleed. He says, "What do I do now? I have another eye I can give you but I don't know where to put it. Because once I take the eye out, I cannot see. Where will I put it?" So he puts his foot out and with his big toe he marks the place for the eye on the Śiva *lingam*. As he's about to take the other eye out Śiva comes out of the *lingam* and says, "Stop, Kannappa!!"

And from that point he's known as Kannappa.[3] And the brahman priest and this guy both have a vision of the Lord and are given *vibhuti* [sacred ash as a blessing].[4]

Listening to the story, I thought I knew what was coming. I could already hear the moral Aiya would apply when he finished: the laws of purity and pollution that the brahman scrupulously observes pale in the face of true faith. Since deep devotion overrides orthodoxy, Śiva is pleased with offerings the brahman considers defiled: water mixed with spittle; flowers embedded in hair; cooked, pretasted flesh; and even a foot planted on the god's face. Śiva, anticipating the great sacrifice born of Thinnan's endless devotion, produces blood from the eyes of his *lingam* form and teaches the hiding brahman priest a lesson. Since a theme running through Aiya's discourses so often involves suspicion of brahmanical privilege, I was ready to hear it again. What I did not consider was the audience. Returning to the slightly scolding tone he set at the beginning of the story, Aiya offered the moral I was expecting but from a very different angle: "And the moral of the story: Lots of Sri Lankans who come here, especially people from Jaffna, they come and ask me, 'Aiya do we have to be initiated to do these things?' I say, 'Yes, you have to.' And they lose their enthusiasm. If you are going to go the same route as Kannappa, to take your eye out, dig one eye out, then you can go and do. But can you? You won't. So that kind of devotion is very difficult, much more so than what we have here."

While Aiya could have crafted the story's moral to be an endorsement of faith-filled unothodoxy, he focuses instead on the need for maintaining discipline. In a seemingly uncharacteristic stance, Aiya invites the listener to identify with the brahman priest rather than the renegade devotee. Although I did not anticipate this moral lesson, it is perfectly consistent with temple practice. There are ways the Rush temple *does* identify with the brahman priest. Aiya tenaciously maintains a number of rules and ritual practices considered important by conservative brahmanical standards, some of which are fading in importance at other temple communities, particularly in North America and urban India. Although the previous two chapters have focused mainly on how Aiya breaks with convention, often gleefully so, it is important to note that rules and discipline remain an integral component of temple worship.

When speaking to gatherings composed largely of members of his own Jaffna Tamil community, Aiya often assumes the scolding tone that frames the above story, emphasizing discipline to counterbalance what he sees as a lackadaisical or utilitarian approach to religious practices. For inner-core devotees who tend to maintain impressive levels of discipline, commitment, and even sacrifice, Aiya often encourages a certain mischievous playfulness. If one stands back and views the temple as a whole, it seems to be one big balancing act containing clusters of smaller feats of balance and complementarity.

Cultural Baggage: Selective Packing

As mentioned in chapter 4, one of the greatest earthly concerns driving temple practices and programs is the welfare of the local Sri Lankan Tamil community, most of whom live in the Toronto area across the Canadian border. Aiya does not expect that many of these visitors will become committed initiates and, for the most part, this seems fine with him. He is eager to provide them with a powerful site for worship and a place of calm away from an often tumultuous, sometimes troubled, urban context—a piece of Sri Lankan "home" without the turmoil. The fact that Aiya has a deep affinity for and sense of responsibility toward his community does not mean, however, that he is uncritical of what he considers its negative tendencies. Some Sri Lankan visitors from Toronto offered me similar criticisms, and one might even assume that the growing number of Sri Lankan Tamils coming over the border to the temple reflects a general concurrence with Aiya's critiques. But basic differences in opinion continue between Aiya and many Sri Lankan visitors, particularly those who travel to the temple solely for utilitarian reasons, propelled by its reputation for granting miracles. These are the people, liberally sprinkled throughout weekend and festival crowds, for whom he maintains his soapbox.

An overarching appeal in many of Aiya's public reprimands is that people be more selective about the contents of their cultural baggage.[5] He insists that devotees do away with some habits, keep others and, in all situations, apply more discipline. One Sri Lankan "tradition" Aiya feels would be best left behind is the tendency to treat temple visits as opportunities for socializing. This practice, common throughout South Asia, often relegates temple rituals and the priests performing them to the background. The environment Aiya aims to create is thus more like an attentive church service than a typical temple gathering. As he put it during one weekend address, "You may jabber with your neighbor and find out what television he's got and what kind of movie he's been watching and what green-colored sari, where did she buy it. . . . Is this why you go to temples? We try to prevent that here." Aiya insists that constant chatter distracts serious devotees and, besides, there is plenty of room outside—twenty-three acres, in fact—for those who wish to wander and chat. Seemingly punctuating the point, a sign stating in bold, red lettering "NO NEEDLESS TALKING" glared down from one of the temple walls for several years. The sign was removed during a temple repainting and never rehung—indicating, perhaps, that people are catching on.

Other habits that Aiya encourages his community to relinquish range from an overemphasis on astrology to littering, yet these seem to be of less consequence than the problem of discarding worthwhile cultural habits too easily. Aiya most commonly addresses this issue by noting how parents neglect handing down stories and traditions to their children, but the larger problem, as Aiya sees it, is that people have too readily adapted to consumerist culture. The following excerpt from a conversation in the small temple house during the summer of 2000 speaks to this concern:

> AIYA One day I was criticizing the crowd—the Tamil crowd [in the temple]: "You place so much importance on stupid things like observing birthdays. Where did you learn this tradition of cutting a cake and peo-

ple standing there and singing, not knowing what the words mean? And you'll say something just because you saw the idiot next to you doing the same thing? Where did you learn this? Is this your culture?" And two, three fellows walked out. They don't like it. And I don't care.

CORINNE So are you critiquing the fact that they take on North American culture?

AIYA This is not North American. You go to Oslo, or you go to New Hamburg, or you go to Modena in Italy, or Sicily—the same thing. The Tamils, wherever they are, they go blblbl! [*Aiya makes the sound of entropy, like air escaping a balloon.*] And, I tell them, the English calendar means nothing. That's not your birthday.

And on birthdays, don't expect people to give you gifts. You give to people. That is our tradition. If you can't give too much, feed someone. Give them a meal. And in this country, if somebody comes and tells me, "I can't afford to give somebody a meal," I think they should be thrashed. Not in this country. Not in this country and not in Canada. You cannot say that you can't afford to give somebody a meal. Give a homeless person a meal! If you can't cook it, go to a McDonalds, get a good meal and go give it to the guy. He will eat.

But I see things going in the other direction. In Toronto, there are sixteen Tamil newspapers. If a child like Purvaja has a birthday, one week ahead of time there will be a big ad saying "Purvaja Celebrates Her Tenth Birthday!" with a picture of Purvaja. And uncles and aunts in Denmark and Italy and England and Sweden wish her a happy birthday—and Malaysia and Australia and New Zealand—they print all these names and places and sometimes titles and professions. What the hell is going on?! And at other times they will go to extremes. They'll rent a hall with music and food, just so you can show the rest of the community how important you are. I used to make fun of this kind of thing knowing fully well that some people get upset. So okay.

CORINNE So you're suspicious of the showiness.

AIYA Absolutely. You're breeding consumerism all over the place. It has come to a point where, weeks ahead, the children are sitting there anticipating, "This is my birthday, what will my oldest uncle from Sweden bring me?" It's the same thing as the damn idiot tube showing you so many little toys and gimmicks during the program break. And the parents have to go and get that and this. And you're making this into an institution. This is culture?[6]

During subsequent conversations, Aiya elaborated on this argument, noting that Western nations do not have a monopoly on consumerism or status consciousness (or television). Excessive showiness within the immigrant Sri

Lankan community is, as he sees it, a reflection of certain members' "small-town natures" that manifest as competitive opulence when given the financial means to do so. Consumerist appetites, latent during simpler times, flourish under the proper conditions. Aiya's admonishments hearken back to a simpler time and place that he furthermore realizes is difficult to unearth in today's world. He nonetheless invokes this elusive state of being, it seems, for the sake of challenging a newly adopted lifestyle that he considers unhealthy. By arguing that his audience is losing its grip on tradition—even if it is largely a part of history—he hopes to make his appeal all the more persuasive.[7]

Aiya will undoubtedly continue to dole out admonishments even though they may rub the wrong way and in spite of his knowledge that some attitudes are nearly impossible to alter. Although he would prefer that temple visitors be compelled by devotion—like Kannappa, their distasteful idiosyncrasies might then be overlooked—most come to Rush for utilitarian reasons. Visitors want their problems—whether having to do with business, health, children, or astrological projections—to be fixed, and they set their sights on Aiya and the Śrī Rājarājeśwarī Pīṭham as the cure. Although Aiya does not actively discourage this—indeed, he works hard to ensure that the temple is ritually powerful—he is constantly on the lookout for chances to forge deeper commitment, focus, and discipline. He hopes that by being selective about one's cultural baggage, discarding some habits and holding fast to others, the right balance might be struck, paving the way for deeper devotion.[8]

Temple "Rules" to Keep and to Leave Behind

During the summer of 2002, I did my best to talk to as many temple visitors—non–inner-core devotees—as possible.[9] After learning a bit about their background, I often asked people for general impressions and, for the most part, was not surprised by their answers. Many visitors noted the beauty of the temple, its elaborate layout and gleaming gold *mūrtis*. Others were interested in the fact that women conducted *pūjās* and that rituals often involved synchronized chanting. At one point, however, I happened to have back-to-back discussions with people who related seemingly opposite impressions of the temple. I initially tried to remedy the contradiction by "clarifying" for one of the visitors what he really meant. Later it occurred to me that the temple itself embodies disjunctions that, upon closer inspection, are more complementary than contradictory. These apparent contradictions have to do with another set of "rules" that Aiya selectively keeps and breaks, having less to do with discipline and cultural assimilation than with ritual itself.

One Sunday afternoon at the end of May, a group of three Sri Lankan men agreed to sit and talk with me in the white plastic chairs set up in the temple hallway. All roughly in their early thirties, they had come to the temple from

New York City for the weekend. As a threesome they had been fairly regular visitors since September of 1999 and planned to continue traveling to Rush whenever they had the chance. When I asked what kept bringing them back all this distance (about three hundred and thirty miles), they unanimously agreed that the powerful temple goddess drew them. Once this was established, one of the men mentioned that at other temples you could not touch the main temple *mūrti* or talk to the priest. At Rush, you not only could talk with the priest but he also made you feel right at home. Hearing this, one of the others laughed and added, "Yes, he [Aiya] is always saying, 'Feel free! Feel free!' At other temples you feel like visitors. Here we feel like we're partners, not visitors." The third gentleman added that people are so open-minded at the Rush temple; you can do anything you wish. On second thought he continued, "You really *have* to participate. You cannot just come and ignore what is going on." Together they marveled at the fact that the *śrīcakra pūjā,* so beautifully performed by a Euro American woman the night before, was unlike anything found anywhere else.

I conducted my next informal interview the following day, after the morning *pūjā,* with a local Rochester man originally from Andhra Pradesh, his brother and wife visiting from Florida, and his parents visiting from India. Although the Rochester man was not a regular member of the Rush community, he wanted to show his family the temple. When I asked about their impressions, the brother from Florida stated emphatically that *pūjā*s were performed *just* like they were in India, with such precision and beauty. About the temple in general, he said, referring to its adherence to traditional practices, "No compromise. No compromise." Wondering why he did not mention the fact that a woman had performed the morning *pūjā* and that afterward everyone was invited to approach the main deities and touch them, I suggested that maybe it was a little different from most Indian temples. Not seeing things my way, he insisted that there are indeed places in India, particularly in the north, where one can touch *mūrtis.* And besides, the reason people cannot touch them is because they lack discipline. If a person is properly attuned, it is okay. Left unsaid was the fact that touching the main *mūrti* in a traditional south Indian temple goes completely against the grain, as do women publicly performing rituals.

After we finished talking and the group left the temple, Sudharshan, who overheard the conversation as well as the one the day before, remarked to me, a little surprised, "That's the complete opposite of what those men said to you yesterday!" He and I marveled at the Florida man's sense that the Rush temple did things according to traditional specifications—that there was no compromise—and laughed at my insistence on the "right" answer, that the temple was not at all *just* like India. Upon further thought, we decided that the two very different reactions reflected the way the temple abandons some agreed-upon traditions yet carefully guards others. This latter "conservative" impression in some ways grounds and gives validity to Aiya's maverick approach, functioning like his frequent appeal to the authority of scripture and his guru. The unanticipated interpretations of the man from Florida are not only not "wrong," they represent an integral part of the mix.

The most obvious way Aiya adheres to tradition, noted by the Florida man, is his attention to ritual detail and largesse. Although Hindu "tradition" is an unwieldy, rather subjective entity—as Aiya at times admits—Rush rituals are commonly perceived as "out-priesting" the priests in the region, particularly at Tamil Sri Lankan temples, forcing some of them toward greater diligence.[10] Amid a morning conversation that flowed into a variety of subjects, Aiya expressed his view that maintaining agreed-upon tradition is part of what allows him to break with the same:

> So hopefully people will say, "Oh the Rājarājeśwarī Pīṭham broke with all traditions and they let white and black and Muslim and Hindu and Sikh and every other type into the temple, into the sanctum. They did that." So to get to that point, what I am trying to do now is that I'm trying to bring the temple up to have the reputation that the rituals are pure, the rituals are clear, the rituals are based in the Vedas, and the rituals are authentic. Not a figment of somebody's imagination. They are based on the true teachings and on an authentic and powerful [guru] lineage.[11]

Beyond his attention to ritual detail, there are a number of other ways Aiya sticks to "tradition" against the current of contemporary temple worship, especially in North America. A cluster of restrictions placed on women—who are otherwise unusually unrestricted at the Rush temple—provide a few, somewhat ironic, examples. These practices—the binding of long hair (men's and women's), menstruation restrictions, and taboos against women attending cremation ceremonies—were once fairly widespread in South Asia but are slowly becoming less common, particularly in urban areas and abroad.

Visitors to the temple, after leaving their shoes and coats in the entryway cloakroom, proceed toward the temple through a door displaying the sign, NO LOOSE HAIR INSIDE THE TEMPLE. Immediately in front of them as they pass through this door is an electronic sign displaying a stream of letters running along a narrow screen. During the years 2001 and 2002 it read: "WELCOME TO SRI RAJARAJESHWARI PEETAM. THANK YOU FOR KEEPING YOUR HAIR UP. 2001 CALENDARS AVAILABLE IN THE OFFICE." Although the same letters ran during 2002, a visitor might deduce that current calendars are available in the office and that hair still must be tied up. Hair bands are available for women and men with long hair who come unprepared. During the 1999 *pratiṣṭhā* festival, Aiya explained this entryway request to the crowd:

> Those of you who have walked through the front doors have seen an admonishment that says, "No Loose Hair inside the Temple." I don't care if you're male or female. If you have hair below your shoulders you'd better tie it. Otherwise you don't come into the temple. Why? Two reasons. In our Tamil tradition, a woman lets her hair loose only on the day she becomes a widow—*amaṅgalī*. So in our tradition it is inauspicious for you to let your hair loose. I don't care what your fashion statement is. Second reason, you will notice we don't hide things in our temple. Everything is out in the open. *Nyayyavedyams* [offerings to the deities] are open, flower baskets are open, and you have access to the deity. We do not want loose hair falling in these things. If it falls in there it is considered *ucistam* [polluted]. We cannot use it after that. So please do not think that we are being unduly harsh on you. It's for practical reasons.

As I understand it, Aiya's insistence that people tie their hair back—to the dismay of many first-time female visitors who prefer to leave their hair down and do so at other temples—has more to do with aesthetics and accessibility than tacit support of traditional notions of pollution and inauspiciousness.[12] As the following demonstrates, rationales for maintaining and breaking with other gender-based practices similarly reflect a nontraditional set of concerns.

Aiya's insistence that women follow menstruation restrictions is not advertised through temple signs but through word of mouth. Although many women in South Asia curtail temple visits during menstruation, associating it with pollution potentially harmful to temple ritual, this practice is quickly falling out of favor, particularly among the younger generations in urban areas and in diaspora communities. If a woman nonetheless wants to respect other people's views, particularly elders still concerned with menstrual pollution, the advantage is that, unlike loose hair, no one needs to know when she is menstruating. From Aiya's perspective, this does not let anyone off the hook, since he views menstruation restrictions, unlike loose hair, as having nothing to do with external perceptions and inauspiciousness.[13] During a conversation in the temple hallway involving Anusha, on break from UCLA graduate school, a middle-aged South Asian man visiting from Chicago (whose name I did not catch), Aiya, and me, Anusha broached the seemingly ubiquitous question about menstruation. Aiya good-naturedly offered his explanation, once again:

> AIYA That is a very good question and I have answered it lately only about fifty times.
>
> At that time [of the month], Amma, the uterus will expel blood. Right? Okay? And all the blood vessels that have formed during that twenty-eight day period get expelled along with the blood and everything. For those three or four days, the top layer of the uterus is raw. It's in a very tender state. Especially if you have Śiva *mūrti*s inside the temple,

like a Śiva *lingam*, like a Bhairava, right? The mantras that are absorbed by those are in the alpha to gamma range. So when you walk into the temple, even without doing the *pūjā*, these things are continuously being emitted from them. They are harmful to you.

CORINNE So it's not about women being polluting, it's about being vulnerable.

AIYA They're harmful to you! Not every woman is going to be affected. About one in ten, one in eight will have a problem.

The man from Chicago then asked Aiya to explain more about the transmission of energy from granite stones. Aiya led us into the temple for a lesson on male, female, and complementary stones and their various ranges in tone. He demonstrated by knocking against the three granite *mūrtis* and eventually brought the conversation back to menstruation.

AIYA So to continue, those vibrations emitted between the alpha and gamma range, they can go down to the cellular structure and can cause problems around the mitochondria, in the cells in that region. And then scar tissue in that area will start. Later on you might have endometriosis, prolapse—all these problems will be there. It'll also affect the mesenteries that suspend the uterus. That's one reason—the main reason. You're talking about things that happened 2,000–3,000 years ago. They didn't have sanitary pads, it was a case of sanitation also.

MAN So the question is, can they do *japam* [chanting of mantras]?

AIYA Yeah! Internal *japam*. *Manas pūjā*. No problem. No external rituals.

CORINNE So what you're saying is it's not about pollution.

AIYA No, not at all. But that is exactly how you can convince the peasants: "Now, don't go in there, you'll pollute the temple." So they'll be careful. You see how these things have come about? And then some fellow will take it into his head and write it down and say, in Sanskrit couplets, "Okay, if you go at this time, this will be polluting." And then all the other pandits will now keep chanting that and say, "Oh, see, it is written."[14]

Female devotees having their periods often spend time at Rush with Aiya and other devotees but refrain from going inside the temple building itself. On the temple grounds and in the small house they join the others for lunch, help make the tea, and receive Aiya's blessings—all activities conventionally understood as conduits for pollution.

Another traditional practice that Aiya maintains although it seems to be fading elsewhere has to do with restrictions against women's presence and participation at cremation rites. In diaspora communities, Hindu women often accompany men to the crematorium and, in some instances, they will push the button sending their relative into the fires (Leonard 1997: 111). Women in urban South Asia, particularly in north India, are likely to attend cremation rites and recently, as close kin to the deceased, are designated to light the funeral pyre. Taboos against Hindu women attending cremations still exist in some areas and, although the reasons are not always clearly articulated, they commonly hinge on two types of rationales. One has to do with female pollution's potential effect on the rite itself and the other, more common, rationale has to do with a woman's vulnerability to malignant spirits present on the cremation grounds.[15] Aiya's reasoning relates to the second of these two rationales, that cremation grounds and crematoriums carry forces that are potentially dangerous, particularly to women between the ages of eighteen and twenty-three. He submits that, in worst-case scenarios, these forces can cause insanity.

Typical of Aiya's style of maintaining and discarding tradition, he encourages women to lead *srāddham* rituals to honor their husbands and fathers at prescribed intervals after their death. In most of north and south India as well as in North America, the performance of *srāddham* rites remains primarily the domain of male family members. While people often resist breaking from this tradition, an even more difficult practice to break has to do with removing signs of married auspiciousness after a woman's husband dies. During funeral ceremonies, Aiya often encourages the widow to keep wearing a red *pottu* or *bindu* on her forehead, flowers in her hair and, if she is south Indian, the wedding *tāli* necklace. Women are not always receptive to these suggestions, since removing the signs of married auspiciousness can be a gesture of mournful respect for the deceased. But Aiya, when possible, insists. These outward signs are not for a woman to own or not own, he reasons, they are a means of honoring the goddess, eternally present within.[16]

Aiya's unconventional maintenance of fading traditions and its mirror reflection, his disregard for fervently held aspects of tradition, presents challenges for some, just as it presents opportunities. Female devotees of South Asian descent, some of whom have little interest in conventional temple culture, are willing, to varying degrees, to work off of Aiya's nonconformist grid. They agree, sometimes begrudgingly, to restrictions often not required at other temples in North American in exchange for relinquishing conventional notions of female pollution and widow inauspiciousness and, most importantly, in exchange for access to ritual performance. Although some women concur with Aiya's belief in their vulnerability during their periods or at crematoriums, and therefore comply to restrictions for this reason, some young women with whom I spoke were not so convinced. But, in the end, they prefer this view to one that projects them as unworthy or potentially harmful participants in temple life.

While Aiya's attention to ritual detail gives validity to his maverick approach, the other side of the equation is no less important. Not only are female devotees willing to pull their hair back and refrain from entering the temple during their periods in return for unconventional full participation, devotees in general agree to go the extra mile, to give their time and support to the temple, and to spend countless hours learning difficult chants because at the Rush temple they "feel free" to make the most of their discipline and hard work. Continuing this theme in which freedom from and disciplined adherence to convention are intertwined, I end this chapter with reflections on a related balancing act at the Rush temple: the place of mischievous playfulness amid serious devotion.

Serious Playfulness in Ritual

Aiya would be the first to tell you he was, from a very young age, a naughty boy. One of his earliest memories from childhood in Sri Lanka paints a worthy picture. When he was four, his mother enrolled him in kindergarten where one of his teachers, a Carmelite nun named Sr. Leona, babied her youngest student, who would regularly run off in search of his mother. She often presented him with sweets from her habit pocket and kept him in her lap to console and distract him. Aiya remembers looking up from his perch on Sr. Leona's lap, marveling at her great veiled head, the perimeters of her face encased by a white wimple. Much of the time he spent wondering what might be hidden underneath. He recounts with laughter his occasional attempts to plumb the mystery by inserting, when he thought she would not notice, his crooked index finger alongside her face and under her wimple. Sr. Leona, who Aiya recalls with great admiration, never reprimanded him; she simply tried to keep him otherwise occupied. When outside her sphere of influence, Aiya's other exploratory venture—in a classroom that doubled as the convent chapel—was into a special box located below the crucifix. Aiya discovered flat little wafers inside and, when no one was looking, he ate them. Because he knew full well at the time that he was being naughty, Aiya laughingly finished his story, the last time I heard it, with the assessment, "I was a little scamp."

Gleeful naughtiness is a defining theme in Aiya's life, something he emphasizes in stories of his childhood and teenage years as well as in his current self-assessment as a maverick priest. The temple itself contains reverberations of Aiya's trademark mischief and humor during everyday interactions and, most significantly, during rituals. Rituals are in many ways the heart of seriousness at the temple, providing the basis for its miracle-making reputation as well as its disciplined respectability. It is during rituals, however, that playfulness often breaks through—sometimes dramatically. Ritual provides an appropriate vantage from which to view the mixture of serious intent and mischief at the Rush temple, since ritual is not only central to the serious work of harnessing divine power, according to *Śrīvidyā* theology but because it is also the mode by which the temple most starkly and gleefully defies convention.

Of the various understandings of play and laughter available, the one that I find most relevant to Rush is Mary Douglas's (1966, 1968) proposal that laughter and joking reveal the arbitrary nature of socially constructed categories and, as a result, work to suspend hierarchy, level social differences, and challenge the balance of power. With this in mind, ritual playfulness and laughter at the Rush temple reflect, underscore, and further validate one of the primary aims of the temple and its founder: to challenge power structures by leveling distinctions having to do with caste, gender, and ethnicity. The function of ritual playfulness as reinforcing the temple's aim to bind and level human relations is only a portion of the equation, however. Since the central purpose of temple rituals is to create ties with divinity and divine power, reverent playfulness and laughter enacted during ritual, it seems, further underscore its aim toward human-divine intimacy, narrowing more profoundly the breach between the two realms. It is here that "serious playfulness," so prevalent at the Rush temple, truly hits its stride.

Creating intimacy through ritual playfulness in the widest sense, Aiya regularly evokes laughter by joking in Tamil and English at the expense of participants, both human and divine. This occurs most commonly during *homams*, where Aiya often interjects explanations and humorous asides. Drawing more exclusive parameters, he also plays with Sanskrit words, a joke genre lost on nonseasoned chanters, marking a boundary of belonging around those who understand and laugh. Although Aiya is the master joker, others can play the role as well. For instance an adolescent boy named Dharmam often assists *homams* by walking through the crowds with the tray of offerings bound for the fire, allowing participants to piously touch the tray and its contents. This tradition, unique to Rush, defies convention by enabling all present to offer sacrifice, and Dharmam added his own version of playful deviance, particularly when he was younger, by offering the tray to a devotee and snatching it away before she or he could touch it. Eventually contact was made and Dharmam's mischief rewarded by warm laughter and tweaks of his chubby cheeks. While the Rush *homam* tradition aims at leveling caste and gender distinctions, consequently freeing previously blocked channels between humanity and divinity, teasing and laughter seem to underscore the process by closing the gap between mischief and piety.

Examples of everyday ritual playfulness such as these abound and are significant for their regularity, but there are also instances when levity bursts into ritual space with a flourish. A good example is the *mahā abhiṣekam* "mud fight" of Navarātri, 2002. Unlike Saturday *abhiṣekams*, where participants carefully douse the three main deities with milk, this hour-long *mahā abhiṣekam* is of a much larger scale, involving bucketloads of various substances.[17] Aparna described the intensity of the ritual itself:

> When you're doing the *abhiṣekam* rituals on this level it's almost as if the intensity builds because you're drenching Her. It's as if She's going for a water ride or something like that. And I'm sure it's exhausting for Aiya, because it takes a lot of strength. Because he's picking up and lifting over his head buckets for an hour. So that's physical labor. So you can see that his adrenaline is probably going too, because it takes a lot of physical energy to do that, and spiritual energy. Because it's almost as if, if it stops, it's not going to create the same effect. And so you're building it. And you can feel it.

The point at which the mud fight breaks out, people are performing a gesture typical of Rush's Saturday *abhiṣekam*. Turmeric-colored liquid contained in a *kālasam* (along with cloves, perfume, and pieces of devotees' gold jewelry returned after the ritual), ritually infused with sacred energy, is processed around the temple and poured on the Śrī Rājarājeśwarī *mūrti*. The liquid is contained by a low tile wall surrounding the three main deities, into which devotees put their hands. They then press the yellow liquid onto their eyelids, lightly slap it onto their cheeks, and perhaps onto the cheeks of a person nearby. This sharing of liquid *prasādam* is a loving gesture under normal circumstances, ever so slightly naughty and playful. Aparna describes the transition from the weekly *abhiṣekam* gentle gesture to the *mahā* mud fight that seemingly incited hilarity not only in the devotees but in the Devī as well.

> Now we escalate that, because now we're in an escalated situation. So it started out like in that simple ritual that we always do, that's familiar to us. So all you need is for one person to do the next thing. I don't know if it was Aiya or who, but all of a sudden someone put in their forehead and then someone else's arm went in, then somebody else's other arm went in.
>
> The last substance was the sandal paste. And that was what we started getting into a fight with, because that's more like mud. You can actually pick it up and make a shape and throw it. . . . I didn't feel like we were being sacrilegious to the Devī at that point. She has so much on Her, you have to scoop it off. Aiya's pouring it on Her, but as Aiya's pouring it, other people are there scraping it off, just to scrape it down so that there's more room for him to pour more on. So it starts off as kind of a practical thing. You're part of the worship, you're doing your role, right? So then all you have to do is take one hand that has a little too much on it, and you don't want to put it down, so you put it on someone's arm. . . .

> And so Aiya was right there, and I was right at the Devī and there was a lot of it [on my hand] and it just went on [Janani's] arm. And Aiya looked at me and said, "I saw that!" And then it was like it didn't matter. Even though he said, "I saw that!" as if you were being a naughty kid, you think, "Oh goody, he saw!" So you're almost encouraged and so you take the next one and throw it at him.
>
> And the Devī, normally She's really proper. She has that little apron on and She's basically naked when we do the *abhiṣekam* except for the little apron, but so much stuff is going on, her clothes are falling off too. So normally people are putting them back up again, but in this situation, we didn't care if her clothes were falling off, we were just going for it. It was this idea that . . . it was just really fun.

Rituals that become play, as described by Aparna, do not have to leave divinity behind. She can be an active participant, blessing the event by binding the raucous with the sacred, the naughty with the pious. Aiya's mischievous

Mahā abhiṣekam frivolity during the 2002 Navarātri festival. Photo by Aparna Hasling.

endorsement has a similar effect. Heightened playfulness, rather than being sacrilegious, as posed by Aparna, seems simply to function more effectively in narrowing the divide among humans and between humanity and divinity. The *abhiṣekam* "mud fight" ultimately becomes communal *abhiṣekam*, bringing Devī into the realm of the human and the human into the divine. For some this may seem sacrilegious, but within the context of Rush temple theology, the binding of the mundane with the sacred and vice versa is what religion is all about. If spontaneous play and laughter help perpetuate and validate this process, all the better.

My final example of ritual playfulness involves a mock procession. Although on par with the *abhiṣekam* mud fight in terms of spontaneity and hilarity, this event represents play infused with ritual rather than ritual infused with play. At the conclusion of the first *pratiṣṭhā* festival, Memorial Day weekend 1999, the final scheduled procession had made its rounds and the crowds mostly dispersed. Many of the inner-core devotees who stayed on to help clean up had headed out to the food tent for lunch. As Aiya appeared at the doorway of the temple, also heading out to lunch, a group of young men started shouting "Aro Hara!" and held up the small procession palanquin for him to climb onto. With a grin on his face, Aiya obliged, and the young men set off around the temple, the palanquin on their shoulders, with irreverent shouts of devotional reverence and laughter.

Waiting around the first bend was a group of young women. Jamuna, Aiya's niece in her late twenties, held in her hands a hose used earlier for cooling the excruciatingly hot cement. Egged on by the women around her, she sprayed first the palanquin bearers and then Aiya, provoking more shouts and laughter and a small crowd to gather. After he was sufficiently doused, I saw Aiya frantically motioning for the hose to be passed his way. The young women obliged and he turned the spray onto the crowd, further heightening the hilarity and drenching those who had earlier laughed at his expense. As the procession neared its completion, a group of women wrested the palanquin from the men and carried Aiya into the final stretch. Once back at the temple door, devotees performed perfectly orchestrated *pāñcapūjā* to Aiya, offering flowers, fruit, and fire while shouting Sanskrit in unison at the top of their lungs. By enacting a procession and *pūjā* mockingly outside of ritual time yet in a devotionally accurate manner, devotees honored their mischievous yet serious guru who, in all playfulness and reverence, they positioned as processional deity. The sacred spilling out into the mundane, the water fight became, by association, a kind of raucous group *abhiṣekam*. Laughter, heightened with each new layer of mischief, affirmed and was furthermore fed by a shared sense of sacrality.

Although I was able to witness firsthand the water-fight procession, I just missed the *mahā abhiṣekam* mud fight. I had been in Syracuse for the day and arrived in time to see devotees wandering about in various stages of disarray.

Crossing my path as I got out of my car was Ammamma. A special recipient of Aiya's mischief, she was covered from head to toe with drying sandalwood paste. The previous summer I had asked Ammamma to describe Aiya as a little boy, figuring, as his teacher from kindergarten through second grade, she would have special insight into his character. Not one to waste words, she answered by mentioning two things. One: he was always teasing the girls and making them mad. Two: he was always looking for his mother. While these two activities probably bore no connection at the time, they are now—if I may stretch an analogy—inextricable. As reflected in Rush temple rituals and mock rituals, mischief and intimacy with the Mother not only coexist they also reinforce one another. Breaking with convention helps devotees find their way to divinity. The naughtiness and irreverence of play underscore and are intensified by strains of serious, hard-won devotion.

PART III

Temple Inhabitants

Making Home in a World of Impermanence

7

Grounding the Sacred

Traveling Deities and Sanctified Terrain

The image of a barn nestled in a rural landscape is in some ways a romantic one, conjuring up notions of permanence, stability or, at very least, desires to resist the forces of change. The small yellow barn that houses the Śrī Rājarājeśwarī Pīṭham is by no means an exception, at least from the outside. Its inhabitants, on the other hand, both human and divine, embody histories that defy a sense of permanence and continuity. Most have endured drastically shifting physical landscapes in their lifetimes; others, more culturally at home in the temple's North American environs, have experienced radically shifting religious landscapes. Amid participants' encounters with geographical and religious upheaval, many consider the *pīṭham* to be "home"—a place that, in a sense, grounds them and helps make sense of life's various ruptures. Although the process of "making home" is not typically easy or pain-free, it can offer a means to engage the generous stores of individual, communal, and divine adaptability and creativity of those who partake.

Previous parts of this book explore collisions of mundane and miraculous worldviews and of religious convention and nonconvention, respectively, whereas this remaining section considers the confluence of foreign and domestic cultures and terrains. Like preceding discussions, this final part not only delves into the challenges and creative opportunities inherent in such junctures but also shows how apparent disparities can, at times, be complementary or interdependent. Lines between secular and sacred, renegade and conservative, foreign and home—vivid and vital though they may sometimes be—can also, with proper perspective, blur beyond recognition.

Śrī Rājarājeśwarī Lands in Rush

Śrī Rājarājeśwarī, exquisitely crafted from solid black granite, sits five feet three inches high from the bottom of her pedestal to the top of her crown, and weighs in at approximately six hundred pounds. One of the largest and by far the heaviest of the Rush temple *mūrtis*, She is also the one whose route to Rush has been, ironically, the most circuitous. Most of the other temple *mūrtis* have been carefully commissioned from India, arriving unceremoniously in wooden crates filled with packing materials and a few stray spiders, but Śrī Rājarājeśwarī's story of travel is considerably more involved.

The person most extensively involved with the goddess's journey is Devi Parvati, a devotee referred to in chapter 5, director of a nationally renowned Hindu heritage camp currently operating out of Rochester, New York. A self-proclaimed bridge between East and West for her students, she also acted as a bridge—organizationally and literally—for transferring the goddess from India to an ashram in the Pocono Mountains and from the ashram to Aiya's garage temple. Although I heard snatches of Rājarājeśwarī's story while talking with Aiya and other temple devotees, it was not until a teatime visit in Devi Parvati's home that I heard the tale from beginning to end, fleshed out with images from her photo album.

The Rājarājeśwarī Pīṭham of the Holy Shankarcharya Order ashram in the Poconos, first official home the Śrī Rājarājeśwarī *mūrti*, was established in 1968. Although the *mūrti* did not arrive until 1985, its original commissioning and eventual departure from the ashram reflect significant trends not only in the ashram itself but also in the shifting terrain of North American Hinduism over the past three and a half decades.[1] Briefly described, the ashram began as a center for yoga and meditation, geared toward Euro American tastes. During the mid to late seventies it gradually conformed to the needs of a growing new clientele: recently arrived Indian professionals and their families.

The ashram was founded by Swami Lakshmi Devyashrama, originally Kaylee Rosenberg. Rosenberg grew up in New York City during the Great Depression and, although unexposed to mystical religious traditions, found herself entering, from the time she was a child, states she later identified as deep meditation. She married at a young age, eventually left her abusive husband, and raised their two children on her own while working as a seamstress. She later married an office furniture salesman and, during the mid-1950s, became a student of an Indian swami named Vishnu Devananda, disciple of Shivananda. From his yoga center in New York City, Swami Vishnu offered a context from which Rosenberg could understand and enhance her meditational experiences. Eventually she took the vow of *sannyās* or Hindu renunciation and, with her husband's financial and moral support, Swami Lakshmi opened an ashram retreat center for yoga and meditation on a thirty-five-acre farm in the

Poconos. When she advertised the new ashram retreat in the *Village Voice* in 1968, the response was overwhelming. As Devi Parvati observed, the timing could not have been better: "A huge influx of flower kids came out. The place just grew and kept growing."

In 1973 Devi Parvati, then a Spanish teacher in New Jersey, started attending weekend retreats at the ashram. Possessing eclectic religious inclinations throughout her life as well as an interest in other cultures, Devi Parvati was first introduced to Indian philosophy when she lived in Spain for a number of years. But it was not until her ashram experiences that, as she put it, "I just had a major revelation that this is what I was supposed to do with my life—to be involved in yoga and meditation and work with the spiritual teachings rather than the secular. So I just gave up everything, gave away everything I owned. I just said 'good bye' to it." During her first few years living at the ashram it thrived as a yoga and meditation center, housing about fifty permanent residents, thirty-five of whom were initiated swamis, all Euro American. The ashram also kept ties to India by hosting a steady stream of teachers and holy men. Starting in 1976, when immigration from India to North America began to escalate, the ashram sponsored rituals and festival events, attracting newly arrived immigrants for weekend visits.

During the late seventies, as this shift in ashram activities continued, Euro American devotees more interested in yoga and meditation than Indian culture and ritual began drifting away. Devi Parvati considers this to be a natural sequence of events; the ashram's intention was always to educate and send people into the world to live the tradition. Devi Parvati, on the other hand, was one of the few initiated Euro American swamis for whom ritual and cultural events added richness to the ashram atmosphere. She learned basic Sanskrit and ritual mechanics from the series of priests who lived at the ashram and became one of the main ritual officiants, performing *pūjā*s whenever an Indian priest was not available. In 1983, a young priest from Andhra Pradesh taught Devi Parvati the more elaborate *śrīcakra pūjā* as well as the *Lalitāsahasranāmam*. The Hindu Heritage camp, established in 1976 and geared toward immigrants' sons and daughters, also focused more on Indian rituals and philosophy than on yoga and meditation.

In 1978, Swami Lakshmi decided the ashram's increasingly ritualistic and devotional emphasis warranted the official installation of a temple deity. She also felt it important to identify and honor the divinity whose presence she already sensed at the ashram. Because the ashram followed the tradition of a Śaṇkara *maṭh*, Swami decided to ask the advice of one of the esteemed leaders of the four Śaṇkara *maṭh*s in India. She instructed her disciples to write to these four men, explain their predicament, and request an audience. Abhinava Vidhyateertha, the jagadguru of the Śriṅgeri *maṭh* at the time, responded immediately to their letter and invited Swami Lakshmi to meet with him in India.

En route to Śriṅgeri, Swami and her small entourage stopped at a fishing village where she often rested when traveling in India. There Swami met with the head *stapati* or temple craftsman, Subramania, someone she knew and respected, and described to him the divine energy she perceived at the ashram. Subramania asked her a series of questions, consulted his book cataloguing the various goddesses and their attributes, and deduced that the ashram divinity was Śrī Rājarājeśwarī, the goddess who encompasses all other goddesses. When in Śriṅgeri, Swami passed on the *stapati*'s assessment to the jagadguru. He went into meditation and then agreed that Swami install Rājarājeśwarī at the ashram. He gave her a picture of the goddess to be used as a devotional focus.[2]

In 1981, Swami Lakshmi died of a heart attack and was buried according to tradition on the ashram grounds.[3] At that time, only five of the original swamis were left at the ashram. By 1984 the number further dwindled to three. Responding to the ashram's increased ritual emphasis as well as the needs of their growing Indian congregation, the remaining swamis, including Devi Parvati, decided it was time to install a full-sized temple *mūrti*. Without Swami Lakshmi to guide them in this significant step, the three traveled to India to consult with the Śriṅgeri jagadguru, who had become for them an important spiritual authority. Before meeting with him, the American swamis agreed among themselves that the ideal Rājarājeśwarī *mūrti* would look like the one installed at the Śrī Cakra temple outside Bangalore, artfully chiseled from black granite. The jagadguru, accustomed to white marble *mūrtis* typically stationed at Śaṇkara *maṭhs*, had a different image in mind. Devi Parvati recalled the meeting with the jagadguru in which, after some discussion, he pronounced enthusiastically, "You are white—so She must be white!" Devi Parvati recounted the quick-thinking diplomacy that followed:

> I thought, "Oh God, no!" [*We both laugh.*] Then somebody said, I think it was Rajasubramania Aiyar, a very wealthy businessman devotee who took us under his wing, he said, "You know Guruji Holiness, when you ship white marble, a lot of the time it gets damaged. It's really very soft and there are a lot of problems shipping it. They're really afraid to ship it." So the jagadguru thought about this and said, "Oh. In that case, She'll have to be granite." And we all went, "Phew!"

After establishing that Rājarājeśwarī would be chiseled from the stone that the Euro American swamis (and Aiya) considered the most aesthetically and ritually appropriate for their temple, the jagadguru grandly proposed she be as beautiful as the *mūrti* in Bangalore—the same *mūrti* the swamis had earlier admired. As Devi Parvati recalls, the jagadguru then turned to Rajasubramania Aiyar and told him, "You call Muthiah Stapati who carved that statue and you make sure that they make one just exactly like that one." A request from a jagadguru is as good as done, and in 1985 the granite *mūrti* of Śrī Rājarājeśwarī, carved by the famous temple craftsman and identical to—although slightly smaller than—her Indian counterpart, arrived in the Poconos.

Aiya's first exposure to the Pocono Śrī Rājarājeśwarī was in 1989 when he and Guruji visited the ashram. He did not realize at the time that, although the ashram hosted regular festivals and rituals as well as a successful Hindu Heritage summer camp, the shortage of full-time staff and support made it increasingly difficult to keep the ashram afloat. Because of its remote location, steady assistance from the Indian community was also out of the question. After this first visit, Aiya and an entourage of devotees from his Rochester garage temple regularly made trips to the Poconos to perform ritual and musical offerings to Rājarājeśwarī. Aiya relished the opportunity to offer worship to such an exquisite temple *mūrti* and to a goddess so central to the Śrīvidyā tradition. Because this kind of access was not typically available to him at other temples, he was grateful for Devi Parvati's blessings and encouragement. Meanwhile, worried about the ashram's future, Devi Parvati anxiously searched for avenues of support to keep it open. She described how, finally, during Navarātri in October 1990, she received a clear message that the future of the ashram and its goddess had been determined in spite of her efforts. "I was sitting in meditation and there were some absolutely crystal clear words that I got. I mean, when you hear something like that, it's internal and you sometimes think, 'Is it me? No, it isn't me.' This was just so clear that there was no way I could doubt it. No way. [They were,] 'This place has to rest. It needs to sleep. Sell this property. Move me to Rochester.' And I thought, 'What?!' Rochester is like the last place in the world I'd pick, weather-wise. I was thinking, 'I want someplace warm! And beautiful!' " After her experience, Devi Parvati phoned India to ask Guruji and the Śriṅgeri jagadguru their advice, and both agreed that moving to Rochester was the right thing to do.

Aiya also recalls receiving a message while sitting in front of Rājarājeśwarī at the Pocono ashram, something that foreshadowed, only in retrospect, future events. He had come to the ashram with two young students to perform a *śrīcakra pūjā*, arriving later than expected due to a severe ice storm. No one else had braved the mountain roads to the ashram, and so Devi Parvati and one other resident were the only others in attendance. Aiya described the messenger arriving halfway into the four-hour *pūjā*,

> Around two thirty or so, I was sitting there and I felt somebody do this to me. [*Aiya taps himself on the shoulder with his index finger.*] And I turned around, "Yes?" There was this little girl, typically Indian, with nicely made up eyes and all that, flowers in her hair, skirt and nice blouse. She smiled and I smiled. And I thought, "Somebody has come. Some Indian family has come for the *pūjā*." And I'm sitting and doing *pūjā* and thinking, "How nice. I'm doing the Devī's *pūjā* and the bala has come." Bala is the little girl. The

> Mother must be blessing me and saying, "I approve of what you are doing."
>
> After another forty minutes or so I feel this. [*He taps himself again and turns around.*] It's the same person. She gives me a nice smile and then says in Tamil, "Uncle, I am coming with you." I looked at her—and it didn't strike me. I was thinking, "It is a little girl saying something nice probably because she is fascinated by the clothes I am wearing or how I am seated and doing this. I smiled back at Her and continued to finish the *pūjā*. When I finished I asked Parvati, "Where is the little girl? I want to put some *kumkum* on her." She said, "What little girl?"

Three weeks later, Aiya returned to the Poconos to conduct another, shorter *pūjā*. When he finished, Devi Parvati asked if she could have a word with him. They went to her next-door apartment where she described to him the ashram's financial difficulties, explaining that she could no longer continue to run it by herself and was going to have to sell it. Her remaining concern, she told him, was for the future of the *mūrti*. She had tried contacting various temples around the country, hoping they could continue her worship, but when they heard the deity in question was Rājarājeśwarī, they all refused. Many reasoned that she could not be a peripheral deity and that making her a central deity would be impossible in an already established temple. By the time Devi Parvati spoke to Aiya she was, as he told me, worried the *mūrti* "would be auctioned off [by the IRS]. Somebody might buy it and put it in their garden as a centerpiece. Or maybe it would end up in a museum. I'm not kidding, Amma. It would end up in a museum. She was concerned."

When Devi Parvati asked Aiya if he could accommodate Rājarājeśwarī in his garage temple, he felt he was being presented with an opportunity of many lifetimes. Worried about the responsibility of caring for such a powerful temple *mūrti* in a converted garage, Aiya told Devi Parvati he needed first to speak with his guru. Devi Parvati handed Aiya the phone, he dialed India, and Guruji answered. After Aiya explained the situation, the line went dead for about twenty seconds while Guruji went into meditation. He then said, as Aiya recalled, "If the Divine Mother wants to come to your house, who are you to say no? Let Her come."

The transfer from ashram to garage temple took place around four months later, on January 19, 1991, during *dakśiṇāyaṇa*, an auspicious period when the sun turns from the south to the north. Guruji, Aiya, and a group of around twenty temple devotees came to the Poconos to assist the move. Before the movers packed the *mūrti* into its custom-made crate, Guruji unceremoniously transferred the goddess's energy to Devi Parvati. Reflecting on Guruji's style as a ritual minimalist, Devi Parvati described the transfer—the *prāṇa pratiṣṭhā*—as uneventful, performed before she was aware it was happening. She described feeling slightly disoriented but still able to drive to Rochester and to direct traffic for people leaving the Poconos. Once at Park Circle, back in Aiya's garage, devotees returned the *mūrti* to its platform, and Guruji transferred the goddess's energy from Devi Parvati's body to the granite image. The efficiency of the move was such that, as Devi Parvati put it, "She never missed one *pūjā*."

For two years Devi Parvati commuted between Rochester and the Poconos, finishing the emotionally draining job of transferring the ashram to new management. Although the Pocono ashram no longer maintains a full-fledged temple, periodic festivals and weekend rituals continue today under the direction of a group of Indian-born businessmen from New Jersey. Devi Parvati is ultimately relieved that the ashram remains a religious institution, honoring its legacy and her beloved Swami who lies buried there.

As for Rājarājeśwarī, Devi Parvati is pleased to have found such a good home for her. Elaborating on this, she cites two important aspects of the Park Circle/Rush temples, central to maintaining the power of the deity and the devotees' connection to her.

> First of all, She's open. She's available. You can be right in front of Her face. I mean, where do you find that in other temples? They're enclosed, there's a little vestibule, you can hardly see them, and the priest is doing the *pūjā* and nobody is allowed near. In our temple, there is no inner sanctum. The whole thing is the inner sanctum. There is no me/you. It's us. It's us. So that's the first thing. Everything, everybody is included.
>
> And the second piece is that all the devotees are chanting. How many temples do you go to where people know the chants? Nowhere. You all sit there and listen to the priest and maybe two other pundits who sit there and chant. So here we have a *chorus* of people chanting. There's no priest, there's no you and me. Everyone has the opportunity to learn.

Many devotees, Devi Parvati included, consider the final leg of Śrī Rājarājeśwarī's journey—her ceremonious transfer from Park Circle garage to Rush barn on Memorial Day weekend 1998—to be inevitable and important. The goddess's new, more public place of residence allows her to be properly honored by and accessible to an even larger group of devotees. At the same time, many miss the intimacy and focus of the garage temple days.[4] Indeed, each time the Devī has moved to a new home, devotees have had to adjust. Whether relinquishing the idea of a white marble *mūrti*, catering to a changing ashram complexion, negotiating the cramped quarters of a one-and-a-half-car garage, or acclimating to an influx of less focused clientele, reconfigured expectations fill the wake of her travels. Yet overriding the long and varied list of human adjustments is Śrī Rājarājeśwarī's ability to sanctify and transform the places where she lands. The site most radically transformed by the introduction of her divine energy is, perhaps, her current rural residence. The goddess does not have to work entirely from scratch, however. Like the ashram and the garage temple, the barn and its terrain appear to bring a sacredness all their own to the mix.

Sanctifying Land: Hills, Creeks, Trees, and Pilgrims

The arrival and installation of the Śrī Rājarājeśwarī *mūrti* in Rush on Memorial Day weekend 1998 was, as one might expect, a ritual extravaganza. For over a year leading up to the event, a few hired workers and dozens of devotee volunteers gave countless hours of their time to prepare the grounds and building structure. The point at which Śrī Rājarājeśwarī was carried with fanfare into the building during the *pratiṣṭhā* festival was, by all accounts, extremely moving. As Aiya put it, "There wasn't a dry eye in the house. You should have seen the grown men crying." This was for many the greatly anticipated moment when barn transmuted into temple. Yet it also belongs to a larger process involving and invoking terrain that both sanctifies and is made sacred by divinity.

According to local, regional, and Sanskritic Hindu traditions, physical terrain is rarely without religious significance. Many South Asian mountains, rivers, and the subcontinent itself are considered sacred and, moreover, associated with female divinity. In the *Devī-Bhāgavata Purāṇa* (7.33.21–41), Sanskrit scriptures written between the seventh and ninth centuries CE, Devī literally embodies all of creation. Her bowels are the oceans, her bones the mountains, her veins the rivers, her body hair the trees, and the sun and moon are her eyes.[5] The link between South Asian landscape and the sacred is so strong that some orthodox brahmans, particularly before the era of mass travel, worried that crossing the ocean could unhinge them from their high-caste status. Although very few South Asian Hindus today restrict travel for this reason, emigration from India and Sri Lanka does mean leaving behind a sacred landscape not easily duplicated. Diaspora Hindus thus often concern themselves not only with establishing temples fit for their gods and goddesses but also with imbuing the surrounding new-world landscape with old-world sacredness.[6]

Before describing how some Hindu communities, particularly at Rush, make new lands sacred, it is worth mentioning that the North American continent does not simply provide a blank slate. In his book describing North American sacred geography from a variety of angles and traditions, Belden Lane argues that although American culture is often characterized by rootlessness, it is precisely this quality that makes place so important. As a result, the linking of locale and sacrality, beginning most explicitly with Native American traditions, has been practiced throughout North American history (2002: 6).

As for the rolling hills of western New York, this area experienced a particularly strong religious jolt, referred to as the Second Great Awakening, during the early to mid-1800s. Aglow with images of a fiery spirit blazing, the region was dubbed the Burned-Over District.[7] The religious revival movements that sprang up during this era were characterized by emotional fervor, experimentation, and ideals of egalitarianism and self-reliance. Church attendance and lay participation increased, while traditional authority was regularly undermined through the movement's association with abolition, its receptivity to female leadership, and its preponderance of charismatic priests who lacked formal seminary training (Johnson 1989: 9, 53; Tweed 1997: 69; Brodie 1976: 14; McElroy 1974: 9–10). The term "Burned-Over District" was most specifically associated with the region west of the Catskill Mountains, the logistical and activist heart of which was Rochester, New York.

The Second Great Awakening was anti-authoritarian, lay empowered, and appealed to people recently uprooted from foreign countries or disenchanted with religiously traditional settings—themes that reverberate at the Rush temple today. Although it is tempting to speculate about the demographic and philosophical foundations of these reverberations, I draw this rough sketch of the Burned-Over District to make the religiously pertinent point that the Rush temple sits on holy ground. Although it is true that Aiya could have successfully established his temple in a number of locales in the United States, the reality is that it has flourished in the heart of the Burned-Over District—first in a suburb just outside Rochester and now in an adjacent rural area. Since sacred geography is so foundational to Hindu temple traditions, particularly goddess traditions, the fact that the Rush *pīṭham*—literally the "seat" of the goddess—rests on previously designated and strikingly familiar sacred terrain cannot help but be reassuring. When I first mentioned to Aiya the ideological and geographical overlap between his temple and the spiritual fires of the Burned-Over District, he nodded approvingly and said, "See? History is repeating itself."

The process of (further) sanctifying land for Hindu diaspora communities is, in most cases, an attempt to repeat history or, more precisely, to replicate onto new soil holy terrain from the Indian subcontinent. When building temples in North America, Hindu communities, whenever possible, give added significance to their endeavor by linking surrounding mountains, rivers, and other geographical formations with Indian holy sites and topography.[8] At the Penn Hills Shri Venkateshwara temple, for instance, its brochure proclaims the similarities between its surrounding hilly terrain and the land surrounding the Venkateshwara temple in Tirupati, India. A 1986 temple statement also notes how the Indian Prayāg—the holy confluence of three Indian rivers, the Gaṅgā, Yamunā, and the underground Sarasvatī—is duplicated in Pittsburgh through the meeting of the Allegheny, Monongahela, and a subterranean river brought to the surface through a fountain downtown (Narayanan 1992: 162). The Shiva-Vishnu temple in the suburbs of Lanham, Maryland, near Washington, D.C., takes this theme and runs with it, reproducing on its grounds virtually the entire sacred landscape of south India, from Tirupati to Trivandrum (Eck 2001: 126).[9]

The Rush temple's most conspicuous duplication of an Indian holy site is its very own Banaras, most commonly known to devotees as Kāśī, situated on the banks of a small creek running through the property. In India, many consider Kāśī, Śiva's city, to be the holiest of locations, blessed in particular by its proximity to the goddess Gaṅgā in the form of the Ganges River. The Rush creek thus becomes a surrogate Ganges, its banks the ideal location for a Rush Kāśī, designated by the installation of a Śiva *lingam*. At different points during the year and at least once every weekend, Rush devotees make the short trek to the bottom of the hill behind the temple to perform rituals to Śiva at Kāśī. Because one of Gaṅgā's main functions in India is to sanctify and release the spirits of the dead, Rush devotees gather at Kāśī most particularly during seasonal and anniversary rites for the deceased.

Other features of the Rush property that sanctify and in turn are sanctified by the temple and its rituals have nothing to do with duplicating practices or attributes found only in South Asia. For instance, the fact that Devī currently resides in what used to be a barn is not, according to Aiya, irrelevant to temple worship. In one of our first conversations, barely two weeks after Rājarājeśwarī was installed, he enthused about the fact that the Mother was physically connected to soil that for many decades had animals living on it. He brought me to the front of the temple and explained how the pedestal upon which the Devī was seated made direct contact with the earth, adding that scriptural injunctions for temple layout, found in the *Śaiva Āgamas* and the *Tantras*, suggest that Śākta (goddess) temples install the deity in a setting inhabited by animals.[10] I heard from Aiya and other devotees that the animals' urine and feces, stomped into the soil over the years, enhance the area's electromagnetic conductivity and thus the power of rituals performed in their proximity. Aiya claims that the intrinsic power of the land is such that, even before Rājarājeśwarī was ritually installed, he could feel her presence in the barn/temple.

Before the temple was completed, Aiya reports having a meditational experience in which the goddess asked him to install a trident near an oak tree that sits in the northeast corner of the property overlooking the temple. South Indian temples honoring Bhairava, whose emblem is a trident, typically station him in the northeastern corner of the building, often for the sake of protection. The request and placement of the trident thus made good sense to Aiya. After installing the trident, as Aiya circumambulated the tree, he noted an old trident-shaped scar on its trunk—further affirmation that Bhairava and the other temple deities were long destined to settle on the Rush property. The apple trees lining a good portion of the landscape likewise express the temple goddess's sanctification of prior agricultural life on the Rush property. No longer bearing much fruit when Aiya bought the property, the trees have ap-

Bhairava's outdoor shrine. Sandalwood paste blesses and accentuates the trident tree scar. Photo by author.

parently become increasingly heavy with apples each autumn since the temple was consecrated. Continuing the cycle of blessings, the fruit is harvested and offered to the temple deities during *pūjās*. The leftover blessed apples, or *prasādam*, are then cut up and spiced by Amma and other devotees, made into Sri Lankan–style pickle, and sold by the jar at the temple office.

A ritual innovation practiced at the Rush temple further affirms that its terrain is sacred in its own right, independently of South Asian associations. This innovation involves modifications to the traditional *saṅkalpam*, a Sanskrit invocation recited at the beginning of rituals, locating and sanctifying the time, space, and intention of the rite (Eck 2001: 127). In the traditional *saṅkalpam*, the officiating priest locates the ritual's position on the map by first invoking Mt. Meru (also known as Kailāsa) in the Himalayas and the land south of Mt. Kailāsa, namely, the Indian subcontinent and Sri Lanka, as sacred by association. He then invokes a list of the sacred rivers on the Indian subcontinent.[11] In an attempt to maintain ritual authenticity, most temple priests at diaspora temples recite the *saṅkalpam* in its original form. Variations of this ritual, practiced at Rush and at some other diaspora temples as well, interject local geographical features into the traditional formula. At Rush, the officiating priest invokes in Sanskrit the North American continent, situating it north of Mt. Meru. He or she then specifies the town of Rush, located near the holy river Genessee. The consecrated sanctum of the Śrī Rājarājeśwarī Pīṭham is then invoked as the site of the ritual to be performed.

The expanding network of Hindu temples spread throughout North America also has the effect of validating the intrinsic holiness of "foreign" terrain. Established pilgrimage networks, prompting family vacations and chartered bus tours since the early 1980s, further sanctify the New World continent (Bhardwaj 1990: 225). Surinder Bardhwaj, writing in 1990 before the Rush *pīṭham* was established, identifies the two most popular pilgrimage routes at the time. One includes the Ganesh temple in Flushing, N.Y., the Shri Venkateshwara temple in Pittsburgh, and New Vrindaban in West Virginia. The other circuit runs from temples in Montreal or Toronto to the Pittsburgh temple to New Vrindaban. Bhardwaj notes that pilgrims on both circuits often make side trips to Niagara Falls, as well (1990: 224).[12] Based on the increasing number of out-of-town visitors every year, it seems the Rush temple is becoming a regular addition to some U.S. and Canadian pilgrimage circuits. Since pilgrimage is part sacred journey, part vacation, it probably does no harm to Rush's pilgrimage status that it is located just off the interstate, about two hours' drive east of Niagara Falls.[13]

One weekday afternoon in late spring of 2002, I gave a tour of the temple grounds to four couples on pilgrimage outings—two couples from Boston and one each from New Jersey and New York. The tour spontaneously materialized in response to one couple's two young sons who were antsy from the day's driving. The 12:30 *pūjā* would not be held for another hour, so I offered to show them the outdoor shrines and give the boys a chance to run around. As we were heading out the door, Sudharshan ushered over another couple interested in a walk, and two other couples, recently arrived, joined the flow. As we mucked our way through the grounds (it had rained heavily the day before), we discovered that each couple, from various parts of north and south India, had independently come to Rush, all had been or were going to the Pittsburgh temple, and all had been to Niagara Falls. I seemed to be the only one struck by this, and when I suggested it was a surprising coincidence, people disagreed. In addition to Pittsburgh and Niagara Falls, the Rush temple, people felt, was becoming an important link within many pilgrimage circuits.

Rush temple terrain connects with and contributes to the sacred in fairly regular, somewhat unremarkable ways, as well. One such instance involved another walk on the temple's grassy acreage. Small part ritual and large part evening stroll, it took place one August evening in 2001, after the completion of Ganeś's annual *Caturthī* festival. As participants were lining up for dinner after the final procession, I saw a group of eight devotees, all in their twenties and thirties, head back out into the dark with Aiya. Sudharshan spotted me and asked if I wanted to come along. Not knowing where we were going, but not wanting to be without my camera, I ran into the temple to fetch it and caught up with the group outside.

As we headed down the grassy slope behind the temple, I saw that Aiya was carrying a handful of votive candles. Our mission, it turned out, was to give light to the little outdoor shrines that mark the landscape.[14] We stopped first at Ganeś's shrine under a maple tree, then Śiva's down by the creek, then back up to Bhairava's beneath the oak tree near the *homam* pit. At each shrine someone lit a votive candle and placed it in a nearby hanging lamp. As we walked and lit candles, I found myself astounded that, although our task was meant to benefit the deities, no one was chanting. Instead, the darkness was filled with joking and laughter and giddy comments about lurking snakes. At one point we all stopped in our tracks to appreciate the new sliver of a moon, the sound of chirping crickets filling our momentary silence. After making our rounds, we paused again at the top of the hill to admire our work. Kumaran mentioned that the flickering candles looked like little twinkling stars from afar, which they did. As we contentedly returned to the temple, Aiya happily remarked to me that young people like it at the temple because it feels like a village.

Although I did not know exactly what Aiya meant by this, I did not want to spoil the moment by asking questions. On the one hand, he may have been referring to the village of deities who dot the rural landscape with their shrine homes, enhancing the temple terrain with their warmth and blessings. He may also have been referring to a village in the sense of a close-knit human community who feel at home with one another and share an appreciation for ordinary things in life. Or maybe it was both. Setting out into the night, bound by the simple purpose of giving a little light to the hillside shrines, it seemed the small band of devotees honored their affiliation with the land, its deities, and one another with their laughter and camaraderie. In this case, the simplest and homeliest of acts—absent of elaborate rituals, ancient associations, or cross-country networks—sanctified a chain of connections between the temple, its community, and its terrain. Once back inside the brightly lit temple, I remember looking down at my hand and rediscovering my camera. The twinge of disappointment over missing some lovely photo opportunities was quickly replaced by a sense of gratitude that I been too swept up by the event's simple sacredness to remember my role as chronicler.

Sanctifying Bronze, Vision, and Flesh: Rush's Divine Ambassadors

Keeping with the theme in which "foreign" terrain blesses and is blessed through contact with temple practices and communities, we return to the subject of traveling deities and explore how gods and goddesses—manifest as *mūrtis*, visions, and human beings—transform and are transformed by contact with new territory.

Arriving at the Rush *pīṭham* during special occasions, acting as a kind of divine ambassador between countries, traditions, and regions, is the Viṣṇu Durgā *mūrti*. Like the Rājarājeśwarī *mūrti*, she has a traveling story to tell. Standing about three feet tall and made of bronze, Viṣṇu Durgā took up permanent residence quite unexpectedly in St. Catherine's, Canada, at the home of Santoshimata and the late Sagar in 1994. The unusual chain of events leading up to this began with a priest who brought the *mūrti* from Tamil Nadu to North America with instructions to deliver her to a temple in Toronto. Before reaching Toronto, he was scheduled to help officiate at a three-day festival in Hamilton, Canada. En route to Hamilton, the priest became stranded at the train station in Buffalo, New York, and Sagar and Santoshimata, members of the Hamilton temple, were asked to pick him up. The priest and the *mūrti* thus ended up staying at their house for the duration of the festival.

When the Hamilton festival ended and it was time for the priest to move on, he informed the couple that the Devī did not want to leave their house. Her installation at the Toronto temple, he insisted, must be called off. Initially shocked and then convinced it was the best thing to do, Sagar and Santoshimata bought the Viṣṇu Durgā *mūrti* from the priest for several thousand dollars.[15] The priest performed a *pūjā* in their shrine room, installing the Devī there. He also installed a *śrīcakra meru*, a three-dimensional *yantra*, placing it in front of the goddess. Devī worshippers, particularly Śrīvidyā *upāsakas*, consider the *śrīcakra meru* to have immense power. In spite of this, it seems the priest left behind the *meru* and the Viṣṇu Durgā *mūrti* with minimal explanation. The couple nonetheless honored her as best they knew how, with an *āratī* flame and familiar prayers. Coming from northwest India, their exposure to Devī worship was nearly nonexistent; they were not even sure of the goddess's name. The *meru*, furthermore, was a complete mystery.

Sagar and Santoshimata met Aiya about four months later at the home of friends. Aiya and a group from the Park Circle garage temple were staying overnight at the house after performing devotional hymns at the Hamilton temple. Aware that Aiya was a Devī *upāsaka*, Sagar approached him to learn more about his *mūrti*. Sagar described for him what she held in her hands (a *cakra* discus and a conch shell) and what lay at her feet (a buffalo head); thus they determined that the goddess was Viṣṇu Durgā. Thinking someone perhaps had given him a small statue, Aiya was stunned to hear the *mūrti* was temple-sized, originally bound for installation in Toronto. When Sagar described the conical-shaped object that came with the Devī, Aiya recognized it as a *śrīcakra meru* and, as he put it, "That's when I got really excited." At Aiya's request, Sagar and Santoshimata brought him to their house, where he instructed them in the fundamentals of Devī *pūjā* and gave them initiation. In due course, the couple became highly dedicated *upāsakas* and regulars at the Park Circle garage temple. Sagar played a major role in preparing for Rājarājeśwarī's installation at the barn temple, chanting the fifteen-syllable *pañcadasi* mantra two and a half million times to charge the *yantra* that sits beneath the goddess. Chanting for up to eight hours at a time, the task took him nearly four years to complete.

Beginning with the Rush temple's one-year *pratiṣṭhā* anniversary festival in 1999, St. Catherine's Viṣṇu Durgā has traveled, at least once a year, from her home in Canada to Rush during festival occasions. She ceremoniously arrives in the family van decorated with brightly colored paper flower garlands and is greeted by temple participants at the end of the driveway, who grandly usher her into the temple on a palanquin. Once in the temple, she receives *pūjā* three times a day in the company of the other deities. During the *pratiṣṭhā* festival, when devotees honor a different deity each day—Ganeś on the first, Devī on the second, and Dattātreya on the third—the culmination of the three-day weekend features Viṣṇu Durgā's chariot procession around the temple.

Aiya has a many-sided rationale for orchestrating Viṣṇu Durgā's celebratory travels to and around the Rush temple. Most simply, he wants to honor the goddess present in the *mūrti*, something he earlier did on a smaller scale at Sagar and Santoshimata's home. The new Rush temple allows her to be celebrated by more people and with greater panache. The other more explicit side of Aiya's rationale is that Viṣṇu Durgā represents an important bridge between countries, religious traditions, and cultures. Most basically, by coming to Rush the *mūrti* links Canada with the United States. Also, by celebrating a deity from the Vaiṣṇava tradition, Rush's Śiva-Śakti temple deliberately and publicly breaks sectarian barriers. Finally, because she resides at the home of

Sagar and Santhoshimata with their Viṣṇu Durgā *mūrti* and offerings of *kumkum* powder. Photo by Pathmanathan.

Punjabi devotees, her celebration in Rush by a mainly Sri Lankan Tamil crowd provides a link between north and south India. One of the most common sources of temple tensions in North America hinges on South Asian regionalism, something Aiya wants to symbolically deflect. Although the reality of the Rush temple is that it is uncompromisingly sectarian and largely Sri Lankan Tamil, the explicit place of honor given to Viṣṇu Durgā helps to assure people, as Aiya sees it, that all are nonetheless welcome.

Although Indian deities reveal themselves on North American soil most regularly and reliably in *mūrti* form, divine visions can also act as cultural ambassadors, albeit indirectly, through their appearance on and adaptation to foreign terrain. In the account in chapter 3 of the little girl goddess who appeared to three Euro Americans, the van-riding outsiders understand her as someone of Indian descent whose immigrant parents do not fully comprehend the dangers of nighttime neighborhoods and roads. Devotees who hear the story, expecting the Devī to look Indian, are not so much struck that the vision is that of a slightly confused foreign youth as by the fact that she rides a bike. Not used to hearing about goddess apparitions who ride bikes, a number of people I spoke with interpreted this as a whimsical adaptation to North American culture. Just as her appearance in the temple vicinity helps endorse the ritual life of the temple itself, the bike-riding variation on a familiar theme reflects, for some, how North American culture provides a worthy setting in which the goddess can make herself at home.

Presenting a more dramatic instance of divine adaptation and tacit endorsement of North American culture is Aiya's account of meeting the god Dattātreya in a 7-11 store. Following the Dattātreya *homam* on the third day of the 1999 *pratiṣṭhā* festival, Aiya stood by the smoldering fire pit and regaled the festival-tent crowd with traditional stories about the deity, concluding with the following local account:

> I will tell you about an experience I had some time ago right in this country. I was traveling somewhere to do a *pūjā*—I can't remember where. And the whole time, throughout the journey, I was chanting "*Om, hrīm dram Dattātreya. . . .*" [*Aiya continues chanting in Sanskrit.*] Like this. I was singing, and the tape [of prerecorded mantras] was playing continuously. And I remembered reading that if you keep chanting this mantra all the time, this *stotram*, you're supposed to see Him.
>
> I stopped at a 7-11 to get a cup of coffee. I went inside—it was evening in wintertime. A hunter walked into the store with his gun and fishing boots and all that. Along with him two dogs came inside. And he was looking at me as he took some beer from the case. He was not looking at the counter clerk; he was looking at me directly like this. [*Aiya demonstrates his somber stare.*] Then he walked past me and out the door. I got a whiff of camphor and I remembered, "*Katpura gandhi dehaye . . .*" [from Dattātreya's *stotram*]. I thought, "That is Dattātreya! He has come!"

A few days later, I made a joking comment to Aiya about Dattātreya liking beer. He responded that Dattātreya always comes to his devotees in an undesirable form, as a rogue. His presence at 7-11's domestic beer case (he chose a six-pack of Old Milwaukee), along with the fact that he was accompanied by dogs, animals typically associated with the deity, further confirmed for Aiya, beyond the smell of camphor, his identity. Divinity is recognized, in this case, in a person who does not look or act particularly Indian. Like Devī on the bike, a North American Dattātreya not only validates the faith of his devotees but, in some ways, by association, the cultural trappings of a "foreign" land.

A final type of traveling deity linked with and explicitly supportive of the Rush temple, its terrain, and its devotees, is not a statue or a vision but rather a human female invested with divine attributes and knowledge. Hindu traditions on occasion associate exceptional individuals with particular deities, attributing to them divine powers and understanding. Akka, as she is popularly known, was recognized at age nine by the Śaṇkarācārya of Kāñcāpuram as the goddess Akhilāṇdeśwarī incarnate.[16] She was visiting the Kāñcīpuram temple with her parents at the time and, when the Śaṇkarācārya caught sight of her, he received a powerful vision of the goddess. He conveyed his discovery to her parents, paving the way for her recognition by others. Akka, now in her sixties, has never married and currently lives in Chennai with her mother and a small group of devotee residents. She has a substantial following in south India and has built a small Krishna temple where devotees can meet with her. Devotees in California, mostly south Indian immigrants, have established the Nandalala Mission in her name, sponsoring outreach projects and hosting her periodic visits.[17]

During a trip to Chennai to conduct a wedding in early 1997, Aiya learned about Akka from Delhimammi, a woman he had met through the distribution of his Śrīvidyā book. He was moved by her account of having three consecutive dreams about Akka before she met her. Impressed by stories of miracles he heard from other devotees in Chennai, he requested an audience with Akka to ask if she could help an eight-year-old girl he knew who suffered from leukemia. When he was in her presence, he felt, as he described it, an incredible power. After discussing the little girl, Aiya told Akka about the property he had recently purchased in the United States and his plan to build a temple. He asked if she might visit some day to grace their new venture. Without deliberation, Akka said she would.

In the fall of 1997, amid a seemingly futile struggle to get town council approval for a building permit, Aiya learned that Akka was in California and arranged for her to visit upstate New York. Park Circle devotees excitedly anticipated Akka's arrival, constructing a royal seat for her in their small garage temple. Akka was sincerely impressed, in her quiet way, by the devotees' rapt attention and by their ability to perform extensive chants in unison. Akka agreed to Aiya's request that they visit the future temple property the following day to, as he put it, "bless it with the touch of her feet." The next morning in Rush, Akka walked onto the grounds, faced the different directions, and affirmed to Aiya in her quiet voice, "This is good." She then sat in the main entrance to the barn, on the dirt, and requested that Priya perform with her a *bhumi pūjā*.[18] When they finished, she told Aiya not to worry about his current difficulties; the temple would manifest.

In a matter of two months the permit was secured, and within six months the Rush temple celebrated its opening *pratiṣṭhā* ceremony.[19] Akka's ties with the community continue—whenever possible, she makes it a point to visit—and her Nandalala Mission funded the new temple kitchen, completed in 2003. In spite of Akka's naturally reserved nature, she expresses high praise for the temple privately to individuals as well as during public events. Particularly impressive to her is the attention the temple gives to ritual performance and to the training of its participants. Akka detects a level of divine energy, fueled

Akka sitting in front of Navagṛha *mūrtis* (nine planets) with Aiya and Amma offering *pūjā* to her feet. Photo by Pathmanathan.

by elaborate and accessible rituals, that she does not experience at other North American temples. This energy is further heightened, she feels, by the fact that devotees make themselves so at home at the temple, as does she. This sense of home is what seems to prompt her regular returns as well as her tendency to mingle with and talk to devotees in ways she typically does not at her centers in Chennai or California.[20] For Aiya, this multilayered endorsement of the Rush temple by an embodiment of the Devī herself is beyond his wildest dreams. The thrill he receives from Akka's visits and support is palpable.

During the final few days of the 1999 Navarātri celebration, Akka flew from California to upstate New York to join the Rush festivities. On Sunday evening she formally announced, at Aiya's request, the release of that year's *Navarātri Malar*, a compilation of religious commentary produced by the temple each year. She continued talking for about thirty minutes, on her own accord, praising the ritual power and style of the temple. On Monday, the final day of the festival, Akka unceremoniously arrived at the temple during the afternoon *homam*. With the sound of chanting in the background, she began walking from person to person, anointing their foreheads with strongly scented oil she had brought with her. When enough people noticed what she was doing, a long line quietly formed to receive her blessings. After everyone had been anointed, the *homam* still continuing, some devotees suggested that Akka sit in her designated place of honor some distance from the fire. She pleasantly waved them off and remained standing nearby, watching the ritual. About twenty minutes later, a small explosion burst from the *homam* flames and a burning ember flew directly into one of Aiya's eyes. Aiya, blinked and, to his amazement, found himself unharmed. He looked up to see Akka, who smiled at him, then turned to find her seat.

The rest of the afternoon and evening Aiya seemed particularly beside himself with gratitude and excitement. At one point he passed by my mother, who was visiting from California, and me and blurted out, "Can you believe this? It's what I've been dreaming about since I was nineteen!" During his afternoon address, he had to stop several times, fighting to keep his tears in check. With Akka, goddess incarnate, endorsing his work at the temple and saving him from bodily harm, the depth of his appreciation seemed to know no bounds. At one point, after describing the overwhelming sense of humility he felt when basking in the Mother's abundant grace, he stopped short. Silent for about twenty seconds, he started up again. Still composing himself and speaking softly, he reminisced about the instance, two years prior, when Akka visited from India and cleared the final obstructions that kept the temple from becoming a reality.

> This place was just a barn. Dirt floor. And Amma [Akka] graced this place. She didn't even wait or look for an *āsanam* [priest's seat made from cloth or animal skin]. She just sat down on the dirt [and performed the *pūjā*]. Devī is called *Avyāja Karuṇā Mūrti.*[21] She Herself does not know why She is giving Her grace. I saw this in action on that day. And She blessed this place and said, "The temple will manifest."
>
> Every time I think of that I shed tears. Never tears of sadness; they are tears of happiness. And I know there are lots of devotees in this *pīṭham*, every time they go and look at that picture [of Akka], tears come. It's love and devotion that is given to Her as a tiny token.

The final event of Navarātri 1999 was a procession featuring Devī in the form of Akka leading the way. Although this weekday event involved fewer participants than had attended during the weekend, it was no less grandly orchestrated. Flanked by devotees carrying the requisite regalia fit for a deity, Akka walked on red carpet spread before her. Bringing up the rear, majestically stationed in the temple's *tēr* chariot and pulled by a raucous group of female devotees, was the goddess in her Viṣṇu Durgā *mūrti* form. As they circled and blessed the barn temple and its grounds, these traveling deities helped link and sanctify terrain and traditions old and new, far and near. As such, they tempered apparently insurmountable divides and barriers—not least, the perceived abyss between divinity and humanity. Rush stories and experiences of sacred travel and transport thus demonstrate that quests for holiness and home are, at times, indistinguishable.

8

Expanding Turf for Racial and Religious Others

We move now from tales of divine travelers and sanctified terrain to accounts of traveling humans. Although the introduction of new kinds of people and religions opens possibilities and opportunities not previously imagined for those living in zones of contact, so also can it stretch uncomfortably the worlds of those who resist change. The following thus explores human frontiers that, unlike the deities', can be rather uneasy yet, sometimes unwittingly, are not without their miraculous moments.

Race and Racism on a Shifting Planet

The short and rather tumultuous history of South Asians in North America began only in the late nineteenth and early twentieth centuries.[1] In the United States, what little immigration occurred during these early years—about seven thousand new arrivals between 1899 and 1914—was soon brought to a standstill.[2] Responding to widespread anti-Asian sentiment, Congress passed a 1917 Immigration Act designating an Asiatic Barred Zone that prevented new arrivals from India and Southeast Asia (Richardson 1985: 18). In 1923, the Supreme Court ruled that Indian immigrants were not "free white persons" within the law and thus not eligible for citizenship. Certificates of citizenship earlier issued were withdrawn. A reversal of these early laws began in 1946, when the Luce-Celler Bill removed India from the barred zone and gave the remaining 1,500 immigrants the right to become citizens, but limiting new citizens to one hundred per year. In 1965, a new Immigration Act proposed by John Kennedy and signed by Lyndon Johnson turned the tide completely. For the first time since the 1920s, a person's right to enter the United States did not depend on country of origin or race. In 1980, the peak of South Asian immigration, the Immigration and Naturalization Services reported 22,607 arrivals for that year alone (Williams 1988: 15).

Mirroring U.S. patterns, Canada's first South Asian immigrants arrived in British Columbia around 1900. A subsequent wave of immigration during a severe economic depression in 1907–1908 became known as the "Asian Menace," and in 1909 the government banned further immigration from South Asia. South Asian residents were barred, furthermore, from full social, political, and economic rights and participation (Buchignani 1980: 122). By 1920, wives and other dependents of earlier immigrants were allowed into Canada, but by then most had either returned home or moved to California. The population at this time had stabilized at around 1,100 from an earlier peak of around 5,000. Up until 1947, immigration was barred, and South Asian Canadians were unable to vote or become citizens. Not until 1967 did immigration laws formally disregard race, ethnicity, and nationality (126).

The South Asian immigration boom, beginning in earnest in the mid 1970s and peaking during the early 1980s, in some ways reflects North American governments' newfound openness to non-European citizenry. Yet such openness did not guarantee a similar receptivity by citizens whose ties to North America go back for generations and whose understanding of home turf, disrupted by recent immigration, has undergone radical reconstruction. The prevalence of "native" resistance to new immigrants is such that Rush devotees of South Asian descent have, without exception, experienced racial tensions while living in North America. Accounts of racism cut across the generations, yet they seem to flow with particular ease and poignancy when young adult devotees describe their North American grade school experiences. While listening to these accounts, I found myself alternately disturbed by their uniformity—it seems no one was immune from childhood cruelty—and in awe of each storyteller's sense of equanimity. Without watering down their memories of pain, all seemed to have come to terms with their imperfect society.

Muralee, Kumaran, and Vijitha, now in their twenties, left Sri Lanka and settled in Toronto with their parents in 1985. They reported that for their first three to four years in Canada, their neighborhood and school were predominantly Euro Canadian and Chinese. Since their family was part of an early wave of immigrants who left Sri Lanka and its troubles, they were met by a particularly acute strain of racism upon arrival. Muralee described being blindsided by childhood taunts when he joined his new school in the fourth grade. In retrospect, he understands their cruelty as having less to do with the children themselves than with a larger problem.

> When I started school, it was hard because my name was different. They couldn't say my name. My color was. . . . They would call me "Paki." It's like saying "Nigger." Before, when I was a kid, I didn't know what it was. I didn't know about anything. But after a while you realize, "Oh, this is what's happening!" And you come to understand that, okay, this is the way it is. Gee, what the hell, there's no difference between you and me except for my skin coloration! Our body parts are the same. It's not like I have something that makes me different than you. It was bad. Even younger kids, people like younger than me would call me that. It was sad to see, but I couldn't do much about it. It was the way they were brought up, right? I now blame the parents. It's not the kids' fault.

After three to four years, the Sri Lankan community had established itself in the larger Toronto area, keeping overt and persistent racism at bay. As Kumaran put it, "Four years later, there were more and more people coming, so they realized that if you talk such and such about this person, he's going to get support from his other friends—like that. We're in the same boat. So [racism] just started to die out. It's become more and more multicultural in Canada since the nineties. It's much better now." In spite of the large numbers of Tamil Sri Lankans who have moved into their neighborhood, Vijitha, Muralee, and Kumaran consistently cultivated friends from a variety of backgrounds. Muralee's playful attitude regarding race and color emerged in a story he laughingly told me involving his Euro Canadian college friends who, due to his darker complexion and curly hair that he keeps very short, thought he was of African descent. Their assumption was embarrassingly exposed when they came to study in Muralee's room and saw his posters of Ganeś, Devī, and other Hindu deities. Muralee, who knew they thought he was Black, reflected on their astonishment at the deities, "I kind of walked them into it." Now, as Muralee describes it, misguided perceptions of race and color are a joke they all share.

Abhi, Aiya and Amma's niece, was seventeen when we discussed the subject of racism. Born in the United States, she entered the public school system in Webster, a predominantly white suburb of Rochester, in the late 1980s. From first to fourth grade she was regularly teased, especially on bus rides to and from school. Athletic and outgoing, she made good friends at school as well, but the name-callers were relentless. Keeping her troubles to herself at first, she eventually told her teacher. The teacher asked Abhi to tell her the names the children were calling her, made a list of the names, and informed the principal. Abhi was henceforth assigned an adult "guard" who shadowed her during recess and on the bus. When she reached the fourth grade, her parents decided attitudes were not changing at her school and enrolled Abhi and her sister at a very small private school in Rochester. The two sisters were the only South Asians enrolled but, according to Abhi, the school's ethical teachings, its size, and its slight racial diversity helped keep blatant racism in check.

Like Kumaran, Abhi currently feels that racist attitudes are subsiding somewhat in her area, based on the fact that the population is more diverse and also that her brother, six years her senior, had a much rougher time at the local public school than she. Although it may be true that racism toward South Asians in many schools is less severe than it was a decade or two ago, younger, school-age temple members related to me accounts that suggest problems with racist bullies on the bus and playground are not entirely over.[3]

Dipi, a Sikh devotee in his early twenties who, in accordance with tradition, kept his hair long and wore a turban until he was seventeen, recounted his particularly dramatic encounters with racism. Born in the United States, Dipi grew up in Connecticut and Syracuse in the eighties and early nineties and experienced, as he put it, "double the problems" since his difference was marked by both his ethnicity and his turban. A soft-spoken and thoughtful young man, Dipi portrayed his upbringing in broad strokes: "My whole childhood was pretty rough. Growing up was hard. My family life was okay—I had a good family life. But socially, my life was terrible. Going to school, I got picked on. I didn't have many friends, anyone to relate to. I got beat up sometimes." At sixteen, Dipi, at his wits' end, informed his parents that he planned to cut his hair and stop wearing a turban. Because he knew this would come as a shock, he kindly gave them six months' warning before taking action. Once he no longer wore a turban and blended better into his surroundings, Dipi's social life slowly began to improve.

Trained in psychology and philosophical by temperament, Dipi reflected on how his past informs his present: "Everyone has their tragic spots. The main thing is to learn from them. Maybe not even learn from them, just grow from them. That's the main thing. Some people can get stuck on these things and let them ruin their lives. It's sad. But as I see it, it's all part of a process." Since he was thirteen, Dipi occasionally attended Aiya's garage temple with his parents and in the three years before our interview had become a more fully committed participant. Dipi reflected on how, in the past several years, Aiya and the temple have helped him work through his earlier trials. "I feel like I'm slowly starting to transcend my humiliations. I'm trying to get rid of the duality that everyone lives in. That happiness/sadness, good/bad, judgment. All that. I feel I am coming along, and I am grateful for that."

Although present-day demographics may quell overt racism somewhat, and adult status may provide valuable perspective, they are not perfectly effective shields. Aiya, for instance, narrated an experience of his own to the temple gathering during the 2002 Gurupūrṇimā. Driving to a temple function in Toronto a few weeks earlier, he stopped at a Mobil station where he went inside to prepay before pumping his gas. He was wearing a long tunic kurta and loose cotton pants, traditional Indian attire for men, causing the two men working at the shop, drinking coffee behind the cash register, to look him over as he entered. One of the workers asked if Aiya was an American and he responded that yes, he was an American citizen. The man then asked why he did not dress like an American, to which Aiya responded with another question: "Are you American?" The man answered that he was. Aiya then asked why he did not dress like one. The gentleman, confused, stated that of course he dressed like an American. Aiya pointed out that, in fact, he did not. He dressed like an Englishman. If he truly dressed like an American he would be wearing a loincloth and a feather headdress. With that, Aiya left to fill up his car elsewhere.

Although Aiya is quick to recognize and remark on racism leveled at his community, he is also quick to note racial discrimination aimed in the opposite direction. This is most strikingly the case when non-Indian Hindus are denied access to Indian temples. In response to a male student's exclusion from the Kāñcīpuram Kāmākṣī temple, Aiya requested an audience with the Śaṇkarācārya of Kāñcīpuram during the summer of 1998. Aiya recounted for me his argument that although the official rationale for barring white people from temples has to do with religion it is actually about skin color. Aiya's words to the Śaṇkarācārya, as he recalled them, were as follows:

> I'll tell you, the intensity with which [Euro American students] do *japam* and *pūjā*, you cannot match in this country. I have *seen* it and you cannot. We [at the temple] talk about Kāmākṣī so much, they are dying to see Her, but when they come to the Kāñcīpuram temple, at the entrance they are told that they are not Hindu and they should not come to the temple. What kind of injustice is this? [*Aiya whispers.*] I think it's not fair. Let me paint you another scenario. Let us say I'm a Muslim from Bangladesh. I come here; I take my shirt off and walk into the temple. Do you *know* that I am not a Hindu? What is this?

Aiya remarked that, at this point, the Śaṇkarācārya's aids began trying to usher him away or, at very least, to get him to quiet down. But he persisted, demanding a response. Finally, the Śaṇkarācārya spoke up, stating that, in the future, non-Indian Hindus would be let into the Kāñcīpuram temple. When I expressed enthusiasm at his victory, Aiya shook his head and said, "It's not going to be implemented, Amma. No way." Then with a big smile he dramatically thrust his finger in the air and continued, "But I have found another way! The chief priest has now become one of my good friends. So I told him, 'Aiya, when any of my Western disciples come, they are not going directly to the temple; they are coming to your house. You take them inside.' " As related in chapter 5, Aiya's plan was a success. In 1999, Kathy and Steve entered the Kāñcīpuram temple, escorted by Aiya's friend. The following summer Aiya told me he made his peace with the Śaṇkarācārya, who seemed aware of and supportive of his Euro American students' entry into the temple. Aiya thanked him, and the Śaṇkarācārya assured him he was happy to help.

At the Rush temple, Euro American devotees represent a small minority, creating for some a feeling of being on the periphery. Often this has less to do with race than with not being part of a Tamil-speaking culture. Non-Sri Lankans and certainly non-Tamil-speaking devotees from India sometimes express a similar disconnect, particularly during weekend and festival events. Complicating this perception of center and periphery, as we have seen, is Aiya's tendency to place Euro Americans—better yet, Euro American women—in the spotlight during major ritual events. The deliberate display of competent non-South Asian chanters promotes an agenda of equal access, but Aiya also hopes it inspires people born into the tradition to reach for levels of proficiency that those "foreign" to the tradition have achieved. Although this plan can backfire—some South Asians express embarrassment and shame that they cannot chant as well as the featured Euro American devotees—it provokes in others greater effort. At very least, Aiya admits, Euro Americans adept at ritual draw people to the temple for the "show."

At the Chennai Śrīvidyā conference, described in chapter 5, a number of Indian women approached Aparna and Kathy to thank them for demonstrating the possibilities they did not realize existed. Kathy and Aparna, sharing Aiya's agenda to inspire devotion, were pleased by these exchanges but realized nonetheless how their incongruent whiteness inspired, from others attending the conference, plain curiosity. Aparna painted the picture: "There's the element of shock. There's the element of us walking in. Not only are we white women, but we were the only Westerners who were there from start to finish. And along with Aiya we were the only nonbrahmans. And I don't think they ever considered the idea that we would have the interest or the ability to learn chants. . . . So we created a stir. Aiya said that attendance rose because we were there. Indian women were coming to see us. So we were a kind of circus item on that level."

Also offering shock value were the various opportunities Kathy and Aparna took while in Chennai to chant *rudram*, an extremely challenging mantra typically performed by men. Kathy, whose mastery of the chant is particularly exceptional, remarked that although she enjoys chanting *rudram* for its intrinsic value, she particularly enjoyed doing so in India because of the dissonance between her white femaleness and traditional expectations. Seeing and hearing a white woman so expertly chanting *rudram* indeed shocked many people but, as Kathy experienced it, no one seemed upset. She described an enthusiastic reception that resulted in her being put up for display—this time not by Aiya: "During this conference I chanted *rudram* and the conference organizer grabbed me and made me chant it in front of his leading *purohit*, like the oldest man who everyone has the greatest respect for, the lead chanter. It was like this old brahman man in Madras who was their *purohit*. And this head guruji

Kathy performing *śrīcakra pūjā*. Photo by author.

of the conference who had organized the whole thing, he made me sit down in front of his *purohit* and chant *rudram*. And the *purohit* was very pleased."

Sudharshan reflected on this event during one of our conversations, distinguishing it from instances when Aiya uses display to inspire people. Although he admitted that the conference event may have inadvertently inspired some, he felt this was not their intention.

> So I think the Pharisees and the Scribes of India were shocked because she was female, she was white, she was nonbrahman, and how the hell did she learn this? Because [*rudram*] is very challenging. It's very challenging. My god, I have a hard time with it and I've been doing it for seven years! But there she is and it's kind of odd, y'know? It's just such a freaky picture. [*We laugh.*] So of course they're encouraging it because it's sort of nonthreatening. You do realize that is why they're encouraging it. Because how is she going to threaten their access to privilege? She's white, she's a woman, and she's not brahman. But if it were a nonbrahman Indian male doing it, I think they'd be very threatened. They'd be afraid that someone was going to take their jobs away.

Motivations for staging such displays seem be the desire to sensationalize difference, on the one hand, or to demonstrate the irrelevance of difference, on the other. While sideshow appeal and genuine challenge to religious exclusivism often seem to work at cross-purposes, they can overlap and reinforce one another, as well. To what extent an event will shock and/or inspire is ultimately up to the spectator. Aiya's commitment to promoting the irrelevance of gender and race for ritual practice creates displays that, he hopes, open a range of possibilities rather than suggest the freakishly impossible. The fact that adept white (female) chanters nonetheless make a stir at Rush and that South Asian children still cannot ride the school bus in peace are testimony, however, to an imperfect world not always receptive to such possibilities. Amid shifting cultures, Rush temple devotees of all backgrounds strive, on a variety of levels, to transcend ideas of racial difference. And most would agree that race as a category continues to receive far more relevance than is its due.

A Hindu Temple Moves into the Neighborhood

While late twentieth-century South Asian immigration has forever changed North America's ethnic landscape, so also has it changed its religious landscape. Paving the way for Hinduism's arrival into the mainstream were the nineteenth-century writings of Transcendentalists Emerson and Thoreau, as well as Vivekananda's famous address at the Chicago's World's Fair in 1893. The countercultural movement's fascination for Asian religions during the 1960s and 1970s, as well as an influx of spiritual masters from India during that time, further laid the groundwork for waves of immigrant Hindus in the 1970s and 1980s. Reflected in the shifting clientele of the Pocono ashram described in the last chapter, the ritual and temple-based religion of diaspora Hindus was not, however, what many Euro Americans had in mind when they earlier embraced Indian philosophy and meditation.[4] When South Asians began establishing places of worship across the continent during the 1980s and 1990s, they represented decided variations on prior North American Hindu themes.

Not surprisingly, the recent steady emergence of North American Hindu temples has been unsettling for some "natives," and not without incident. Most commonly, temples have struggled to secure local acceptance and permission for construction. A Krishna temple in New Jersey finally opened in 1994 in a former YMCA building after years of community resistance and a court case. Once it was consecrated, the temple was defaced, spray-painted with "Get out Hindoos! KKK." The community has repainted and resolutely remained (Eck 2001: 131). Gangs of young men have harassed South Asian residents living near the Flushing temple and vandals have pelted the building with eggs, yet it as also has persevered. On the other hand, an Elmhurst temple finally relocated after failing to stop similar types of harassment (Richardson 1985: 49). Several days after the September 11 attack on the World Trade Center, vandals set fire to the Hamilton temple in Canada (mentioned in Viṣṇu-Durgā's story in the previous chapter) in the early hours of the morning. By the time devotees rushed to the scene and firefighters began their work, the entire building was ablaze with no hope for saving it or the *mūrtis* inside. As of this writing, the community is still raising funds for a new temple building.

Aiya's temple at Park Circle and later at Rush has weathered its share of community welcome and resistance, as well. At the garage temple, neighborly relations strained as the temple community grew and as many as one hundred cars lined nearby streets during large festivals. Friday nights, the main weekend event at Park Circle, would regularly draw twenty-five to thirty vehicles. The crowded streets tested the patience of many residents, some of whom had begun to complain, but the final straw was during an ice storm that coincided with the 1995 Śivarātri festival, when parked cars blocked the passage of an emergency vehicle. Soon afterward, Aiya received official notice from the city. As he tactfully put it, "They were kind enough to let it go on for a while, but they finally wrote and said that perhaps it was time to look for a new place." For the next two and a half years, while the Rush property was located, bought, and approved for public use, Park Circle devotees organized a shuttle bus between Aiya and Amma's house and a public lot.

In retrospect, Aiya and other devotees seem genuinely sympathetic to the Park Circle neighbors' trials with congestion and commotion in their otherwise quiet neighborhood. One spring morning, as we walked from the temple to the small house, Aiya told me about an exception. During a weekend event while the shuttle was in operation, a few devotees nonetheless parked their cars on the road, prompting a particularly volatile neighbor to call the police. The police arrived at Aiya's door and mandated that no parking whatsoever be permitted on the road anymore. Violators would be ticketed and towed at the owner's expense, costing as much as four hundred dollars. A few nights later, the same neighbor had his nephew for dinner. When the young man parked his car on the road rather than in the driveway, it got towed. The neighbor, although furious, had to pay the bill. This demonstrates, Aiya explained, that Devī has a sense of humor.

Once the Rush property was located and purchased, attempts to prepare it for use as a temple met with a variety of obstacles, not least of which was community opposition. One problem was that the neighborhood was zoned as residential, and thus a special use permit was required for additional construction and plumbing to make the building, in essence, public. Aiya figured that the town could not deny him a special use permit since a church operated just down the road, one-quarter mile away. He was wrong. On Gurupūrṇimā of

1999, Aiya told the story of the permit, granted eventually by the town council. In his view, of course, the decision was ultimately Devī's—sense of humor or not:

> Not many of you know that when we presented the plans, there was an ultraconservative town council in place. Later on I heard that there were moves to table the project. This means that we would have been delayed by three years. We presented the first time in September, November the elections came and every single one of those members lost their elections. And in December I went to present it again and all the processes were waived and a special use permit was given to me on a golden platter. And a building permit was issued. In January, the board that gave me the permit was defeated, and the same ultraconservative board returned in midterm elections. By that time the Devī decided She was going to move here.

Since the establishment of the Rush temple, most of the surrounding community has been either neutral or supportive, and overt harassment has been minimal. Resistant neighbors who spoke out against the temple at the town meeting have tended, ever since, to keep complaints to themselves. Explicit or implicit critiques, such as there are, circulate primarily in the form of printed matter, the most dramatic being a series of notes found in the mailbox shortly after temple construction began, stating such sentiments as, "Hindus, go back where you came from!" Less directly confrontational was a fairly regular supply of Christian leaflets found under car windshields during the temple's first couple of years, appealing to non-Christians to embrace conversion rather than eternal damnation. For the most part, those who distributed the leaflets went undetected. One festival weekend in October 1999, however, an elderly woman stood at the foot of the temple driveway passing out leaflets to arriving cars. Two men preparing the chariot saw her and politely asked her to leave. Contemplating a double standard, Mohan, who described the scene to me, said he could never imagine someone from the temple standing outside a church handing out leaflets about the goddess. Even if it were part of their tradition to proselytize—which it is not—someone would certainly have called the authorities.

Aiya, who was half listening to our discussion at the time, chimed in that he had had a number of positive experiences with law enforcement and felt they would be fair. A few months later, in September of 1999, while we were eating lunch in the little house, he shared some of these encounters. He opened the subject by telling me that a police car had driven into the temple parking lot the day before. When Aiya went out to ask if there was a problem, the officer explained that he was just doing his rounds and that he regularly checks places of worship. He added that recently some hoodlums had painted swastikas on Jewish synagogues in the area and so the police were on the alert.

This led Aiya to relate another incident of police support in response to the hate mail found in the temple mailbox during building construction. When Aiya reported the notes to the Rush police, one of the officers suspected he knew the perpetrator. He tried a number of times to visit this gentleman at his house, but his wife kept answering the door to tell him he was not home. One day, as he drove toward the house, he saw the man go inside. When the wife again told him her husband was not home, he insisted she go get him. When the man came to the door he denied writing the notes, but the officer argued that if he were innocent he would not be avoiding him. He proceeded to tell him that he was lucky people at the temple were not pressing charges and that if he ever did anything of the sort again he would be facing a jail sentence. This put an end to the notes. When Aiya later thanked the officer for his persistence, the latter told him about an experience he had while in the service in Germany in the 1970s. A Jewish American friend of his had become the target of verbal and, later, physical harassment by a group of young skinheads. Fearing for their friend's safety, this man and some other servicemen decided to take matters into their own hands, warning the teenagers to leave him alone. Shaken by the experience, religious and racial harassment have been a concern for him ever since.

Although anti-Hindu sentiments have typically arrived at the Rush temple in the form of leaflets and anonymous notes, on rare occasions visitors have been messengers as well. For the most part, non-Hindus who visit the temple—whether out of curiosity or as spiritual seekers—are respectful if not supportive of the temple and its activities. The following example of an outspoken critic thus represents an exception—instructive, in part, due to devotees' responses and reactions to such blunt criticism.

According to Mohan, Vijitha, and Aiya, each of whom related portions of the story to me, the visitor was an elderly relative of someone in the neighborhood. Vijitha was on her way from the temple to the little house after morning *pūjā* when she saw her walking resolutely up the temple driveway. The woman approached Vijitha and brusquely asked her when the next service was scheduled. Vijitha, a bit startled by her demeanor, explained that "services" had just finished but that she would be glad to give her a tour of the temple instead. During their rounds, Aiya overheard bits of their conversation from the temple office and joined them in time to see the woman standing, hands on hips, in front of Dattātreya, who sports six arms and three heads. The woman asked Vijitha, in a demanding voice (as Aiya described it), why the god had so many arms. Aiya interjected that it was to show his power and that this kind of imagery was helpful for some people.

Once the woman finished her tour, with not much else to say, Mohan asked her what she thought of their "church." (Since he felt she may not have been able to understand "temple," he translated.) She responded, paraphrased by Mohan, "Your idols don't hear you; they don't talk. They're dead. You should worship the living God." Mohan asked who this was and she said it was Jesus. Mohan responded, attempting another translation, that his Jesus was the Devī. When the woman replied that his Devī was not living, Mohan insisted that she was very much living. She was his Mother. She said, "But your mother's dead!"—which in Mohan's case is true—to which Mohan calmly replied, "No, She's standing right here in front of me," referring to the temple *mūrti*. This seemed to confuse the woman and so, rather than responding, she handed him a pamphlet that she said would explain to him the living God. Mohan thanked her and promised to read it.

After she and Mohan finished their exchange, the woman drew Aiya, at the ready, into a debate. She insisted that people who worshiped at his temple were sinners, to which Aiya responded that everyone was a sinner, adding, "Who of us are not?" The woman could not refute this, responding that the difference is that his temple-goers are going to hell. In his usual debating style, rather than insisting they were not going to hell, Aiya confounded the argument by asking more questions: "Where is your God? Is He in a particular place? Up in the clouds, wearing a nice silver suit and sporting a gray beard?" Not to be taken in by such simplification, the woman interjected that God was everywhere. Aiya thus concluded, "Well, God must be in hell too!" Appalled at the idea, the woman suggested that Aiya read the Bible. To this Aiya spun out more questions: "Which Bible? The King James version, the Catholic version, the Book of Mormon, which one?" King James would be just fine, she replied. Aiya kept his course, "Okay, which one? The 1902 version, the 1945, or the 1995?" The woman seemed unaware that King James had so many editions, and also seemed surprised at his knowledge of Christianity. At this Aiya stopped asking questions and suggested she read other people's scriptures. If she had an open mind she might find truths there too. She replied that she'd found her savior in Jesus and that this was the Truth. Aiya then sternly noted that since her mind was completely closed there was little point in visiting the temple. With that, she left, striding back down the driveway the same way she came.

When Aiya, Vijitha, and Mohan related pieces of the above account, the mood was playful. Aiya enjoyed reflecting on the woman's apparent shock at encountering the multiarmed deities around the temple, laughingly adding that she probably figured that Mohan, seeing Devī standing before him, was "off his rocker." Apparently not worth discussing were the theological arguments she proposed. It seems reactions to outsider disdain often switch between dismissive laughter and angry indignation, depending on the context, and this incident called for the former. There are times, however, when the response is more philosophical in tone. For instance, when a fresh batch of leaflets had been left under people's windshields during a weekend event, I asked Aiya how he felt about it. He did not respond, as I sometimes heard, that people ought to mind their own business. Instead he chose to view the big picture, framed by the goddess, thus refocusing ideas of Christian supremacy: "If I believe that there is this Divine Mother who is behind all this intelligence and everything else the scriptures tell me, and if I have complete faith in that, then She is the one who is moving these people. For what reason, who knows? Maybe six hundred years from now, after they've gone through several cycles of births, what they may have accidentally imbibed here may blossom out onto something. Who knows what Her plans are? So I'm not mad. Let them do what they have to do."

Aiya's policy with his neighbors who do not approve of the temple is to respect their need to keep a distance. One elderly woman living across the street has been particularly upset by the temple because of her religious views, exacerbated by the fact that the property once belonged to her family. Aiya realizes this and tries not to get in her way. On snowy winter mornings during his first winter in Rush, however, he would ride the temple's small snowplow to the end of his driveway and, seeing the woman removing her snow, shovel by shovel, asked if he could clear her driveway. Without making eye contact she always refused. One morning, after the region received a record dumping of forty-six inches of snow overnight, Aiya plowed to the end of his driveway and simply continued into hers. He said, "I didn't even make eye contact with her; I just kept going and cleared her path as well." After he finished and was heading back toward the temple, a car followed him. The woman had sent her son after him with fifteen dollars' payment. Aiya refused the money, insisting it was no trouble at all—just a matter of forging straight ahead. He told me that the next time he drove past the house, he received a small wave from her, and demonstrated for me a tiny, tentative wave. The rest of that winter, he cleared her snow on a regular basis (her son subsequently bought his own miniplow).

For the most part, neighbors who are not overtly upset about the temple still choose to keep their distance. Curiosity kicks in from time to time, as Aiya has seen people viewing temple festivities through binoculars from their porches. Among the several neighbors who have ventured onto temple property to pay friendly visits was Ray, an elderly man who died a little over a year after the temple was consecrated. Ray apparently enjoyed talking with Aiya, advising him on such issues as the property's spring drainage and the maintenance of large machinery—topics about which Aiya gladly gathered advice. Ray apparently relished working with his hands and constantly kept himself busy at various neighborhood homes. Near the end of his life, however, he suffered from emphysema and became increasingly frustrated by the limits the disease put on his naturally active lifestyle. Ray became so miserable that he asked Aiya, during one of their last conversations, to pray for his peaceful and speedy death.

By far the most visible and supportive of the temple's neighbors are Jim and Cindy whose land runs adjacent to the temple property. I first met Jim at the 1999 *pratiṣṭhā* festival, where I saw him watching the procession with his two blonde daughters and talking with a Sri Lankan gentleman. Although Jim was willing to meet with me for a formal interview, arranging a time was tricky, since he worked six days a week managing a lumber yard and Cindy worked long hours as a medical technologist. The night of our interview the girls were at their grandparents, and Jim and Cindy were just sitting down to a late dinner. They nonetheless agreed that we talk while they ate. I was somewhat surprised when they then invited me to hold hands with them as they prayed a mealtime blessing. I had imagined that a family so openly supportive of the temple community would be nonreligious or, if religious, at least unconventionally so. As it turned out, Jim and Cindy are active, traditional, Bible-based Christians who attend a Methodist church and commit much of their time to leading Koinonia spiritual renewal retreats.

As the temple's closest neighbors, Jim and Cindy were initially concerned that new construction would drastically change the property. Both were pleased with the way things had turned out: the property was kept tidy, the grounds mowed, and the barn nicely painted. When I asked about the other neighbors' reactions, they echoed Aiya's impressions that most people preferred to keep their distance and that a few elderly neighbors were explicitly disturbed by the temple's presence. Jim mentioned one neighbor who was particularly upset when the special use permit was approved by the town council. He recalled her coming to their house to discuss the matter,

> She came and sat down and started talking. [*Jim whispers.*] "We don't want *them* here." And I said, "Why not?" "Well, they don't know the true God!" And I go, "They don't?" "Oh no." "Well," I said, "look at our street here. On this street there are maybe fifteen houses, let's say. Now, what percentage of these people on the street do you think attend church regularly?" Well, she didn't really know. So I said, "I think maybe ten percent would be high." I said, "I would much rather have a believing group of people here, even if it's not our religion, or whatever, because you know they're going to be good people. I'd rather have that than have some group move in here that might be either dope addicts or criminals or who knows what? I'd much rather have that." Well, she didn't know what to say.

When I asked Jim and Cindy why they thought their reaction to the temple was so different from that of their neighbors, Jim said, "Well, the crux of the problem is that people oppose anything they don't understand. Or anything that's new. No doubt." Cindy agreed, adding that people seem afraid of what they do not know. It is for this reason that Jim, the extrovert of the pair, has repeatedly made efforts to visit and learn about the temple when he can spare the time. He brings friends and relatives to the temple as well, whenever they are willing, and appreciates the fact that Aiya and other devotees are so welcoming.

Although Jim and Cindy said they enjoyed learning about the temple and its traditions, they were also honest about some of the practices that strained the limits of their open-mindedness. Jim described experiencing particular difficulties during the first *pratiṣṭhā* festival. The whole family attended and participated in the *abhiṣekam* milk dousing of the main deities—something that roughly translated for them as a kind of divine baptism. The mystifying part of the festival, however, was the blindfolded *mūrtis*, positioned so that the first thing they would see at the temple were animals—a white horse, a cow, and her calf—brought by nearby farmers. The idea that statues could see or enjoy food offerings was, as hard as they were trying, more than they could appreciate. In any case, Jim and Cindy reiterated how the temple community produced polite and kind neighbors and how they truly enjoyed the novelty. Big festivals made a bit of a commotion but, as they both agreed, at least devotees were not directly disrupting people's lives by pushing their views and knocking on people's doors.

From time to time I have heard Aiya expressing his great admiration for Cindy and Jim, conservative Christians who nonetheless support the temple on many levels. Since the temple's construction, Jim has donated wood every Saturday for the weekend *homams*, something for which Aiya is greatly indebted. Because their property is so close, Aiya is often concerned about the temple disrupting their lives and the valuable friendship they have forged. He was beside himself during the 2002 *pratiṣṭhā* when overflow parking ended up on Jim and Cindy's property and, due to torrential rains the week before, produced deep gullies in their field. During the *pratiṣṭhā* a number of temple devotees went to their house to apologize. Some talked with Cindy and others with Jim and, after the festival, a group of young men delivered a large fruit basket to their door. After Aiya's conversation with Jim, he impressed upon me once again how lucky he felt to have such generous neighbors.

Down the road about a mile from the temple is the Mulligan dairy farm. I arranged to visit Lisa Mulligan in November 1999, after hearing she was the farmer who brought the cow and her calf to the temple consecration. She and her husband had also been supplying the temple with fresh *abhiṣekam* milk for the first year or so—until devotees decided, against scriptural injunction, it would be safer to use pasteurized milk.[5] Lisa, a quiet and careful speaker, held her six-month-old baby boy, Aiden, who gurgled and lunged as we talked in their farmhouse dining room. Lisa explained that she and her husband were raised Catholic but now only practiced sporadically. Although they had no previous exposure to Hinduism, when Mohan contacted their farm in search of animals for the opening *pratiṣṭhā*, Lisa was intrigued and agreed to bring a mother cow and her calf to the festival. Thinking it would be interesting for her young daughters, as well, she decided to bring them along. Seemingly taking the religious rationale in stride, Lisa explained to me that the devotees wanted the cow and calf (and a horse brought by another farmer) to be the first beings the statues saw when their blindfolds were removed.[6] Lisa said she very much enjoyed the splendor of the rituals, the women's beautiful saris, and, most of all, the friendliness of the people.

After giving me her impressions of the *pratiṣṭhā*, Lisa added that her connection to the temple went deeper than her role as supplier of cows and milk. She began by explaining that her two girls were conceived by in vitro fertilization—she and her doctors knew without a doubt that she could not and would never be able to get pregnant without medical intervention. But the weekend of the *pratiṣṭhā* she conceived. As she put it, "It is just a medical miracle. I wasn't trying to have another child, but it happened. So I found a connection there. And when I went [back to the temple after Aiden was born], a little girl said to me, "Oh, you're the one!" I mean, they've talked about me at the temple. And there were a few other women [Aiya is aware of six] who became pregnant at that time."

When Lisa told Aiya about her baby, he invited her to have him blessed at the temple. Lisa remembered the ritual as being simple and beautiful. Aiya laid Aiden in the center of the temple on peacock blue silk fabric, chanted his blessing over him, and administered whitish-grey *vibhuti* ash and red *kumkum* powder on his forehead. Afterwards Aiya gave Lisa a shawl, and she and Aiden remained in the quiet temple for a while, soaking up its peacefulness before heading home. Although she had not returned since, Lisa said she wanted to bring her girls back. She explained that they would not become members or anything—"I just think it's a nice, spiritual place to go."

In the final analysis, it seems Rush temple neighbors should expect, at some level, to meet the unexpected. Standing outside the temple door beside her cow and calf, symbols of sacred motherhood, a neighborhood farmer has no idea she is being bestowed with blessings in kind. A local man who sends threatening notes does not expect to be pestered by a policeman with a story of religious intolerance of his own. A woman equipped to debate the supremacy of her tradition finds her arguments confounded and deflected by a deftly knowledgeable opponent. Even when choosing not to engage, people may find that proximity itself renders the choosing moot. In other words, there is no telling what might strike the neighbor at the small end of a binocular lens. Although there is value in surprise itself, the real question, for me, is whether it opens for participants the means to complicate and/or reduce division—racial, religious, and otherwise. Whether through binocular lenses, theological debates, or temple miracles, encounters with religious Others have, at the very least, the capacity to generate otherwise inconceivable ways of thinking and behaving.

A View from the Temple: Negotiating Pluralism

For Aiya and most South Asian Rush devotees, encounters with Christianity are far from novel. The convent schooling Aiya received in Sri Lanka, for instance, is fairly commonplace throughout the region. South India and Sri Lanka, the area of origin for most temple devotees, furthermore contain a significantly larger percentage of Christians than do many other parts of India.[7] The Rush neighborhood's experience of first contact with a Hindu temple thus stands in sharp relief to the multireligious worlds inhabited by most South Asian temple devotees.

For Aiya, one of the repercussions of his many decades of exposure to Christianity is that it helps him substantiate his view that divinity cannot be boxed in. For example, the star of his Catholic education experience, his kindergarten teacher, Sr. Leona, was not only a source of religious inspiration for him but also a beacon, as he now sees it, of divine light: "The simple faith she had, the intensity with which she used to sit and pray and teach the children, that taught me something when I was only five or six years old. I used to look at her and think, 'My God, this lady, she's beaming!' There was so much inner light. Now I know what that was. Why not learn from everybody? That's what it's all about. If you're willing to accept that God is an open book and that God is universal, then God is going to teach you through different means."

One of Aiya's more recent experiences of divinity in a Christian context occurred when an Italian Śrīvidyā *upāsaka*, Roberto, flew him to Italy for two weeks during the summer of 2000. Roberto and a group of fellow *upāsaka*s had recently parted ways with their guru and, searching for a new teacher, found Aiya on the internet. During Aiya's stay, Roberto and his parents led him on tours of some nearby churches. Aiya described to me how impressed he was by the tremendous power of these Italian churches, particularly by the divine maternal presence he felt at the San Luca Church in Bologna, famous for a painting of Mary attributed to St. Luke. To top it off, he recalled that, while strolling through the church, the face of his own mother suddenly appeared to him with eyes like the goddess's. Overwhelmed by a presence so immediate yet powerfully divine, he resumed his walk around the church with tears streaming down his cheeks.

The philosophical context from which Aiya frames and makes sense of these interreligious experiences—in which inner divinity shines forth from a Catholic nun and the divine Mother appears to him in an Italian church—is primarily neo-Vedantic. In a question-and-answer period with a group of thirty visitors from a Catholic parish I attended while living in Syracuse, Suzanne, a parishioner, asked Aiya about the non-Hindu religious symbols that he, against convention, prominently displays on the pillars inside the temple.[8] Aiya responded with one of the better-known neo-Vedantic metaphors relating the value and unity of all religions:

> Okay, it's simple. You know that the earth has five or six continents. And there are rivers starting somewhere and they're flowing in all directions. Where do they go? They reach the ocean. And this ocean, you may call it the Pacific Ocean, Indian Ocean, Atlantic Ocean—it's one mass of water, isn't it? We believe that every faith that is practiced on this earth ultimately is going to lead you to that ocean of mercy. What does it matter what you call it? And we recognize that people from different lands and divisions, that means their seers from different lands, their prophets, their incarnations, whatever you may call it, were placed there because of the Compassionate One. And every one of them has a spark of divinity in them. [*As he continues, Aiya points to the various religious symbols stationed around the temple.*] We say that the Christian tradition is a valid path to God, the Jewish tradition is a valid path to God, the Buddhist path is a path to God, the Islamic tradition is a path, the Sikh tradition is a path to God.

This view that values all religious paths is common among some South Asian traditions and is typically held by Rush temple devotees. Satyajit and Indu, Sikh by tradition, live out this philosophy most tangibly. When I asked them during an interview at their home whether they felt tension between their tradition of origin and the Rush temple tradition, Satyajit answered, "True religion is to serve all and love all. For this you don't have to change your religion and become a Hindu. Because what is Hindu or Sikh and what is Christian or Muslim? We're all children of the same God. If we believe in God, God is our father and mother. So therefore we are all children, all the same religion."

Speaking from a very different context, Lily, a Puerto Rican American raised primarily in the Pentecostal Christian tradition, considers ideas of religious supremacy to be fundamentally problematic. As she put it, "If I talk about my religion, I'll talk about it, and I'll answer anybody's questions. And if they're interested they can come. But that's one thing I couldn't stand about the Church—everyone was trying to convert you. And they were often bad examples of Christians telling me, 'You're totally on the wrong path. You're doing everything wrong. This is what you should be doing.' So I was like, 'See you later.' " When Lily was first involved in the temple nearly a decade ago, she largely rejected the teachings of her original tradition but now, demonstrating consistency of thought, she feels that had she been more patient with its flaws she might have remained Christian. Lily's response to her younger sister, disenchanted with Christianity at the time of our interview, was therefore not to persuade her to join her at the temple but to focus on her current practice and realize that every religion has its shortcomings.

Offering another angle on religious inclusivity, Sudharshan grew up with a Hindu father and a mother who was a member of the Anglican-influenced Church of South India. As a boy in Sri Lanka, Sudharshan was a choir member and youth leader in his mother's church and, at the same time, actively participated in support tasks at several Hindu temples in the area. He described having an appreciation for both traditions and does not remember feeling conflicted by his dual involvement. Realizing how overly idealistic his perspective might sound, Sudharshan supplied the added assurance, "I'm not just saying that because it sounds good." Although Sudharshan identifies himself currently as Hindu, focused on practices learned from Aiya, he feels his Christian past, a formative part of who he is today, is not something from which he consciously breaks.

The three Sri Lankan visitors from New Jersey who appreciated Aiya's "feel free" attitude, described in chapter 6, demonstrate a similar crossing of religious boundaries. Of the threesome, two were Hindu and one was Catholic. The Catholic man always accompanied the other two on their trips to Rush, and the three of them would on occasion go to special Catholic churches and events, as well. When I expressed my appreciation for their interreligious collaboration, they seemed to think it less than remarkable.[9]

Although perhaps idealistic (as Sudharshan intimates), this approach to religious pluralism is not necessarily unrealistic—the idea that God is found in all religions does not lead those mentioned above to consider religious distinction irrelevant. The two Hindus and one Catholic in the Sri Lankan threesome readily identified themselves as such in spite of a relative lack of discrimination about the religious sites they visited. As Lily suggests, religious traditions, flawed though they may be, provide an important focus for their followers. During an afternoon conversation at the temple house, Aiya expanded on this point, reasoning from a different angle that religious tolerance is in some ways a religious duty, since it is the Devī who guides her children into their traditions. Nonetheless, respect for other religions should not make us lose our grip on our own traditions and practices.

> If I don't respect their wishes and their ways of worship, then I am questioning the Mother. As far as I'm concerned, I want to show people when they come into this temple that it is a temple that respects other people's point of view. But that doesn't mean that someone can come in here and say, 'Okay, you have a crucifix, let's say Mass in here! That's not what it [the crucifix hanging on the temple wall] means. In this temple we have done certain mantras and rituals and so we have a particular focus and power. That's the tradition.

During another conversation, Aiya elaborated on this point by arguing that when people are "running from pillar to post," dabbling in various religious practices at the same time, they will only find frustration. As he put it, "What you're trying to do, in other words, is to experience somebody else's bliss. That's all. If you apply yourself, stay with one tradition for some time, you begin to tap that inner spring. Once you begin to tap that, nothing will dry it out."

Aiya's understanding of the temple's main goddess, Rājarājeśwarī, sheds a different light on his philosophy that is religiously all encompassing yet promotes practical focus. Typical of Hindu goddess traditions, devotees understand her as the One from whom all other goddesses manifest. Moreover, Rājarājeśwarī, queen of kings, empress of all creation, is, as Aiya put it, "the primordial cause of this entire universe and millions of them like it." She is thus not limited to encompassing Hindu goddesses, or even gods. Aiya once described the goddess's breadth to me in the context of explaining, once again, the various religious symbols displayed around the temple: "Durgā and Kālī and all those emanated from Her. And Śiva and Rudra and Viṣṇu and Brahmā and the six hundred and forty Hindu deities came from Her. And Jesus and Mary and Muhammad and everybody else. That is why you will see all the symbols here."

Viewed in this way, Aiya gives value and respect to the religions represented on the temple pillars yet subordinates them to the Supreme One who rules the universe. When pushed, Aiya is nonetheless refreshingly fair about the issue of religious supremacy and subordination. When I asked him to explain how he reconciled his different views of the temple's interreligious symbolism—as representing the equality of religions on one hand and their subordination to the Goddess on the other—he answered by summarizing what he considers the center of Śāṇkara's eighth-century teachings:

> [Śāṇkara argued that] you should become what you're praying to. You should become what you're worshiping. That means that the worshiper and the worshiped, or the act of worship, must merge. That means you become God. Period. Now, after saying this, various commentators [responding to Śāṇkara] have put in little footnotes saying, "Ah, but you have to belong to this kind of tradition to become like this. . . ." Like even me, I'm saying, "Okay, you have to practice Śrīvidyā to become one with God!" B.S.! That's *my* idea. Because that's what I'm exposed to.

Because Aiya's faith centers so strongly on tangible experiences of divine power, the events in his life that demonstrate for him most convincingly that divinity resides in all traditions are interreligious miracles. The most vivid example for Aiya is a miracle he attributes to a recently canonized Italian priest, Padre Pio. Aiya spun his story with verve one morning in late March 1999, while he, Anusha (on break from graduate school), and I sipped sweet tea in the little house near the temple. The incident took place during Aiya's second year studying architecture in Columbo, Sri Lanka, when he lived during the academic year with his sister, Sulochana, a teacher at a convent school. She had a very close colleague friend named Bibiyana, a young Catholic woman who was orphaned and who was treated as family by Aiya's mother and sisters. Aiya, likewise treating Bibiyana as he would a sister, teased her mercilessly. Once he discovered her fear of cockroaches, his favorite trick was to catch them in bags and ceremoniously give them to her.

During the summer, Aiya, along with eight other second-year students, joined a dig with the government's Archeological Department to fulfill a college requirement. The site was in dense jungle—reached by walking about fifteen miles from a remote village. Here, they cooked their meals with meat they caught in the wild. Aiya, a vegetarian since his conversion two years earlier, brought dal to eat instead. Each day a different student remained at the camp to help cook the meal and, when it was Aiya's turn, one of the workers caught about six or seven rabbits, cut them up, and gave him the meat to cook. He also gave Aiya a green plant that had been drying in the sun and told him to put a little in with the rabbit curry. Not knowing what it was, Aiya put the entire plant into the pot. He learned only later that the worker had given him a large quantity of *ganja*, or marijuana, meant to be used sparingly to enhance the food's flavor. When the young men came back from the dig and began eating they became ravenous and proceeded to consume the entire stew. The worker, suspicious, asked Aiya if he had put any of the green leaves into the curry and learned to his horror that the whole plant was used up.

While his fellow workers slept off their spiked rabbit curry, Aiya, the vegetarian, had the rest of the afternoon to himself. He brought some books to a nice shady flat rock by an ancient water tank, read a bit, and dozed off. While sleeping, he had a vivid dream in which a white Catholic priest appeared before him, smiling. He patted Aiya on his left shoulder and said, "Don't worry, I'm with your mother." So vivid was the dream that Aiya made note of the unusual details in the priest's clothing and of the fact that he wore bandages on his hands. When he awoke, Aiya was startled and concerned for his mother but, because the nearest phone was fifteen miles away, in the village, he pushed the dream from his mind. That was Wednesday, and four days later the group finished their work and left the site. Aiya arrived at his mother's house around ten thirty that night, expecting her to greet him, as usual. Instead his sister met him at the door and told him to come in quietly. She explained that on Tuesday their mother had suffered a heart attack. Until Wednesday afternoon, things were touch and go, but since then she had slowly begun to improve. Now she was at home resting.

Aiya remembered the dream and figured perhaps a Catholic saint, someone he did not recognize, had come to his mother's aid. Several months passed, his mother regained her health, and Aiya was again pestering Bibiyana during one of her visits, teasing her and pulling her hair. Amid the commotion, her purse fell over, spilling some of its contents. Aiya noticed a holy card among her

Framed photo of Padre Pio blessed with *kumkum* alongside popular image of the goddess Bhuvaneśwarī in the temple's business office. Photo by author.

belongings, picked it up, and discovered that the image printed on it was, without question, the man he saw in his dream. Awestruck, Aiya stopped his teasing and asked Bibiyana about him. She told him about Padre Pio, explaining that his bandages covered the wounds of a bleeding stigmata he received when he prayed or said mass. When Aiya then described his dream to Bibiyana, she burst into tears. She insisted he keep the card, which he did for many years.

Aiya gave his holy card away long ago to the mother of a dying Sri Lankan friend (with this comes another miracle story).[10] He now memorializes Padre Pio in the temple office with an eight-by-ten inch framed photo of the priest. Although the photo is not stationed in the temple itself, Aiya and other devotees periodically dab red *kumkum* paste between Padre Pio's eyebrows, as they do for images of deities and gurus in the temple. Set apart by his position outside the temple sanctum as well as by his Franciscan cassock, the fact that the Christian priest is marked in the same manner as a Hindu holy figure—or that he deigns to heal a Hindu woman—does not flatten religious difference. It simply assents to the possibility of divine power outside the fold. Accepting possibilities that lie outside conventional constraints of race, culture, and religion, exposed by the perpetual shifting of our planet, requires not just an open mind but, perhaps for the most resistant, a leap of faith.

9

Making Home at the Śrī Rājarājeśwarī Pīṭham

It should come as little surprise that the temple, poised in the midst of various types of shifting terrain—geographical, cultural, and religious—provides for devotees an invaluable sense of belonging and, ultimately, of home. Whether Aiya and Amma are invoked as parental figures, the community as a type of family, or the temple and Devī herself as offering unqualified acceptance and peace, much of what draws committed devotees is not access to the extraordinary but to that which is reassuring and familiar. This final chapter thus brings us home—to an entity that is sometimes difficult, often elusive, and ultimately comforting for those who claim it as such.

Growing Pains: From Private Garage to Public Temple

The single most difficult temple issue experienced by long-standing inner-core members of the Śrī Rājarājeśwarī Pīṭham has been the move from the explicitly homey, intimate setting of the garage temple at 33 Park Circle to the more overtly public Rush temple. Because I first arrived in Rush during June of 1998, barely two weeks after the move from garage to barn, my knowledge of this earlier phase takes the form of devotees' reminiscences. As most people described it, the shift from intimate setting to public arena has meant, most significantly, a change in community makeup and tone. Not only does the new temple regularly host large crowds of less-than-dedicated devotees but a few of the old guard have decided, their needs no longer being met, to discontinue regular attendance.

Group photo before returning *tēr* chariot to its shed. Navarātri festival, 2002. Photo by Muralee with Corinne's camera.

Those inner-core devotees who remain, including Aiya, readily admit that moving to Rush has meant the loss of a certain level of intimacy and focus. Some people continue to struggle with the transition, hoping the temple will eventually recapture, to some degree, its earlier form. Others have, over time, come to accept the fact that the temple has a life and flow of its own, and are doing their best to flow with it.

During a typical Friday evening at 33 Park Circle, the main weekly event, devotees would arrive around seven in the evening in time for a lengthy *pūjā*, many after driving two to three hours from Buffalo, Syracuse, or Toronto. Around eleven o'clock, after the *pūjā* finished, Amma would serve a meal. From midnight until as late as three or four in the morning, the group, typically including a number of instrumental musicians, would sing *bhajans* to the deities and engage in "chat sessions" in which people posed questions and Aiya regaled the group with his endless supply of stories, both personal and traditional. The group would also discuss Śrīvidyā philosophy in considerable depth. Aiya's learning curve was still quite high at this time, and since he is not one for learning alone, he vivaciously brought the group along with him on his exploration.

In Rush, the intensity of inquiry and intimacy experienced at Park Circle has been nearly impossible to duplicate. On weekends, Aiya spends most of his time accommodating the steady flow of first-time and casual visitors, welcoming them and meeting their ritual needs, causing some longtime devotees to feel pushed to the side. Contributing to this, some non-south Indians and non-Sri Lankans find themselves excluded from much casual conversation, as it is often conducted, particularly among newcomers, in Tamil. Some devotees furthermore feel that the increased yet necessary focus on temple maintenance in lieu of deeper learning has created an overemphasis on duties, contributing to squabbles over task territory. Since many believe this imbalance can be corrected by providing alternative learning opportunities, a number of devotees have organized, in the last several years, *pūjā* and *homam* workshops led by Aiya. Other types of workshops have run as well, such as refresher courses for longtime participants and "Devī Vogue," which introduced participants to the art of dressing temple *mūrtis*. Although these events cannot replicate the old Park Circle days, they allow for learning to continue formally.

Nine months after the Rush temple opened, Aiya described to me how he missed the intimacy of the garage temple days. With increasing numbers of visitors requiring more of his time, he felt sorry he could not interact with the old guard as he used to.

> AIYA They work on weekdays and Saturdays and Sundays are too busy. There are demands. Somebody will call and say, "I want this done or I want that done or I want to sponsor this at the *pūjā*." I can't say no. That's exactly why the temple was built. And when I start doing things for people who are strangers, the usual crowd who expects to have undivided attention, they don't get it. And they miss those days when we used to sit and shoot the breeze and pull each others' legs. Those days are gone.
>
> CORINNE Entirely?
>
> AIYA Not really. But y'know, invariably it is difficult for me to do anything like that right now. Because by the time I finish the temple *pūjā* and everything and then I come here [to the little house to relax], I'm exhausted. Because it's far more demanding than it was inside my house.

Many devotees try to look at the bright side of an admittedly difficult transition, emphasizing how people literally had to be packed, particularly during festival events, into Aiya and Amma's one-and-a-half-car garage. On such occasions, an overflow of devotees was often left to watch the *pūjā*, live on video, from the television in their living room. Although many are grateful to have been a part of this exciting early stage of temple life, it was clearly time to move on. With regard to learning, some argue that it continues in a variety of ways at Rush, far more than at conventional temples, and although the level of intimacy experienced at the garage temple seems irreplaceable, a sense of familylike community among inner-core members is still very strong.

As a devotee who maintains, with her husband Vish Uncle, one of the longest-running ties to the temple and to Aiya, Saroj views the shift to Rush as difficult but inevitable and necessary. During our conversation about the transition, she reflected, "I think we have to go with the moment, to move on. Instead of just staying in one place. Things were not the same fifty years ago. In fifty years, everything has changed. Fifty years from now, things have to be different." Regarding the fluid makeup of inner-core devotees, Saroj continues: "It's evolving and evolving. It's like a journey and people are there with you. Some people get off because a station comes up and they're gone. We think about them, but we don't see them. But there are some people who are still on the same track, and we still see them. And those people are something we hold onto. I think that's the way it is." Sudharshan expresses similar sentiments about the inevitable flow of people and place: "It's a necessary stage. You play your role and it moves and evolves. The temple has its own momentum, its own life. It's like a river. Nobody is central. Maybe Aiya is at this present time, but even he will pass."

In spite of reservations, devotees tend to agree that the most important consequence of moving out of their cozy Park Circle confines has been the offering of their tradition to the larger community. Although Aiya would be the first to argue for the importance of reaching out to more people, he nonetheless does not want weekend and festival events to grow too much. He worries that with too many people things will get out of hand and feels, furthermore, that preoccupation with temple growth is as unhealthy as pining for the days when it was smaller. Shifting membership of inner-core devotees also allows for increased access to the tradition. Several summers after the temple settled in Rush, Aiya described in positive terms the changing inner-core composition, arguing that it gave new *upāsaka*s a chance to learn while preventing the group of regular students from getting too large: "See all these people, some of them will lose interest. Some of them have grown so that they don't feel the need to be going to Aiya's temple all the time, to sit in the front and chant. There are those people. As I see it, moving out makes room for others to come in."

Homing Devices: Dreams, Desires, and Happenstance

If Rush and Park Circle were more typical of American Hindu temples, they would be products of local efforts and finances and run by a temple board. Regular participants would most likely be Hindus living in the immediate vicinity. Formed under very different circumstances, Rush and Park Circle have typically drawn devotees who are not from the Rochester area, and many of them spend a good deal of time traveling to temple events.[1] What follows are accounts of the motivations and circumstances that propelled some of Rush's inner-core members into their commitment to Aiya and the temple. Although temple rituals portray a community in sync—featuring chants and ritual gestures gracefully performed in unison—a view into individual histories reveals a community that is anything but uniform.

As committed as Rush temple devotees often are to learning complicated chants and rituals as well as to the endless tasks required for temple upkeep, not everyone arrived at the temple looking for such commitment, let alone with an interest in religion at all. In many cases, arriving at the temple was more a matter of happenstance than conscious design. A number of highly committed young adult devotees, for instance, originally came to the Park Circle temple at their parents' instigation. Abhi, Amma's niece, has been a part of the temple community ever since she can remember. Although she described feeling, from the beginning, a strong sense of warmth and safety at the temple and accompanied her parents happily, Abhi's own commitment to learning the tradition and its rituals began the summer before leaving for college in Boston. During those months, she came to the temple every chance she could, joking that she often appreciated things when it was nearly too late. While attending college, Abhi met for *pūjā* every Friday evening with Rush devotees living in the Boston area and returned to the temple whenever possible for festival occasions. During summer and winter break, Abhi visited the temple whenever her schedule allowed.

Dipi was introduced to the temple when he was around thirteen. Like Abhi, he also came, although less frequently, at his parents' instigation. His commitment, separate from that of his parents', also began during his first year of college. This shift, more dramatic than Abhi's, happened the weekend his grandmother died, when Aiya performed a *pūjā* at his parents' house. Dipi described feeling lost and depressed at the time and recalled that, during the *pūjā*, something inside him changed, prompting what he refers to as an awakening. From that day on, he began refashioning his life and starting a meditation practice. He became a regular at Park Circle *pūjā*s on Thursdays and Fridays, and during weekends he joined painting and construction crews that prepared the Rush temple barn for its new occupants. Dipi described the relief and elation he felt during this period, something he carries with him, though muted, to this day: "For the first time in my life since childhood, young childhood really, in Connecticut and the beginning years in Syracuse, I could really feel a happiness, and it was amazing. It was the greatest feeling in the world. It was as if someone had just given me the greatest gift. I was so thankful. I had so much gratitude. I knew that this is what I needed to do with my life."

Saroj and Vish Uncle also became dedicated members of the temple community only after unwittingly being pulled into its sphere. The couple first crossed paths with Aiya in 1984, during a hectic period in their lives. Vish Uncle had just joined a pediatrics practice in Rochester, while Saroj, trained in India as a dentist, took classes at Buffalo State University to get her U.S.

credentials. At the time, Vish Uncle was primary caretaker of their two small children, while Saroj, living in Buffalo, commuted to Rochester on weekends. Aiya had recently arrived in the Rochester area at the time and was looking to form a worshiping community. He searched the phone book for south Indian names, found and called Saroj and Vish Vishwanathan, and invited them to his home. Vish recalls being so distracted by his busy life that Aiya's phone call did not prompt much further thought, nor did he think to mention the conversation to Saroj.

Their paths crossed again when Saroj began practicing dentistry in Rochester and Aiya, Amma, and their daughter, Charu, signed on as patients. In 1986, Charu required treatment with a specialist, and Amma scheduled an appointment that did not allow enough time for her dental x-rays to arrive by mail. Saroj offered to drop the x-rays by their home, but Amma insisted she pick them up at Saroj's house. Amma arrived with Charu and Aiya accompanying her, Aiya carrying small packets of *kumkum* and *vibhuti* ash *prasādam* from *pūjā*. He gave them to Vish Uncle and invited him and Saroj to his home for *pūjā* and *bhajans* on Friday. Vish describes his reaction: "It touched my heart. Right away I felt so moved. I felt that it was a gift. I would not have been so touched if he had brought me something else. It was a simple thing. I felt so moved by his gesture. I didn't know if he knew whether I was religious or not." Vish and Saroj described themselves as being religiously observant at the time, but not having much structure in their practice. They would light a lamp every morning in front of a picture of the goddess Kāmākṣī, stationed in their kitchen, and pray for everyone's safe return at the end of the day.

Vish and Saroj went to Aiya and Amma's for *pūjā* that Friday and have rarely missed a Friday since. During the first year of Saroj and Vish's involvement, Friday *pūjās* and *bhajans* were held in a house in Ontario, N.Y., in an attic shrine room that fit only ten people. One year later Aiya, Amma, and Charu moved to 33 Park Circle, and the temple was transferred to the slightly larger one-and-a-half-car garage. Although Vish and Saroj are both from brahman families, they insist that Aiya's nonbrahman status was never an issue for them, even from the beginning. The only time Vish Uncle felt Aiya's caste was of potential concern was when his religiously orthodox brothers and their wives, visiting from Bombay, accompanied them to 33 Park Circle. Initially worried that the foursome might disapprove of his guru and the garage temple, Vish Uncle described the outcome of the visit:

> They were so moved. I would have thought that they were not that broad-minded since they had never been out of India, never saw anything different. I thought they would not take to Aiya and that they may even look down upon me and think I was following the wrong method. But they were so wonderful—even the women, who are not as worldly. They were so moved by Aiya, by his magnetism, and by

> his sincerity and knowledge. Because knowledge has no caste barriers. If somebody is knowledgeable, you have to respect them. I was so happy.

Like Vish Uncle, Sudharshan's lasting commitment to the Śrīvidyā tradition was not sealed after his first invitation from Aiya. Sudharshan was in his early twenties when he first met Aiya at Jeya's wedding registration ceremony in Toronto. When he approached him afterward to tell him how impressed he was with the ritual and its accompanying explanation, Aiya rummaged through his bag, pulled out a mantra tape, and earnestly told him, "I want you to have this." Aiya then showed him his address printed on the back of the tape and explained that he had a temple at his house where he should come visit and learn some more. Sudharshan agreed to come but did not show up until four years later. It was May of 1993, and Aiya was holding a three-day festival to celebrate the consecration of his *śrīcakra meru*. The *meru*, a three-dimensional *yantra*, had newly arrived from India; it was crafted to correspond precisely to the dimensions of Aiya's body. Its consecration was a rare and grand occasion. Sudharshan heard about the event from a friend and, intrigued by its novelty, decided to attend. He described walking into 33 Park Circle and into something he did not expect:

> SUDHARSHAN I walked in and Aiya was doing the ritual. And there were all these older young men in their thirties, virile young men, chanting. They were like pillars of the community, sort of thing. And all these young women who I was so enamored with. They were like progressive university students. I came in and saw this and there were tons of people, about two hundred people. People were in the house, *packed* in. People were in the shrine room, so that was packed. There were tents pitched all around the house. It was overwhelming. So I walked in. Aiya was doing the rituals. I guess he had to stop. He didn't do . . . [*Sudharshan gives me a shocked look*]. No he didn't do any of that. He just turned around very casually and said, "Oh! It took you four years to come, man!" And I was stunned. It freaked me out. [*We both laugh.*]
>
> CORINNE What did you do when he said that?
>
> SUDHARSHAN So I just smiled very coyly and tried to hide in the crowd. Because everybody's eyes were on me. I sort of tried to make myself look busy—which was impossible. [*We laugh.*]

Sudharshan ended up staying for the duration of the festival, at Aiya's request, and on the last day he, along with a few others, received mantra *dīkṣā*, or initiation. It was at this point that he became a committed member of the temple community.

Other inner-core devotees' search for and discovery of Aiya and the temple community were decidedly more deliberate, tied into long-established interest in or quests for religious practice. Sheela's search was particularly tailored to Aiya, his temple, and to Guruji. Before coming to the United States, while living in Chennai, she had been trained in the basics of Śrīvidyā. The brahman gentleman who taught her did not mention Śrīvidyā by name, but simply said she was doing Devī *pūjā* and instructed her not to tell anyone about it. As far as Sheela was aware, she was one of the first people to whom he passed on these mantras, yet the man told her specifically that he was not her guru. He assured her that she would eventually find someone who would formally initiate her. Sheela came to the United States soon after this event, facing what seemed insurmountable odds against ever meeting her guru. She described her state of mind: "I was like a madwoman. I had nobody to talk with. Every week I used to write to this person and he used to write to me saying that there is nothing to worry about. When the correct time comes I will meet somebody."

The people indirectly responsible for Sheela's reconnection with Śrīvidyā, one and a half years after she arrived in the United States, were Sheela's sister Charu and Charu's husband Danny. They had a friend in Buffalo who, knowing of Sheela's interest in goddess devotion, introduced the three of them to Aiya. Aiya was astounded by Sheela's knowledge and explained that her mantras and practices were from the Śrīvidyā tradition. Guruji visited the United States shortly afterward and officially initiated her. The profound relief Sheela felt upon meeting Aiya and later Guruji was, as she put it, "like puzzle pieces fitting into place." As for Charu and Danny, they had always considered Sheela rather extreme in her insistence on performing *pūjā* at her home. Sheela laughingly recalled Charu resisting her invitations to join her in the shrine room, saying things like "You are a crazy girl! If you want to do this, you do it. Don't make me sit here and do all these things." But, after their introduction to Aiya, Charu and her husband were, as Charu put it, "hooked" as well.

Jeya, like Sheela, described himself as religiously inclined long before meeting Aiya. Unlike Sheela, Jeya did not set out in search of Śrīvidyā practices or even devotion to Devī, since he had, from a very young age, an affinity for Lord Ganeś. When Jeya was around five or six years old, living in Sri Lanka, he constructed a makeshift shack behind his house into which he stationed a small Ganeś *mūrti*. Since he didn't know any mantras—and felt, as a non-brahman, that he was not meant to chant Sanskrit—he simply performed *abhiṣekam* by lovingly pouring milk over his Ganeś *mūrti* at least once a day. His mother did not approve of Jeya's daily routine but, worried that her skinny son would not eat until he had performed his worship, humored him by setting aside a bit of unpasteurized milk each morning for Ganeś. Jeya soon built a reputation for playing the priest and, during the ten-day period when the local temple held its festival, neighborhood children and cousins attended Jeya's "temple" as well. He continued his backyard ritual up through the age of nineteen, eventually hiding his practice from his peers who, in their teenage years, teased him rather than joining him for worship.

When Jeya came to Canada as a refugee in his early twenties, experiencing a rather harrowing trip through Europe before finally arriving in North America, he brought with him, along with the bare essentials, his *miruthangam* drums and his small Ganeś *mūrti*. Once in Canada, he met and married Aiya's niece but did not seriously take up with Aiya as a guru right away. As a musician, he enjoyed playing drums at Park Circle *bhajan* sessions, but that was the extent of his connection. His disinterest in Śrīvidyā was in part due to his devotion to Ganeś, yet Jeya also admitted it was difficult for him to let go of the idea, in spite of his playing priest as a child, that Sanskrit chants should be reserved for brahmans. After repeated trips to the temple and exposure to its rituals and teachings, Jeya slowly shifted his focus from Ganeś to Devī and took up Śrīvidyā as a practice.

Lily also described herself as being religiously inclined from an early age. Once she entered high school, her dedication to her Pentecostal upbringing waned and was exchanged for less conventional religious and philosophical paths. In 1993, while attending a Zen Buddhist center and taking yoga classes, she enrolled in a Rochester community college where she met Charu, Aiya and Amma's daughter. The two young women worked at the college student services center and quickly became friends. Lily discovered that Charu lived in a home regularly filled with devotees, chanting, and incense when the two of them were working on a school project and Charu invited her to the house. Lily described this first visit, which happened to fall on a busy Friday night:

> So I came to her house and I met her parents and they were really nice. I remember going into the shrine room and it was right before the *abhiṣekam* and I just felt—Wow!—like I was in India. This was one of my dreams, actually, long before I ever came to the temple or anything. I always thought I'd really love to go to India someday. So I was right in the *abhiṣekam* and she was just telling me, "Do this, do that" and I poured the milk and everything. I remember being in awe of the place. It took me back somewhere. It was not Rochester; it was somewhere else.

Lily became a regular at 33 Park Circle, both as Charu's good friend and as someone with an increasing interest in the garage temple. Eventually she received initiation from Aiya and dedicated herself to learning chants and rituals. Although Lily's temple encounter took place after several years of dabbling with different religious paths, she has not looked back since.

Bruce also practiced a variety of religious traditions before discovering Śrīvidyā in 1996 when he, Aparna, Kathy, Steve, and Kalidas drove together from Philadelphia to 33 Park Circle. Prior to their trip, Bruce, a factory foreman from Allentown, had been practicing Zen Buddhism and was looking for a tradition with more of a devotional focus, preferably one that highlighted a female divinity. During his search, he befriended Aparna, who was working at a New Age bookstore in Philadelphia at the time. Because she had seven years' experience as a Ramakrishna nun, Bruce often found himself at the bookstore with questions or, as he put it,

> Pretty much, I bugged her. I mean, she was trying to get her work done and I would go there like for an hour, an hour and a quarter, drive down there, buy something and ask her a lot of questions until she finally handed me off to her other friend who was an ex-Ramakrishna monk. He was a disciple of Aiya's—so that was the connection. And they were both saying that you really should be initiated into a mantra to help your spiritual progress. And so I thought, "Well, I've been doing this long enough, why not check it out?" And so we came up and got initiated into the mantra.

While the rationale behind the Rochester excursion was fairly straightforward for Bruce, it was not for Aparna, Kathy, or Steve. Tied through various mutual friendships, they understood the trip as a lark and had no intention of getting initiated. Kathy had spent a year in northeast India as an undergraduate and had been interested in Indian culture for some time.[2] She had just finished a short stint, along with Aparna, at a Tibetan Buddhist center and was not particularly interested in taking up a new religious tradition. Kathy described the lighthearted mood of the Philadelphia-Rochester road trip that, as it turned out, fell on the sixth night of Navarātri, the most sacred festival for the Devī:

> It was October 1996, like a Tuesday. All of us, Bruce, Steve, Aparna, Kalidas, and me, all our burdens lifted that day. Like I got out of class, they got out of work and everybody on a random Tuesday had this space open up. And we all just hopped into Steve's van and drove up here. I had no idea what was about to happen. I was more just thinking, "Oh, it's a road trip!" I had no inkling that this was about to change my entire life. That this was going to be *it*. [*Kathy laughs.*] And Aiya of course was just so low-key, like he always is, in regular street clothes. I didn't realize anything. I just thought, "Oh yeah, here's this guy and his wife."

Aparna's decision to come along to Rochester was last-minute and without much expectation. Because the Ramakrishna Mission to which she belonged for many years is a monastic tradition, she was unused to envisioning a married householder—like Aiya—as a religious teacher. Considering their collective mission to be retrieving a mantra for Bruce, Aparna nevertheless was impressed by Aiya's sense of fun and ease with his visitors. After their introductory conversation, Aiya suggested that, since there was plenty of time before the evening *pūjā*, they visit some new property he had recently purchased. He asked Steve for the keys to his van, jumped behind the wheel, and everyone else piled in. In Rush, as they walked out onto overgrown farmland, Aiya announced that he and his Park Circle students were soon going to build a temple in that very location. Thinking to herself that this man must be half crazy, Aparna remembered saying something like, "Oh yeah, right! Maybe in ten years you're going to build a temple!" That night during *pūjā*, although Aiya was aware that the group's intention was to get a mantra for Bruce, he suggested that whoever else wanted one could repeat after him as well. Swept up by their whirlwind day, they all repeated after Aiya and received initiation.

While Bruce had in essence committed himself to learning from Aiya even before their road trip, Kathy and Aparna describe different moments after their initiation when they consciously committed to the Śrīvidyā tradition. For Kathy, this happened the morning after their initiation, before the group headed back to Philadelphia. She woke up before the others, showered, and headed to the shrine room where she started reciting her mantras, for the first time, in front of Rājarājeśwarī. She described being engulfed by an overwhelming sense of love emanating from the Devī, so unexpected that she broke down and began to sob. After that experience she vowed to chant the *Lalitāsahasranāmam* daily, her dedication to learning chants and rituals increasing with each passing year. Aparna, on the other hand, described a delayed reaction. After initiation she continued a loose connection to the temple that, a year and a half later, reached a turning point:

> But then I watched Kathy. I went to Kathy's house, I watched her do the *pūjā* and again, I had seven years of training in the Ramakrishna Mission; I thought I knew what it was like to do *pūjā*. I didn't really have my eyes open enough to know how much I didn't know and how much to *pūjā* there really was. I felt like I was sitting in the presence of an ancient *ṛṣī* [sage]. I felt like she was an embodiment of a tradition that was deeper than my Ramakrishna tradition. And it kind of blew my mind. I knew that all she was doing was following the really basic instructions of this guy that we all still have the tools from, and I hadn't really paid attention to him. And I gained a deep respect for the process that we were all given, but that she was taking seriously. Beginning to take seriously. And I think that seeing this transformation in her created a yearning in me.

Aparna then wrote a letter to Aiya renewing her connection to him, expressing her desire to seriously begin learning. When they next met, Aiya assured her that he would teach her. Bruce, Kathy, and Aparna continue, after eight years, to dedicate themselves to Aiya and to the Śrīvidyā tradition while Kalidas, soon after the road trip, found a Tibetan Buddhist community that better met his needs. Steve, looking for a community with more social outreach, became a disciple of Ammachi, an internationally known female guru from Kerala, south India.

The fact that Indu and Satyajit, a Sikh couple, would consider learning from a non-Sikh has to do, as they explain it, with the fact that they were raised in regions of north India where their religious community was a tiny minority. Their families were, as a result, very broad-minded and cosmopolitan. Still committed to their tradition of origin, Indu and Satyajit have been founding members of *gurdwaras* (Sikh temples) in all the U.S. cities where they have lived (Philadelphia; Richmond, Va.; Connecticut; and Syracuse) since arriving in 1972. In 1982, when Indu suffered from migraines, they supplemented their Sikh practices by taking up TM meditation.[3] They also became devotees of the famous Hindu god-man Sai Baba, and in 1991 and 1993 Indu traveled to his ashram in Andhra Pradesh, India, in search of peace of mind for herself and healing for their oldest son, Nupi. Born with disabilities that prohibit speech development, Nupi, now in his late twenties, is one of the primary reasons Indu and Satyajit pursue so vigorously various religious paths. During our interview at their home, I asked the two of them if they thought they would have found and joined a community like Aiya's if they had stayed in India. Indu insisted that their dedication and subsequent profound religious experiences have had nothing to do with geography, but with their son:

> INDU Let me put it this way. If I never had this kid I don't know if I would have had those experiences at all. He is a gift. From God. Because of him I'm near Aiya and Swami [Sai Baba] and my religion. Otherwise I would be like other people, in my own ego. I'd have this and that material possession and would not want to go [to the temple].
>
> CORINNE Although you were raised in a religious environment.
>
> INDU Sure. We did our practice every day when we got married. We did that. But still we had that force coming from outside, like friends and all. The minute [their son Nupi] came along and had those problems, we were more close. We were more close to God. And we wanted to . . . whenever we could get help, or wherever we could find peace. It didn't matter which religion.

Indu and Satyajit first encountered Aiya when he performed a *pūjā* at the home of Syracuse friends. That night, Indu had a vivid dream in which Sai Baba told her that Aiya was to be her guru. Satyajit and Indu subsequently asked their friends Charu and Chauhan if they could accompany them to 33 Park Circle. As TM participants who had earlier paid thousands of dollars for their spiritual advancement, Satyajit and Indu were impressed that Aiya's powerful mantras and teachings came without a price tag.[4]

Barbara, like Indu, credits her discovery of the temple, on Memorial Day weekend, 1999, to supernatural guidance. For a year Barbara had been hearing about a new temple in nearby Rush and, as a nominal Catholic with keen spiritual curiosity, had been searching without success for a templelike structure when driving through town. On Monday morning, her mother read to her from the local paper about the Rush temple's first anniversary festival. Later that morning, when Barbara drove to get potato chips at the local Wegman's grocery store, she recalls hearing a voice directing her to the temple. With the help of the voice, she ended up at a yellow barn with a blue-and-white striped tent set up behind it.

Having minimal exposure to Indian culture, Barbara felt unsure of herself as she approached the festival crowds and even more uncomfortable wearing shorts among women in elegant saris. She felt people were nonetheless welcoming, so she stayed. Although confused by the ritual, she was impressed by Aiya, particularly by his informality and sense of humor. Interested in receiving a mantra, Barbara visited the temple two days later. Aiya gave her a blessing and instructed her to go home and meditate. When she did, she had a dramatic *kuṇḍalinī* experience, feeling energy moving up her spine followed by a sensation of light coming through the top of her head. The next day Barbara returned to the temple, recounted her experience, and received initiation. Although she continues to feel a certain disconnect with temple culture, she maintains her ties to Aiya and to her practice.

Making Home

Although devotees initially find themselves at the temple for a host of reasons, the key to its lasting appeal for many is the sense of home it evokes. For some, however, efforts to make themselves at home is less than smooth or simple. Barbara's experience, particularly among non-South Asians and after the Park Circle temple moved to Rush, is not, in other words, unique. A few non-South Asian devotees who continue their affiliation with the temple are not only not bothered by the temple's emphasis on Tamil culture but find the cultural trimmings a bonus. Lily spoke of her appreciation for the reverence with which temple participants practice and pass on their traditions, something she feels is lacking in her own cultural upbringing. Aparna, as described above, admires the depth of Śrīvidyā's historical roots, although she admits that accurately anticipating cultural cues has taken her a few years to master. Kathy, who lived in Calcutta in 1992 for nine months, is director of a textile company that requires regular travel to India. She is married to a Bengali man and finds the temple to be a comfortable extension of a life theme.

Regular devotees who at times feel like fish out of water find a variety of reasons to continue their ties to the temple. Barbara, in her usual understated way, reasoned, "As I got to know [Aiya], I thought he was the most intelligent, enlightened, compassionate person I'd ever met in my life. So I figured the more I hang out with him, the more it might rub off on me." Like Barbara,

Bruce also admits that he is not particularly at home with Indian culture and ritual. When he first started coming to the temple he was particularly bewildered by cultural differences and lived in fear of unintentionally committing a serious social faux pas. He stays dedicated to Aiya and the temple primarily because of his desire to be a part of a living goddess tradition. He also feels commitment to a religious teacher is important in itself. Although not originally interested in Śrīvidyā's ritual emphasis, he forged ahead, trusting Aiya. Bruce's affiliation with Aiya requires him, as he views it, to take on the whole "package." Citing one of Aiya's sports analogies, Bruce asserted, "If you're going to enter the game you have to play by its rules."

Illustrating the tension between the "rules" of the game and Bruce's allegiance to Aiya and Devī is an event that occurred one Wednesday in November 1998. Bruce had driven from Philadelphia early that morning to work on the temple greenhouse. During nine thirty *pūjā* attended by Ram (Aiya's nephew visiting from southern California), Bruce, and me, Aiya deviated from his usual routine by filling a small conch shell with water. He walked over to Bruce and poured the water from the shell into his hand, instructing him to drink it. He then intoned a name to Bruce, his *pūrṇadīkṣā*, establishing for him the next and rather significant step in his initiation process. After *pūjā*, while we made our clockwise trip around the inside of the temple, Kāmākṣī's big red *pottu*, secured to her life-sized framed image, popped off her forehead and onto the temple floor—a rare sign of blessing in the eyes of most devotees. Aiya picked it up and, handing it to Bruce, said it was her gift to him.

I was unaware of the exchange and so wondered, as we walked across the parking lot toward the little house, why Bruce was walking with a slight hunch, hands carefully clasped together. When I asked what he had in his hands, Bruce answered, "It's Devī's *pottu*. She even gives it to dopes like me." Back in the house, as Aiya energetically spouted Sanskrit terms and explanations, Bruce quietly interjected, seemingly out of the blue and to no one in particular, that he could not even pronounce things correctly. At this, his eyes brimmed and he said, "I'm sorry, I get teary just talking about it." Not realizing Bruce was still reverberating from the morning events, I asked if he was upset over his inability to pronounce things or moved by the fact that the Devī (and Aiya) would honor him in spite of his shortcomings. As I asked the question I realized, based on his comment in the parking lot, that it was the latter. Bruce's perception of not quite feeling at home with temple traditions makes Aiya's and Devī's blessings seem all the more astounding and potent.

By contrast, Kathy's comfort with temple culture as well as the sense of family she shares with many members of the community creates for her a natural sense of belonging. The language she used to describe her dramatic feelings the morning she first said her mantra, sitting before the Rājarājeśwarī *mūrti* at Park Circle and reducing her to tears, furthermore evokes a palpable sense of coming home:

> I felt that the Devī had put one thousand arms around me and just held me in Her arms. I felt completely that I had found my home. She had just taken all of my longings and my desires and all my burdens, all the weight off my shoulders, and she just took it into her lap. She just removed all of that. Like a painful longing where you're just seeking and seeking and seeking and trying so hard to find your home and find your place in the world and find the meaning of life—all of that. She just lifted that right off my shoulders and said, "This is your home." And it was just this incredible feeling of relief and release. I felt like, "This is my home!"

A number of devotees similarly expressed how the temple was for them a type of refuge—a place where they felt unequivocally accepted and released from life's burdens. Vish Uncle and Saroj wove a commentary remarking on the temple's peaceful pull as well as the sense of family it provided:

> VISH UNCLE See, when you come here, you lose all your worries or anxieties about what you have to do. More important recently, I would say honestly, are the people who are with us.
>
> SAROJ Everybody.
>
> VISH UNCLE The devotees.
>
> SAROJ Not just Aiya and Amma and Guruji.
>
> VISH UNCLE It's like a family reunion every week.

Many devotees also spoke about the temple community as an extended family, often portraying Aiya as a benevolent father figure. In Jeya's description of the temple as home, he made reference not just to Aiya, Devī, and the community, but to the Rush scene in its entirety as transcending the impersonal category, "temple":

> My interpretation is that this is not a temple. This is your heart. When you go to other temples, you know you're going to the temple. Every time I come here, it's not that I'm coming to a temple. That's not the feeling I get. It's like it's my house. This is where I belong. It's a party. *Pūjā* is party time. You chant and there's music and food there. It is like this is where you belong. Aiya is trying so hard to make it a temple [*Jeya laughs*], but it's not a temple. This is our house, our home.

Jeya also recounted Aiya's ability to accept people unconditionally, to make them feel welcome and loved regardless of their background or idiosyncrasies. His commentary then flowed into the ways Amma, more subdued and practical than Aiya, cares for temple devotees and visitors alike. He related an experience in which a friend of his was kept in Amma's memory for years:

> You have to only tell her once, "This is what I like," about the food and she will remember for, I can't imagine how long. I had an experience where my friend came here for the first time and he happened to mention to Amma, "I like this food, this kind of food." And then he came back after five years. When she saw him, she went and made that food and offered it to him. Correctly. And she said, "I know you like this." And he didn't even remember that he told Amma! That kind of memory power and that kind of love—it's amazing.

For many devotees, the temple has become home in no small part due to Amma's role as a supportive, no-nonsense mother figure and master cook. Aiya regularly asserts that people come to the temple not for the rituals, but for Amma's food. But, as he sees it, at least that gets them in the door. Vish Uncle and Saroj noted how Amma's low profile at the temple camouflages her exceptional nature. As Vish Uncle put it, "Her heart is very pure, it's like gold. There are very few people who understand and know." Amid Amma's reserve, she often offers honest opinions without the rhetorical padding Aiya so adroitly applies—something that can catch people off guard. Acknowledging the care and wisdom behind Amma's unembellished speech, Sudharshan likened it to medicine: "Sometimes it's hard to take, but it's good for you."

Sudharshan, who enjoys quiet talks with Amma back at her Park Circle home, often marvels at the fact that she, a far more private person than Aiya, has never had much time for herself or alone with her husband except during the first few months of their marriage. Once Aiya learned the *Lalitāsahasranāmam*, their relatively quiet home life ended for good. As Sudharshan put it, he would have "gone berserk" a long time ago if he were in Amma's shoes. Speculating as to how she can possibly manage, Sudharshan felt that Amma was groomed her entire life for her "colossal" job—not just of holding down full-time employment and cooking for the temple masses, but of holding things together, in general, at the temple and at home:

> She is the powerhouse. Not just in the temple, but in this whole ethos. Because she, first of all, bottom line, she's a good administrator. Her whole life experiences have trained her for this position. She was in boarding school from a very young age, disciplined to the letter, by the rule, very type A personality, a leader. Then she became the prefect of her school, head of the netball team, all of that. And she went to a private school where there were houses and she was the head of her house. Team captain, athlete—all of that.

Sudharshan also pointed out that not only does Amma keep the current temple afloat through her stabilizing influence and seemingly superhuman efforts and abilities, she is the one responsible for sending Aiya off, practically speaking, on his spiritual path in the first place. After Aiya's conversion experience at the feet of the Untouchable Devī, Amma steered him toward his first guru, Mataji. Amma, at the time a border at Aiya's mother's house, studied at a local teaching college and during holiday breaks traveled to work at Mataji's ashram orphanage. When Matiji initiated Aiya, Amma had already been her student for two years.

Amma illustrated to me her young adult interest in spiritual matters in very plain terms. As she put it, her mother died when she was five, her upbringing was difficult and, in such instances when one is deprived of material and other benefits, a longing for the peace and comfort of God is only natural. A woman named Kalyanasundaram, a teacher at her college, inspired Amma's initial religious inclinations. As Amma depicted her, the young teacher was a kind of revolutionary who dared to view the world differently from others. Kalyanasundaram apparently found a kindred spirit in Amma when, during a class exercise, she asked each member to name their favorite color. After most of the young women had recited their color of choice, Amma spoke up by refusing to name one. In all honesty, she felt each color had its own beauty. After this, the teacher, only five years her senior, sought out Amma's companionship and, as she put it, turned her whole life around. Two years later, when Amma was twenty-one and had completed her exams, Kalyanasundaram brought her to Mataji's ashram for Gurupūrṇima. Amma was so enthralled with the ashram and orphanage that she did not want to leave. She stayed for four months until her father sent an aunt to retrieve her and bring her back home.[5]

Amma's commitment to the religious path along with her no-nonsense manner seem to define who she is today. Her dedication to the Rush temple is equaled only by Aiya's, yet her approach could not be more different. The most obvious difference, even to casual observers, is the way Amma actively shuns the limelight that Aiya so animatedly occupies. I discovered this most concretely when filling up tape after tape of Aiya's anecdotes, philosophies, and opinions, finding Amma resistant to being interviewed at all. Dashed attempts to engage her in formal discussions about the temple during my early years at Rush became a kind of a joke between us.[6] Closing one door and opening another, Amma eventually allowed me to help her in the kitchen—typically the domain of seasoned cooks—in spite of my culinary deficiencies. Knowing my interest in cooking was matched by a lack of expertise, she generously demonstrated for me various cooking techniques. We also chatted about a variety of topics while in the kitchen, most of which did not directly relate to the temple. After I moved to Wisconsin, Amma always made sure, in spite of my protestations, that I never left for home without taking massive quantities of food with me. When I traveled by air and insisted there was no room in my suitcase, she simply sent someone to the parking lot to help muscle away the goods.

One of Amma's greatest concerns besides feeding people, often surfacing during our conversations inside and just outside the kitchen, is the successful launching of young adult temple members into the working world. The only thing Amma ever explicitly asked of me was to assist devotees with résumés and job application letters. While her temple kitchen work supports the adage that a person cannot pray on an empty stomach, Amma's concern for young people in the world reflects the even more practical fact that a one cannot fill one's stomach without an income. During the summer of 2001, Amma described for me her current, especially urgent, concern for one temple member's future career. As we stood just outside the kitchen, Amma's voice mingling with temple chanting in the background, kitchen smells mingling with temple incense, it occurred to me with a certain clarity that her role at the temple is to provide balance—to keep Aiya's students, reaching for spiritual heights, grounded.

Although sometimes at odds—Aiya may claim that Amma is too analytical for her own good, and Amma may surreptitiously prevent Aiya from throwing gallons of ghee into the fire at once—they make a good team. Aiya's vision and exuberance propels the temple forward, and Amma's more cautious nature helps keep ritual largesse from spinning out of control. Aiya provides the spiritual pyrotechnics, while Amma offers a stable "home" for temple participants, making sure the masses are fed and that certain individuals' worldly futures are in order.

Consistently with the rest of this book, one might view Aiya and Amma's very different approaches to temple life, complementary but often admittedly in tension, as part of a creative force that contributes to the temple's momentum. As demonstrated throughout the preceding chapters, potent opportunities often arise at meeting points between seemingly disparate worldviews, traditions, and cultures. A notable paradox that somewhat parallels Aiya and Amma's teamwork dynamics is the Śrīvidyā teaching that transcendence can be accessed through the material world. Practitioners are encouraged to cultivate expertise in bodily practices and rituals in order to discover divinity. Likewise, if it were not for Amma's Herculean efforts to create a stable home at the temple, it is possible, as Aiya readily and regularly admits, that things would never get off the ground.

Pushing the point further, one could also argue that the perceived incongruence between a grounded "home" and spiritual heights is ultimately misleading. When viewed through the lens of Śrīvidyā, there is something foundationally sacred about "home" itself. Temple rituals, elaborate and dramatic though they may be, are designed not to take us away from ourselves but, ultimately, to bring us back to our essential core, to divinity within. True, unmitigated "home"—centered in bodies and worlds that are perpetually changing and transforming—is the final, dramatically familiar, destination.

Conclusion

A Good Place to Start

The straightforward yet multifaceted goal of the Rush temple is to realize divinity within humanity, to access transcendent power through bodily practices, and to find "home" prepared and powered by the grace of Rājarājeśwarī. Put another way, the temple promotes, on a variety of levels, human-divine interdependence. It not only helps to create links between goddess, guru, and devotees, in the end it also presumes their essential inseparability. The temple tripartite—Devī, Aiya, and temple participants, featured in the book's three sections—are a Rush temple team, their interconnectedness forming both the means and the end to the Śrīvidyā goal. In a final meditation on the temple's purpose and its overarching theme of complementarity and interdependence, this conclusion briefly considers how reading or writing a book (particularly this one) fits into the mix.

Luckily, this strain of thought allows me to retell yet one more tale from Aiya's seemingly endless repertoire. I heard this story one afternoon in July 2000 when my friend Susan (who teaches at Nazareth College in Rochester), Aiya, and I sat outside eating lunch on the wooden planks surrounding the *homam* fire pit. The three of us discussed a range of topics as two small twin girls shuttled back and forth across another set of wooden planks just behind us. Susan had raised a question about the use of imagery during meditation, to which Aiya simply responded that some people found images helpful while for others they only got in the way. This led him to comment to the two professors sitting on either side of him, eating with our hands a south Indian meal of rice, dal, and spicy vegetables, that one of the greatest impediments to encountering divinity is too much education. He explained that while professors tend to get lost in their analyses of religious events, the "village idiot" meanwhile finds his way to God. Eyeing my dormant tape recorder, Aiya announced, "There are stories," and began:

> There is this temple, a beautiful temple in south India. Every day the services would start at nine thirty or ten in the morning. And a brahman bachelor, a young guy, used to come and bathe in the temple tank. Exactly as it is enjoined in his *dharma*, he would cleanse himself before sitting during the *pūjā*. And he would have visions, and there would be this glow about him. So nice. He was simply unaware that the service was going on. This went on for many—two, three, four—years. And it became a habit for the priest to do the service and then come out and give the brahman boy some *prasādam*. A ball of rice was offered. So he would eat it happily and then go home.
>
> One day, it so happened that the village idiot, who was slightly handicapped—mentally handicapped—came to the temple and saw this young man sitting there, beaming, with a beautiful face that reflected his inner countenance. And when the priest came from the sanctum after the *pūjā*, and gave the brahman boy his ball of rice, this fellow was next to him. [*Aiya, with a goofy grin, wiggles his hand out in front of him.*] So he gave him a ball of rice. From that day on, every day, the village idiot was there. His first attraction was this boy, and after that it was the food.
>
> This was going on for some time and then one day, before the *pūjā*, the brahman boy was seated and this village idiot was seated next to him, as usual, and a *beautiful* woman walked into the temple. It was Her. She approached this brahman boy, patted him on his head, and he opened his eyes. And She said, "I have *taṁbulam* [a mixture of betel leaf and betel nut for chewing]. I'm chewing betel leaf in my mouth. If you open your mouth I'll give you some." And he thought [*Aiya makes a disgusted face*], "How can this be?!" Notions of purity and all these things passed through him in a flash and he felt revolted. He said, "Hey! Go away! This is not the place for this!"
>
> This village idiot who was sitting next to him, he said, "Give it to me!" and opened his mouth. So She took the ball of stuff that was in her mouth and gave it to him. And as they were both watching, She walked into the sanctum and disappeared. *Then* the brahman boy realized who She was but by that time it was too late! And this so-called village idiot started composing hymns in the most beautiful Sanskrit. Some of them we still use.[1]

Aiya finished his tale, as usual, with a moral:

> So, the story shows that when you are quote unquote very highly evolved and educated it comes with a pitfall. You try to analyze things. So you're not able to see the simple divinity that an ordinary peasant is able to see in a leaf or a stone or a cat. As soon as you look at it, your mind is going somewhere else. It's trying to analyze and recall what it has read about this type of situation in some book. Before you know it, you've lost the Moment. That's the problem.

As I see it, there are two ways a person could digest this story and its moral. Most directly and drastically, she might focus on the fact that activities such as thinking and reading keep a person at a remove from direct experiences of divinity and its identification with the true Self. (I have heard Aiya exclaim on a few occasions, "You are not your mind!") Overanalysis can block the crucial act of surrender that relinquishes ego and independence in exchange for radical interdependence. She might conclude that writing (or reading) books about the Goddess causes one to sidestep and inevitably lose the Moment.

To back up a bit, she might also note that although Aiya warns us not to identify our Selves with our minds, he considers reason to be one of the many human functions that help us progress along our path, eventually and ideally to a state beyond thinking. This ideology spurs him to give exhaustive explanations of rituals and to wield terms that seem better suited for science than for devotion. The mind, in this context, provides an important means toward discovering the Moment, yet it is not an end. Running parallel to this is the Śrīvidyā philosophy promoted at Rush that considers elaborate, sensual, bodily expressions of devotion to be a vital means for helping participants identify with divinity. Our true Selves are not our bodies, yet our corporeal existence and sensory world can enable our progress toward greater devotion and eventual identification with nonembodied divinity. Devotees eventually and ultimately access nonembodied divinity through inner experience rather than external ritual.

So a second, more palatable, and perhaps more realistic understanding of Aiya's village idiot story and moral is that temple practitioners must eventually transcend reason and, certainly, put their spectacles and books down in order to enter the Moment. Along the way, however, those of us lacking in the capacity of the village idiot need our minds and our bodies, our books and our rituals, to carry us the distance.

The process of traveling the distance toward radical change—armed with books and, perhaps more important, bodies—is, as I understand it, not entirely unlike the enterprise of writing and researching itself, particularly within the field of ethnography. Of particular relevance are interactions with others over extended periods of time—a central component of the ethnographical process. In my experience, lessons gleaned from relationships of mutual respect can lead the researcher to unexpected new places, formed by worldview shifts nurtured by but not dependent upon intellectual exchange. In some cases, such shifts may even defy the intellect. Although the accumulation and analysis of data contribute significantly to ethnographic learning, the ethnographer cannot underestimate the valuable kinds of knowing that arise, more capriciously, from the process of human exchange intrinsic to the discipline.[2] To illustrate, I will tell one more story of my own.

The event took place on a Tuesday morning during the final days of the nine-day Navarātri festival in 2002. Only about fifty participants were present under the festival tent for this final *homam*, although the weekend before it had been brimming with hundreds of visitors. I had newly arrived in Rush, and the regular devotees present already had at least one chance to sit directly around the *homam* fire. So, to my delight, Aiya invited me to be among the eight participants designated to place various items, including beautiful silk saris, into the fire. It so happened that this visit marked my delivery of the first draft of this book's first section to Aiya and other temple members for review. It this portion of the book, as the reader may recall, I describe my initial uneasiness at the sight of devotees pitching gorgeous silk saris into a fire. With the ink just dried and the scenario fresh in my mind, I sat with seven others who chanted in unison around a similar fire. At one point, I watched a sari bundle as it made its way through the small crowd, around our *homam* circle, and into my hands. As Aiya instructed me to lower the bundle into the flames, I could not help but note the tremendous distance I had traveled in four years. The deep sense of honor and excitement I experienced at that moment could not have been further from my first reactions to similar offerings.

The movement from my initial position as a sometimes-startled outsider to sari-pitching insider, made possible through the process of regular, long-term exchange with the temple and its members, seems to me more emotional than cerebral. The honor and gratitude I felt amid the fiery opportunity did not erase lurking concerns about the cost of burning silk saris nor my relief when I learned that temple *homams* after that 2002 Navarātri only received cotton sari offerings. (This switch in textiles occurred when temple members discovered that synthetic ingredients added to modern-day silk were responsible for blackening the walls of the festival tents.) The change of heart that struck me while sitting in front the Navarātri *homam* fire is, as I see it, based upon a series of fundamental and frequently imperceptible shifts in faith and emotion—nonintellectual processes gradually amassed while doing research at the temple.

As dramatic as this Navarātri-day shift may have seemed to me, it certainly is not on par with the existential shift—that of Self-realization—prescribed by the Rush temple. Yet neither is it entirely different. Although undeniably more modest, the cause and effect of transformative ethnographic experiences could be compared to the process of Self-realization in that both correspond with, among other things, relationships of interdependence. In both scenarios, moments of identification and mutuality result in unanticipated modes of perceiving and being and, as such, contain a sense of the sacred, however loosely defined.

As discussed in chapter 1, ethnographers today typically discard traditional claims to a privileged, one-way gaze of scientific objectivity, exchanging them for analyses founded in relationality and multidirectional flows of information. Rather than taking for granted strict divisions between home and field, host and guest, self and other, ethnographic writing since the 1980s often portrays people, cultures, and ideas—ever-traveling, never in stasis—as defying such delineations. The task of questioning traditional oppositions is also assumed by this book when it describes how seemingly contrasting worldviews (scientific and miraculous), religious practices (orthodox and nonconventional), and cultures (foreign and domestic) are often intertwined and complementary at the Rush temple, rather than strictly oppositional. In a different realm, the Vedāntic philosophy promoted by Aiya challenges conventional perceptions that individuals are self-contained and separate from one another. Selfhood as understood through everyday reality is, according to Advaita Vedānta, an illusion, or *māyā*.[3] By breaking free of this illusion, the practitioner discovers that true reality consists only of *Brahman*, or divinity, of which we all are part.[4] It is through experiences of union with *Brahman* and, by association, with all living beings that distinctions between divinity and humanity, self and other, begin to disintegrate.[5]

The Rush temple aim of realizing the unity of Self and *Brahman* and, more immediately, of temple devotee and Devī, anticipates the unmitigated, sacred Moment that Aiya's village idiot encounters. Points of interdependence and interidentification between guru and disciple, humanity and divinity, ideally melting the temple tripartite into one, set the stage for unbounded, often unanticipated, encounters and associations with the sacred. Less dramatically, the meeting places between seemingly separate yet interdependent worldviews, traditions, and cultures explored throughout this book are potentially sacred in that they offer otherwise inconceivable or unavailable opportunities for those caught up in them.[6] Still more modestly speaking, ethnographic encounters found in the midst of interdependence and genuine exchange offer, under proper conditions, a fresh sense of purpose and discovery for those involved.[7]

Because fruitful engagement with such points of "sacred" potential typically involves challenges to convention and sudden leaps of faith, they can be demanding if not risky. Genuine receptivity within contexts of intersection and interrelationship thus requires that the proper set of preconditions be in place, ready for the unplanned. Like the spaces between breaths that Aiya describes as points of meditational focus—precarious moments in which a person is neither inhaling nor exhaling—the potential of these accessible, promise-filled intervals is suspended until realized and actuated. If the Goddess were to surprise us with a handful of prechewed *taṁbulam* to share, we would likely recoil in shocked disgust. Or, if primed to be superlatively receptive and willing to take apparent risks, we might, like the village idiot, accept the soggy wad with awe and gratitude.

This book does not presume to transport its reader—even the most receptive—to the lofty status of the village idiot. Its value is in its portrayal of faith-filled people, events, and ideas dedicated to discovering the Moment and the means for getting there. Although activities such as researching, writing, and reading books may ultimately obscure the Moment, they can also harbor surprises that help disassemble presumed distinctions and allow us to think (or behave) in ways otherwise inconceivable. While making use of tools at our disposal—implements that perhaps eventually and ideally become obsolete—we engage in an ongoing process rather than a one-time event. Moments of humble yet sacred intersection discovered along the way, both constrained by and contained in human limitation, can be good places to start, and start again.[8]

Glossary

In cases when words have more than one meaning or multiple layers of meaning, definitions given are those most pertinent to Rush temple teachings and practices.

abhiṣekam Ritual bathing of a *mūrti* (temple or shrine image), guru, or other human recipient.

Advaita Vedānta Indian philosophy attributed to the eighth-century philosopher, Śāṇkaracārya. Advaita Vedānta argues that all reality is contained by the one absolute *Brahman*. Adherents strive to experience this reality by distinguishing the world of illusion (*māyā*) from their eternal *ātman* (Self, Soul), that which is one and the same as *Brahman*.

Ardhanārīśwara The form of Śiva who is half male and half female. A gold-plated brass *mūrti* of Ardhanārīśwara is stationed in the Rush temple.

Bhairava A form of Śiva who acts as guardian. The Bhairava *mūrti* installed at the Rush temple is gold-plated brass. Behind the temple a trident marks his shrine.

bhajan Devotional hymn sung in honor of a Hindu deity.

bindu A sign of the goddess's concentrated energy worn as a red dot on devotee's forehead or placed at the center of a *yantra* (sacred diagram). Also a common mark of auspiciousness for a married woman.

brahman Traditionally the priestly and most ritually pure of the Hindu castes.

Brahman The eternal, absolute reality that underlies the diversity of appearances.

cakras Understood by most schools of yoga as the six centers of energy flow that line the body's central axis, located in the perineum, the genitals, the solar plexus, the heart, the throat, between the eyes, and at the crown of the head. See *kuṇḍalinī.*

caṇḍī homam Elaborate and lengthy fire ritual (*homam*) based on the *Devī Māhātmaya*, a Sanskrit hymn central to goddess worship.

capparam Tall, conical-shaped festival chariot used to take a deity in procession outside the temple building. At Rush, the *capparam* carries deities during the *pratiṣṭhā* festival.

Dattātreya Deity with faces of Śiva, Viṣṇu, and Brahmā stationed in black granite *mūrti* form near the front of the Rush temple. Considered the head of the temple's guru lineage.

Devī Generic name for the goddess.

dīkṣā Ritual initiation involving the transmission of a mantra from guru to disciple.

Ganeś Also known as Ganeśa, Ganesh, or Ganapati, the elephant-headed deity, remover of obstacles, and son of Śiva and Pārvatī. Two large *mūrtis*, one granite and the other gold-plated brass, reside inside the Rush temple. Another large granite Ganeś sits in a shrine directly in front of the temple building. A small shrine is stationed on a slope behind the temple.

Gurupūrṇimā Full-moon festival annually celebrated in July/August to honor one's guru.

homam Ritual fire offering to the deities.

jagadguru Head guru and teacher of monastic centers of learning (*maṭhs*) purportedly established by Śaṇkara in the eighth century.

japam Repetition of a mantra.

kālasam Metal pot typically containing a ritually charged liquid substance. Often used as a means to transfer the power of a temple deity for procession around the temple building.

Kāmākṣī One of the three goddess who is, according to Rush Śrīvidyā tradition, synonymous with the great goddess Tripurasundarī. A four-by-five-foot framed image of Kāmākṣī hangs on the back wall of the Rush temple.

Kāñcīpuram City in Tamil Nadu, home of an esteemed Vedāntic *maṭh*, religious leader Śaṇkarācārya, and famous temple dedicated to Kāmākṣī.

Kāśī One of India's holiest cities, also known as Benaras, located on the banks of the Ganges River and dedicated to Śiva. In Rush a surrogate Kāśī, marked by the installation of a Śiva *lingam*, is located on the banks of a creek running below the temple.

kumkum Red powder made from lime (calcium hydroxide) and turmeric, used as an offering to the goddess and smudged as *prasādam* (returned blessings) on devotees' foreheads.

kuṇḍalinī Female "serpent power" understood by tantric and yogic traditions as coiled at the base of the spine and activated through yogic and ritual practices to rise through the *cakras*, ultimately reaching the crown of the head and triggering the bliss of liberation.

Lalitā The youngest of the three goddesses who, according to Rush Śrīvidyā tradition, comprise the great goddess Tripurasundarī.

lingam Cylindrical aniconic form of Śiva, commonly found in temples. Positioned inside a rounded womb representation of the goddess, the *lingam* represents the generative powers of Śiva and his consort and the primordial force of the universe.

mantra Sacred syllables invested with divine power.

maṭh A seat of learning often involving the teaching of Vedānta and aligned with an important temple.

meru cakra Conical, three-dimensional form of the *śrīcakra yantra*, ritual device of particular importance to *Śrīvidyā upāsakas*. *Meru cakra* draws its name and significance from Mount Meru, Hinduism's sacred center of the universe.

mokṣa Release of the *ātman* (eternal Self) from the bondage of *saṃsāra* (cycle of birth and death).

mudrā Hand and body gestures performed during ritual.

mūrti Temple or shrine image of a deity that receives worship.

Nandi Śiva's *vāhana* or vehicle, guardian and keeper of the beat. In the Rush temple a *mūrti* of Nandi lies in front of and faces the main deity, Rājarājeśwarī.

Navagṛha The nine planets, designated at Rush as: Sūrya (Sun), Candra (Moon), Maṅgala (Mars), Budha (Mercury), Guru or Bṛhaspati (Jupiter), Śukra (Venus), Śani (Saturn), Ketu (Uranus), and Rāhu (Neptune). The Rush temple Navagṛha shrine displays gold-plated brass *mūrtis*, each accompanied by a female consort and an animal *vāhana* or vehicle.

Navarātri The "nine night" festival celebrating the battle and victory of the great goddess over the buffalo demon, Mahiṣa.

Pārvatī Śiva's wife, whose gold-plated brass *mūrti* is stationed at the Rush temple next to Śiva in his Naṭarāja dancing form.

pīṭham "Seat" of the goddess designating her presence in sacred geography and temple traditions.

pottu Forehead marking of an auspicious woman, traditionally of red *kumkum*. Currently in vogue are decorative stickers of various shapes and colors that may or may not denote a woman's married status.

prasādam Returned ritual offerings blessed by the deity. At Rush these typically include fruit or other foods, flowers, *kumkum*, and sacred ash (*vibhuti*).

pratiṣṭhā Celebration of temple consecration and subsequent annual anniversaries.

pūjā Worship of sacred image or human representative of divinity. Rush *pūjās* occur three times a day to honor the numerous deities installed in the temple.

purṇadīkṣā Advanced *dikṣa* in which devotee is given a new name and initiation into the *Mahāvakyas*, great statements from the Vedas.

Rājarājeśwarī The eldest of the three goddess manifestations of Tripurasundarī and main deity installed at the Rush temple.

rudram Vedic hymn to Śiva.

sādhana Spiritual practice that leads to *mokṣa* or liberation.

Śaiva Family of deities and traditions surrounding the god Śiva. The Rush temple tradition is Śaiva-Śakta, honoring the Śrīvidyā goddess Tripurasundarī in the form of Rājarājeśwarī as well as Śiva, his wife Pārvatī, and their sons Ganeś and Subramaniam.

Śākta Tradition of worship and philosophy that centers on Devī, the great goddess, manifest in a variety of forms and attributes.

śaktipat Descent of divine energy from guru to disciple.

saṅkalpam Invocation at the beginning of worship that locates the rite's geographical coordinates and asks for the deity's blessings.

sannyās Path of renunciation relinquishing worldly goods and values in order to attain *mokṣa*.

***sannyāsi* (female: *sannyāsinī*)** Individual who has taken the vows of *sannyās*.

Sarasvatī Goddess of music and learning. Patroness of poets, artists, and scholars.

sarpa dośa Ritual to correct misaligned planetary forces of Rāhu (Neptune) and Ketu (Uranus) in the body.

Śiva Major deity of the Śaiva tradition, one of the three main deities in Hinduism along with Viṣṇu and Devī. Śiva's Rush temple forms includes Naṭarāja (Lord of the Dance), Bhairava, Ardhanārīśwara, and the *lingam*.

Smārta Subgroup within the brahman caste associated with ritual virtuosity and traditionally understood as guardians of Śrīvidyā.

śraddham Funeral rites for recently deceased and for ancestors.

śrīcakra pūjā Central Śrīvidyā ritual whereby the practitioner worships the goddess through her manifestation in the *śrīcakra yantra* and in his or her own body.

Śrīvidyā "Auspicious Wisdom," a goddess-centered tantric tradition practiced in India and Sri Lanka and at the Rush temple.

stapati Caste name of temple sculptors.

Subramaniam The son of Śiva and Pārvatī and brother of Ganeś, also commonly known as Skanda, Kārttikeya, and Murugaṉ in south India. In Rush, Subramaniam's gold-plated brass *mūrti* is stationed in the back of the temple, flanked by his consorts, Valli and Deivanai.

tāli Necklace with amulet given in marriage and worn by married women in south India. Typically removed when a woman is widowed.

Tantra Hindu and Buddhist traditions involving *dīkṣā* (initiation) and esoteric practices transmitted from guru to disciple. Most tantric traditions incorporate meditative and yogic techniques as well as external rituals involving *mudrās* (hand gestures), the repetition of mantras, and the use of *yantras* (sacred diagrams).

tēr Festival chariot used at Rush during Navarātri for transporting deities in procession around the outside of the temple building.

Tripurasundarī The great goddess and focus of the Śrīvidyā tradition, manifest at Rush as Rājarājeśwarī, Kāmākṣī, and Lalitā.

upāsaka Initiate or adept following a particular religious path.

Vaiṣṇava Deity, tradition, or incarnation (*avatar*) associated with the great god Viṣṇu and his consort Lakṣmī.

vibhuti Sacred ash given as *prasādam* and most typically smeared on a devotee's forehead as a sign of renunciation.

yantra Sacred design mapping and generating cosmic powers. Śrīvidyā's *śrīcakra yantra* has nine interlocking triangles, four pointing upward to represent Śiva, the male principle, and five pointing downward to represent Śakti, the female principle.

Notes

INTRODUCTION

1. From the outset, it is important to know that although I use the term "Hindu" throughout this book, it is not an uncontested term. Many practitioners and scholars argue that there is no such thing as Hinduism because of the diversity of practices the term encompasses and because it was originally a label given by British colonizers to the confusing and multiple non-Christian and non-Islamic religious traditions practiced on the subcontinent. Nonetheless, many today embrace the term "Hindu" as their own. Although Aiya and temple participants regularly use the term "Hindu" when referring to themselves and their temple, Aiya prefers the term *sanātana dharma* (eternal religion or law), a Sanskrit term popularized by nineteenth-century reformers. For clarity and simplicity's sake, I have nonetheless chosen to maintain the term "Hindu" in spite of its difficulties. For more on the various angles of the conundrum, see the thematic issue "Who Speaks for Hinduism?" in the *Journal of the American Academy of Religion* 68/4 (2000). For articles addressing the issue of competing insider claims to define Hinduism, see articles by Narayanan (2000), Sharma (2000), and Brian Smith (2000).

2. Although Aiya prefers "Empress of Emperors," Rājarājeśwarī can also be rendered "Queen of Kings." In either case, the name signifies the goddess as the Ultimate Reality, ruler of all divinities.

3. The Śiva *lingam* is a common aniconic temple form of the god Śiva. Placed in the center of a *yoni*, an aniconic form of the goddess, the two forms represent the male and female principles and together are symbolic of the union between Śiva and dynamic female energy, *śakti*. On a more esoteric level, Aiya understands the *lingam* as the primordial shape and origin

of all creation. As he describes it, the *lingam*-shaped ellipse of light that first emanated from the "big bang" also represents the outer boundaries of the universe—or of many universes.

4. Navagṛha, commonly referred to in English as the nine planets, is more accurately translated as "nine houses." They include the moon and the sun along with the planets, excluding Pluto and Earth. Each house is considered to have a particular effect on the earth and its inhabitants. The Rush temple's Navagṛha display includes foot-high anthropomorphic representations of each house. Exceptions are Kethu (Uranus), who has a hooded snake head, and Raghu (Neptune), who is shaped like a snake below the waist. A bird or mammal *vāhana* (vehicle) accompanies each figure. In the winter of 2004, female consorts were added to the collection, one for each planet.

5. The golden deities flanking the walls in 2001 included, working counterclockwise from the rear of the temple: Śiva Nāṭarāja (dancing Śiva), housed in a station next to his consort Pārvatī; Bhairava (a guardian aspect of Śiva); Ganeś (Śiva and Pārvatī's elephant-headed son); Ardhanārīśwara (the half-male, half-female form of Śiva); and Dattātreya (a god with the faces of Śiva, Viṣṇu, and Brahmā, considered to be the originator of the guru lineage to which Aiya belongs). A granite form of Nandi, Śiva's bull, lay in front of Śri Rājarājeśwarī, facing her.

Since then, up to the time of this writing (early 2005), a number of new deities have joined the ranks. Sitting to the left of the golden Ganeś *mūrti* at the back of the temple is Subramaniam (Śiva and Pārvatī's other son, also known as Murukaṉ or Karttikeya), flanked by his consorts, Valli and Deivanai. Aiya describes these two consorts as representing, respectively, pure, uncomplicated love for God and discipline for prayer and fasting. Kāmadhenu, who has the head and torso of a woman, the body of a cow, and the tail of a peacock, stands directly in front of Rājarājeśwarī. Kāmadhenu is Vaiṣṇava, not Śaiva, but sports a three-lined Śaiva sign across her forehead at Rush and represents the granting of devotees' desires. A gold-plated Nandi has replaced the granite Nandi. As keeper of the beat, Nandi is often given offerings of chanted rhythms by devotees with musical training. A special gold-plated Rājarājeśwarī used for processions sits between Dattātreya and Ardhanarīśwara.

6. Besides flowers, typical daily *pūjā* offerings include water, fruit, incense, camphor flame, and mantras. For more detailed descriptions and explanations of *pūjā* worship, see Buhnemann (1988). See also Courtright (1985) and Eck (1981).

7. "Devī" is the generic Hindu term for goddess, used throughout India and Sri Lanka.

8. The other two goddesses in the Śrīvidyā tradition are Lalitā and Kāmākṣī. According to temple tradition, Lalitā is the youngest of the three, Kāmākṣī is second oldest, and Rājarājeśwarī is the oldest.

Tantrism, practiced within Hindu and Buddhist traditions, contains many branches and focuses on a variety of deities. A common goal for tantric practitioners is that of invoking and uniting divinity with the self through *sādhana*, or practice, involving initiation (*dīkṣā*), by a guru, ritual, and yoga. Tantric practice commonly involves meditation and external worship (*pūjā*) involving mantras and hand gestures (*mudrās*), and a sacred diagram (*yantra* or *maṇḍala*).

9. Śrīvidyā as a practice can be traced to at least the sixth century, although many practitioners, including Aiya, consider it to be older (Brooks 1992: xii).

10. As currently practiced in south India, Śrīvidyā represents an interesting mix of elite brahmanical orthopraxy, on one hand, and tantric ritual transgression of the same, on the other. By ritually transcending conventional distinctions between pure and impure, Smārta brahman Śrīvidyā practitioners can claim, as everyday upholders of such distinctions, to harness through their rituals an unlimited berth of power and access to divinity. Although Śrīvidyā rituals at the Rush temple allude to engagement in *pañcamakāra*—substances forbidden within orthodox Hindu traditions, namely, meat, fish, fermented grain, and sexual intercourse—their explicit transgression of brahmanical values, also occurring during ritual, typically takes a different form.

By extending Śrīvidyā ritual practices to women, nonbrahmans, and non-South Asians, the Rush temple not only lets the privately owned Śrīvidyā loose into the "public" but it also discards, in the process, caste and gender distinctions, based on notions of purity and pollution held dear by traditionalists within the Smārta community.

11. Aiya roughly translated from the Tamil means Sir, and is a commonly used term of respect for Tamil-speaking men.

12. Narayan (1993b) discusses the history and pervasive presence of Western sensationalized images of the Hindu holy man that simplify the wide variations within lived traditions. For a selection of some of these variations among gurus and god men and women, see Babb (1986), Burghart (1983), Hallstrom (1999), MacDaniel (1989), McKean (1996), Narayan (1989), Padoux (2000), Parry (1985), Pechilis (2004), and Van der Veer (1988).

13. Among those whom Aiya initiates, a good number do not become inner-core devotees who are a regular part of the temple community. Among the initiates who wish to be more tightly connected, some cannot maintain regular attendance because they live too far away—typically outside a one-day driving range. Other initiates may have once been part of the temple's inner core, closely affiliated with the temple community, but find their needs are not being met or have shifted. As a result, the number of inner-core members seems to be fairly constant, with membership shifting slightly through the years.

14. From June 1998 to December 1999 I regularly made day visits to the temple, at least once a week, from my home in Syracuse. In late December 1999 I moved to Wisconsin and was able to make trips to the temple, typically two weeks in length, about twice a year. In the meantime, I kept in regular e-mail and phone contact with several core members and have invited Aiya to Wisconsin to guest lecture on three occasions.

15. Although I never pushed the point of conducting formal interviews, Aiya on occasion asserted his authority by laughingly demanding that particular tape recorder–shy temple members allow me to interview them.

16. Along similar lines, Ashis Nandy, when speaking critically about the tendency within the U.S. and British Indian diaspora to create a unified, idealized culture, posits that (real) culture as a way of life is always a form of resistance against homogenization (1990: 104–105).

17. I have, in fact, divided this book into three to the third power (three sections with three chapters divided into three segments each) because I felt it was the best way to organize the material. The fact that three also happens to be a foundational number for the Śrīvidyā tradition itself was certainly not lost on me. The most appar-

ent tripartite aspect of the Śrīvidyā tradition is the centrality of Tripurasundarī, the tripartite great goddess, mentioned above. For the many other complicated ways in which threeness permeates the tradition, see Brooks (1992).

18. See Eliade ([1957] 1987: 21–25) for a discussion of mountains as sacred. In his book, *To Take Place* (1987), Jonathan Z. Smith convincingly takes some of Eliade's theories to task, particularly his identification of a permanent, irreplaceable center as a source of meaning within religious traditions. He argues, instead, for a more arbitrary and complex connection between place and sacrality. Eliade's axis mundi is helpful for my purposes not because it signifies a fixed centrality but because it reflects the sacredness of a meeting point between two distinct realms.

For a discussion of human marginality and sacrality, see Turner ([1969] 1995: 96–97, 167); Ewing (1997: 217), and Eliade (1964: 483–486).

See Bourdieu (1977: 124, 130–135) and Eliade (1957: 25) for more on liminal moments and their ties to ritual performance and the sacred. Historian of religion Tom Driver also refers to rituals as marking boundaries or blazing pathways into previously uncharted territory. He adds that ritual can also perform the opposite function of marking and maintaining the well-traveled status quo. In such cases ritual acts more as a shelter than as a pathway (1991: 16, 50). On a slightly different note, Jonathan Z. Smith understands ritual as mediating the way things are with the way they ought to be. Ritual thus owes its power to a "force where incongruency is perceived and thought about" (1987: 109–110).

19. In her poetic ethnography of a Moroccan village, Stefania Pandolfo meditates on the multidimensional concept of *al fitna* as an ambivalent or paradoxical state of exile that is both the transgression and foundation of God's Law (1997: 5). Along these lines, she writes that fracture—separation and exile—renders us helplessly outside of speech, yet "it is also a passage into another scene. There, like an angel, appears the poetical word" (11, see also 102).

20. Brooks also notes what he refers to as "situational incongruity" within the Śrīvidyā tradition itself. Śrīvidyā's combination of both Vedic and tantric practices and ideologies—at odds within the grid of purity and pollution—seems incongruous for those outside the tradition. For Śrīvidyā practitioners, however, such contradictions are dissolved through the "rules" of Śrīvidyā. In the end, incongruity depends on where one stands (1992: 148–149).

CHAPTER 1

1. Along these lines, Edith Turner's recent efforts give not only coherence but also credence to Ndembu ritual practices and has prompted her to argue, "Which world of logic is the correct one, theirs or ours? We are gradually discovering that there are as many logics as there are cultures, and we are encouraged to at least dialogue with them, if not adopt their way of thought" (1992: 4).

2. These scholars I invoke, mostly in notes, as the story unfolds.

3. Although the short-term visitor often sees what she wants to see, leaving home and returning with a picture of a country and culture still intact, promoted by the tourist industry as well as wishful thinking, this is (one hopes) impossible for the long-term traveler or ethnographer. I unpack this continuum between tourist, pilgrim, and ethnographer elsewhere (Dempsey 2000).

4. I write about my journey to the temple in part because I feel James Clifford is right when he complains that ethnographers do not tend to write enough about their journey to the field—on all levels. They are always just magically "there" in their writings, omitting important contextual information (1997: 23).

5. For a fuller description of the temple's interior, see the Introduction.

6. For an introductory treatments of Latin American liberation theology, see McAfee Brown (1993) and the Boff brothers (1987). Gutiérrez (1973) provides a more classical, technical introduction. For an anthology covering the gamut of liberation theologies, see Thistelthwaite and Engel (1998).

7. Vedānta, meaning "culmination of the Vedas," refers largely to Indian philosophies founded in a collection of sacred texts known as the Upaniṣads, dating between the eighth and seventh centuries BCE to the beginning of the Common Era. For an extensive treatment of Advaita, see Balasubramanian (2000). See J. N. Mohanty (2000) for an overview of classical Indian philosophy that contextualizes Advaita Vedānta within a larger philosophical framework.

8. A good place to start for those unfamiliar with process theology is Cobb and Griffin (1976). See also Griffin (1997) for his proposal that process theology allows for the possibility of paranormal phenomena such as apparitions and out-of-body experiences.

9. This dynamic is chronicled in the conclusion of my book, *Kerala Christian Sainthood: Collisions of Culture and Worldview in South India* (2001); see also pp. 89–94.

10. The *tāli* is a leaf-shaped gold amulet worn by married women in south India. The climax of the marriage ceremony in south India is the tying of the *tāli* around the bride's neck. According to convention, when a woman's husband dies, she removes her *tāli* as a sign of her widowhood. Married south Indian Christian women, particularly in Kerala, also wear *tālis* but these hold a cross rather than an amulet (see Dempsey 2001: 67–74).

11. Thirteen of these fourteen offerings correspond to the thirteen chapters of the Sanskrit hymn to the Great Goddess, the *Devīmāhātmya*. Each bundle, corresponding to each of these chapters, has a specified color and offerings in addition to the items included in each sari bundle. A garland of flowers is also offered into the fire along with each sari bundle.

12. During Navarātri 2002, the temple burned silk saris for the last time, and has since then switched to cotton saris. The reason has nothing to do with the expense of the silk, but rather with the fact that today's silk seems to be blended with an artificial fiber that, when burned, emits black smoke that stains the surrounding area. The tent rental company therefore had to charge the temple thousands of dollars to clean the black film off the inside of the tent. When they switched fibers in 2002, Aiya explained that future *caṇḍī homams* would include the option for people to buy cotton sari offerings from the temple itself. This way, Aiya reasoned, the temple could have ultimate control of the fiber content of the saris and, because of their reasonable price, more people could partake in the ritual offering.

13. In Lawrence Babb's 1986 study of three Indian gurus, he states his position in spite of its limitations: "I was an interested outsider. . . . As such, I could not become an initiate. This was an impediment, because some of the most important practices in the Radhasoami tradition are disclosed only to initiates" (7). Babb does not

explain why an outsider could not be a religious initiate, since such a position seems to reflect academic wisdom of the time. Underscoring the need for scholarly distance, he finishes his point by saying, "Such [religious] commitment would probably be inconsistent with an observer's status anyway, because it is far from clear that the conviction necessary to be a genuine participant in these movements is compatible with reporting in a way that preserves any semblance of detachment" (10).

14. The fact that fieldwork traditionally involves relationships of political and economic disparity has been bothering anthropologists for decades (Clifford and Marcus 1986). Preferring to work within the imperfections rather than silence and ignorance (Suleri 1990: 11–13), many ethnographers continue to go out into the "field," aware of the relative merits of insider and outsider perspectives. Rather than privilege one voice over another, many of these recent writers also conclude that tidy dichotomies such as insider/outsider and home/field are hopelessly intertwined and ultimately misleading (Abu-Lughod 1991, Khandelwal 1996, Kondo 1986, Narayan 1993a). In light of the fact that traveling is the global norm rather than the exception, James Clifford (1997) maintains that we should rid ourselves of such categories, since they imply a false sense of stasis. See also Gupta (2000).

15. Various authors have described in similar ways this gradual narrowing of seemingly separate spheres of "home" and "field" as an extension of the relationships they build. In Meena Khandelwal's portrayal of her dissertation fieldwork with a female renouncer, she recalls the formality of their initial interviews giving way over time: "I began to seek her advice on personal as well as intellectual dilemmas, and within a few months, the distinction between what was for my dissertation and what was for me became hopelessly blurred" (1996: 118). Karen McCarthy Brown (1991) describes a similar dynamic in her relationship with a Voudou priestess (see especially pp. 11–12). Brown's personal involvement in her work leads her in the direction of ritual participation and eventual initiation into Voudou.

16. Kirin Narayan chronicles a similar exchange and reaction in her ethnography of a storyteller swami in India (1989: 59–60).

17. For an excellent description of *śaktipat* in the Siddha Yoga tradition, see Muller-Ortega, "*Śaktipat*: The Initiatory Descent of Power" (1997).

18. Muller-Ortega discusses the spectrum of subjective experiences of *śaktipat* and Siddha Yoga's understanding of these differences. For some, the touch of a guru brings on an intense and immediate reaction, while others experience something much more subtle, yet in all cases *śaktipat* is considered to begin the process of liberation or Self-knowledge. The difference in individual perception has to do with the fact that those who have already worked through impurities either in past lives or during the present life will have a thinner veil of illusion and thus more immediately feel their move toward liberation.

19. For the first several years, the *pratiṣṭhā* was celebrated Memorial Day weekend. Since 2002, Aiya has decided to move it to the prior weekend to coincide with a long weekend in Canada, accommodating the large number of pilgrims who come from Toronto.

20. The temple crew has constructed two major festival chariots. The fall Navarātri festival uses the five-sided *tēr* chariot for processions, and the spring *pratiṣṭhā* uses the tall conical *capparam* chariot. Because devotees themselves designed and constructed these chariots—a process unheard of at other temples—they are believed to

be infused with devotional energy. The group of men who have given—and continue to give—countless hours to the chariots' building and upkeep are, in some cases, more mechanically than ritually inclined. Thus their work offers them a vital means for expressing their devotion to the Goddess.

21. Edith Turner makes a similar appeal on the basis of her 1985 return to a Zambian Ndembu tribe with whom she and her anthropologist husband, Victor Turner, lived thirty-one years earlier. On this recent trip she observed the Ihamba tooth ritual she and her husband previously documented, but this time Turner saw for herself the spirit many Ndembu, particularly Ndembu healers, take for granted. This experience jars her framework and prompts Turner to argue that we must break away from intellectual trends that see ritual as "a wasteful substitute for real action, or at best a metaphor for resistance (which, of course, it is as well as what it is actually all about)." She proposes, "we might yet grant traditional peoples credit for their own kind of religion instead of translating it away" (1992: 16).

CHAPTER 2

1. As described by Douglas Brooks, "Ritual is Śrīvidyā's primary mode of thinking, interpreting, and acting because ritual can transform reality's inherent power into personal power. The world may be divine in origin—a projection of Śiva and Śaktī, just as the scriptures are—but the world gains significance when its configurations and associations are put within one's grasp" (1992: 4).

2. The rug was finally replaced in the fall of 2003, on the occasion of a visit from a south Indian godwoman devotees refer to as Akka, a religious figure who enjoys a special relationship with the temple. For a fuller description of Akka and her role, see chapter 7.

3. Aiya enjoys recounting the seemingly endless ways the Mother miraculously ensures that ritual provisions or a perfectly sized check arrive at the hour of his greatest need, particularly during the lean months—October through March.

4. One devotee told me that she and another temple member proposed selling precooked, packaged food from the temple kitchen, as many other temples do. When Aiya heard their idea, he apparently replied vehemently, "Over my dead body!" A traditional source of revenue that Aiya recently eliminated is the auctioning of Devī's saris during festivals. During its first four years, the Rush temple auctioned saris worn by Rājarājeśwarī, valued not only for their beauty but because they are considered *prasādam*, blessed by the goddess. In 2002 Aiya decided, to the dismay of some financially minded devotees, that it would be better to give the saris away as special tokens of gratitude and blessing.

5. Although Aiya's final offering of silk saris into the *homam* fires was in 2002, due to the damaging black smoke emitted by added artificial fibers, the case of camphor is different. Camphor is scripturally prescribed, whereas offering silk saris, a sign of selfless, generous devotion, is not. Aiya argues that out of the sixteen modes of worship prescribed for *pūjā*, the fifteenth and penultimate is camphor.

6. Another cost of ritual power, slicing across an entirely different set of variables, has to do with its potential for wrecking havoc. Of particular concern for some who keep their distance from the Rush temple is that tantric Śrīvidyā is known to many in south India and Sri Lanka as surrounded by mystery and stories of nefarious

power. As Aiya dramatically remarked the first day we met, "The best way to clear the room in Madras is to tell people you practice Śrīvidyā." Aiya and other temple insiders nonetheless argue that it makes no sense to utilize such powerful rituals for anything but good ends.

7. For a fuller account of Guruji and Aiya's meeting and events leading to it, see chapter 4.

8. See Singer (1972) for a study of the early impact of scientific rationalism on the lives of south Indian Hindu businessmen.

9. For a more detailed description of differences between ashram and temple philosophies, see chapter 4.

10. Narayanan notes that this portrayal of *mūrtis* as "just symbols" is starkly at odds with Śrīvaiṣṇava teachings that the temple deity is totally and completely God. For a description of Śrivaīṣṇava understandings of the temple *mūrti* as divine presence, in some ways different from the Śrīvidyā view, see Narayanan (1985) and R. Davis (1997: 26–33).

As I discuss in chapter 3, the idea that rituals are symbolic resonates with trends introduced not only by Hindu reformers but also by leaders of the Protestant Reformation. One of the most outspoken critics of ritual, pushing the point that it was "merely symbolic," was Ulrich Zwingli, a Swiss reformer. Subsequently, as Jonathan Z. Smith puts it, "a wedge was decisively driven between symbol and reality; there was no necessary connection between them" (1987: 100).

11. Neo-Vedāntic conceptions of the unity of all religions and unity in diversity within Hinduism have gained prevalence in diaspora communities, reflecting, as Ninian Smart put it, "an ecumenical spirit and a new orthodoxy" (1987: 294). Smart notes how neo-Vedānta, furthermore, acts as means for Hindu diaspora groups to formulate their self-identity.

12. When asked for literature that best describes his melding of science with ritual and meditative practices, Aiya typically refers people to Anodea Judith's *Wheels of Life* (1987). See also *Pranayama* (2000) by R. S. Gupta.

13. This process, in which the *yantra*, fueled by mantras, is stationed below and feeds vibrations into the temple *mūrti*, is standard for traditional Hindu temples throughout India, Sri Lanka, and the diaspora.

14. See Madhu Khanna (1979) for a similar view of the *śrīcakra yantra*. See also Brooks (1992) for a detailed description of its ritual use.

15. Black granite is the preferred material for south Indian temple *mūrtis*. In north India marble is more commonly used.

16. A devotee suggested that "gender inclusive" might be a better term to use than "neutral." Whether speaking of deities, forms of granite, or musical tones, the middle range always includes aspects of the female and male sides of the spectrum. See also Goldberg (2002: 133–32).

17. Aiya's drone is set at D# when he conducts *pūjās*. For simplicity's sake my scale begins at C.

18. Richard Davis describes a Śaiva ritual text that incorporates notions of male and female trees used when crafting and invoking divinity into a wood carving (1997: 33–37).

19. Madhu Khanna also discusses this interrelationship between exterior and interior worship: "The practices of ritual and meditation involve an internalization and

externalization of symbols by means of parallel activities, the one inward and the other outward. This constant interplay of inner and outer constitutes the dynamics of *yantra.* For it is held that the energy (*śakti*) of the power diagram remains inert until it is activized and made meaningful through sacred activity. It is through ritual that power descends into the *yantra* and man is able to begin his ascent into a higher realm of being" (1979: 97).

20. Fred Clothey describes how ritual, providing an important means for many South Asian diaspora communities to express their Hindu identity, engages the senses: "For most South Indians (and probably most Indians) religion is expressed primordially as performance. Ritual is pre-discursive and supratextual, experiential, visceral. In ritual one hears, albeit not propositionally, but also senses, sees, even smells, the tradition. In theory at least, it invites the engagement of the entire person" (1992: 128).

21. Aiya often speaks of Śrīvidyā as the fastest path to *mokṣa* or release from the cycle of births. In his book, Brooks mentions that Śrīvidyā practitioners understand their methods to be superior because they are most expedient (1992: 182).

22. The Śrīvidyā tradition, as Brooks puts it, "begins with the theological assumption that the real presence of divinity (*devatāsadbhāva*) is present in the sign beyond the individual or collective imagination" (1992: 82).

23. *Kālasam* pots are regularly used during temple rituals when the officiant transfers energy from the temple deity to something that can be taken outside, typically for a procession around the temple or for *abhiṣekam* of an individual. A *kālasam* pot, made from silver at the Rush temple, is rounded in shape, standing about one and a half feet tall to about one foot in diameter at its widest point. During rituals at Rush it is often predecorated with woven threads, and the presiding priest will often decorate the exterior with leaves and a silk sash, placing a coconut on the top. *Kālasams* used for ritual often contain water and turmeric along with other prescribed ingredients, depending on the event.

Darbha grass is indigenous to the banks of the holy river Ganges. Known to grow to its peak three months before the rainy season, the height of this growth is also believed to correspond to the height of the water during the upcoming rainy season. As the grass predicts the time and amount of rain to come, special, supernatural, powers are attributed to it. *Darbha* grass is also believed to contain trace elements of nutrients that sustain human life and thus is given a place of prominence in Hindu temples, often as a conduit for sacred energy.

24. For a fuller story, see chapter 8.

25. Similarly, Jonathan Z. Smith argues that ritual is, above all, "a mode of paying attention" (1987: 102). He contrasts this with the view of the Reformers, who associated ritual with blind, thoughtless habit.

26. For lengthier, more technical descriptions of the goddess's three forms in the Śrīvidyā tradition, see Brooks (1992).

CHAPTER 3

1. I leave behind the positive or negative associations James ascribes to these categories. In *Varieties of Religious Experience,* for instance, he labels miracles as either "refined" or "crass": refined miracles cooperate with the natural order, whereas crass

miracles do not. Because James understands divinity as working within, not against, nature, only refined miracles can be of divine origin. Crass miracles James attributes to something else, such as trickery or foolishness.

2. It is not clear, when reading this account, whether the insect is a black bee or beetle.

3. See Weber's *The Religion of India: The Sociology of Hinduism and Buddhism.*

4. Babb writes that Sai Baba's devotional community is "notably cosmopolitan, consisting of many people who at least outwardly are as strongly attuned as anyone to the international cult of science and rationality. These people, we are inclined to think, really 'ought to know better' " (1986: 174).

5. Nicely illustrating the power of perspective is Robert Brown's (1998) description of a Marian apparition on a window in a Los Angeles Latino neighborhood. When an outsider claims that he merely sees smudged dirt, the neighbors take him to task.

6. See also Hume ([1777] 1975). Although current Indian uneasiness with "idol worship" can most recently be traced to Hindu reformers, it is part of a much older history. The influential Mīmāṃṣā school of theology argued that God has no body, only sound, and therefore cannot be represented by form. Śaṇkara of the Advaita Vedānta school argued that although God does have a body and can be accessed through external ritual, this was less desirable than immediate realization of unity with the divine. Suspicion of exterior forms was also an important theme for many famous *nirguṇa bhakti* saints, including Kabir and Ravidas (Davis 1997: 44–49, Hawley and Juergensmeyer 1988).

7. This is not to say that Catholic theologians have not tried to rein in a popular fascination with the supernatural. For centuries, the efficacy—or lack thereof—of sacred images has been a particularly contentious issue. Thomas Aquinas nonetheless cautiously proposed a threefold function for sacred images: They provide a source of learning for the "unlettered," they inspire viewers to recall the mystery of the incarnation and the actions of the saints, and they evoke an emotional response "more effectively aroused by things seen than by things heard" (Davis 1997: 32; see also Freedberg 1989). For examples of how popular Catholic supernaturalism and institutional rationalism strain against one another in Europe, see Badone (1990), Bretell (1990), Burke (1994), Devlin (1987), and Woodward (1990: 156–167). For south Indian Christian examples, see Dempsey (2001: 88–114).

8. Ulrich Zwingli, an outspoken sixteenth-century Swiss Protestant reformer, is considered by some to have ushered in the Western scientific worldview or, at least, a revolution in thought through his description of ritual as "mere symbol" that contained outward representation but not inner transformation. Ritual was thus relegated to superstition or habit, not something real or true (J. Smith 1987: 99–100).

9. See Bell (1997: 254–259) for a discussion of the process of repudiation, return, and romanticization of ritual, enacted by religious traditions as well as by the academy.

10. On a related note, Diana Eck describes how the link between healthy mind and body, promoted by ancient Hindu teachings, has moved into the North American mainstream: "By the 1980s doctors in white coats were teaching a simple version of some of the kinds of meditation exercises that Indian swamis in orange robes had been teaching for hundreds of years" (2001: 108). This trend she describes as begin-

ning with the great turning East of the 1960s and 1970s that began "the process of slipping a holistic worldview under the crumbling foundations of American secularism. By the 1980s it would be called New Age, and by the 1990s it would gain the currency of a prevailing way of looking at things" (ibid.).

11. For more on the category and function of the guru, see Babb (1986), Baumer (1990), Butterfield (1994), Gold (1995), Miller (1976), and Narayan (1989).

12. A similar list of powers can be found in Patañjali's *Yoga Sūtra.*

13. Narayan (1989) recounts numerous folk stories and anecdotes describing the existence and danger of guru charlatans. Most of these tales are from the vast repertoire of Swamiji, himself a guru.

14. In her description of the Indian *sādhu,* a religious ascetic who often acts as a guide for others, Narayan describes the multifaceted demands that might lead to incessant phone calls: "A *sādhu,* in short, is someone who may be turned to in times of need, and who serves as spiritual advisor, doctor, lawyer, political commentator, councilor, entertainer, and psychotherapist all rolled into one" (1989: 79). Williams (1986) also writes about the guru's role as guide or counselor and the high demand placed on him or her because of it.

15. According to Brooks, Śrīvidyā literature refers to the Great Goddess through variations on the name Lalitā Tripurasundarī: Tripurā, Tripurasundarī, Mahātripurasundarī, and Rājarājeśvarī (61). In south India, Lalitā is unambiguously associated with Kāmākṣī of Kāñcīpuram. The Rush temple's tradition of Tripurasundarī's three manifestations of different ages is also central to Śrīvidyā teaching.

CHAPTER 4

1. A mark of a good storyteller is the ability to tailor one's tales to particular audiences. Narayan describes how the guru-storyteller subject of her book often adjusted stories to fit the needs of his listeners (1989). See also Laurel Kendall's (1988) description of a Korean shaman storyteller.

2. I have drawn the following account of Aiya's conversion from several renditions I heard while at the temple, including one that Aiya wrote as part of a short spiritual autobiography.

3. *Tēvāram* refers to Tamil devotional hymns composed by Śaiva poet-saints that date between the sixth and ninth centuries CE. (Indira Peterson [1989] dates the Tēvāram between the sixth and eighth centuries and M. A. Rangaswamy [1990] dates the hymns between the seventh and ninth.) Tiruñāṉacampantar, Tirunāvukkaracar, and Cuntaramūrti—popularly known as Campantar, Appar, and Cuntarar—are the three poets to whom the *Tēvāram* is attributed. See Peterson (1989) and Rangaswamy (1990).

4. Brooks argues that, in contrast with other Indian religious movements such as the *bhakti* movement, Tantrism does not typically advance an egalitarian agenda. Tantrism, according to Brooks, is a "reaffirmation of the religious rights of a few over the many and the importance of ritual for living a truly meaningful life without renouncing the mundane. Tantra assumes that privilege and hierarchy is part of the divine plan" (1992: 183). For important exceptions within Tantrism, see Lorelei Biernacki in her work that is forthcoming.

5. The diacritics were eventually written in the Library of Congress format.

6. Aiya's book was the first of its kind not only because it was transliterated into Tamil but also because none of the text was left out. Since the Śrīvidyā tradition is typically secret, written Sanskrit renditions of the ritual often omit lines, instructing the reader to ask their guru for the missing pieces. Aiya's book is also the first to compile both the text of the ritual and practical instructions and explanations.

7. A Śaṇkarācārya is a high-ranking religious official who resides at one of the *maṭhs*, seats of Advaita Vedānta learning. The five *maṭhs* that house India's five Śaṇkarācāryas are Kāñcīpuram in Tamilnadu, Śṛṅgiri in Karnataka, Purī in Orissa, Dvārakā in western Gujarat, and Jyothirmaṭha in the northwest Himalayas. See Cenkner (1983).

8. Aiya's appeal to his guru for validation is typical for Śrīvidyā *upāsakas*. Brooks notes the importance of the Śrīvidyā guru for shaping the content of a disciple's practice. The decision as to which texts or practices will be of importance is often made on an individual basis. Brooks also mentions how gurus defer to their own gurus for their sense of tradition and then, secondarily, to sacred texts (1992: 7).

9. Aiya's assertion that ritual practice is meant for everyone, "women or man, young or old," is backed by his guru and his meditational experiences. This precise wording he found in an introduction to the *Lalitāsahasranāma*—written in Tamil by Anna Subramanian, a Śrīvidyā practitioner. The book was published by the Ramakrishna Mission in Madras.

10. For more on the *bhakti* saints and poetry in Tamilnadu, see Ramanujan (1981) and Cutler (1987). For *bhakti* saints and poetry from Karnataka, see Ramanujan (1975). For north Indian saints and poetry, see Hawley and Jurgensmeyer (1988).

11. Unfortunately, the orphanage was devastated by the tsunami that hit in December 2004. Donations to the Rush temple have helped rebuild and renew supplies for the orphanage and its school. See Tambiah (1991 and 1992) and Daniel (1996) for more on the troubles in Sri Lanka.

12. Although Aiya worships a feminine divinity, he often uses the pronoun "He" when speaking generically, in English, about God.

CHAPTER 5

1. *Arcanas* are individualized *pūjās* performed by a temple priest on behalf of a devotee and his or her particular requests. Rush *arcanas* are distinguished from others in that they begin with an explanation of the ritual, are performed communally, and have no set fee.

2. In his discussion of a Toronto Sri Lankan temple festival, Paul Younger notes the absence of teenagers and young adults. Temple leaders, bemoaning the "lost generation" that includes their own children, were surprised to hear that some of them had enrolled in Younger's university course on Hindu ritual (2002: 158). Baumann, on the other hand, argues that although the cultural habits of current diaspora youth tend to differ from those of their parents in terms of marriage patterns, diet, dress, and language skills, their adherence to their religion of origin largely remains (1995: 26). See also Ballard (1994: 160, 270). My findings, like Younger's, are that second-generation youth are not so disinterested in religion as they are interested in religion on their own, not their parents', terms.

3. Selva Raj (2005) writes about generational tensions among Christian immigrants from Kerala, south India. He demonstrates how intergenerational conflicts have more to do with cultural than with religious differences. For a survey of various generational issues faced by South Asian immigrants to the United States, see Sheth (2001).

4. An unfortunate irony is that the young people for whom first-generation North American Hindus build traditional temples often reject tradition. As one gentleman stated about his recently built community temple, "We have built this for the sake of our children. Are we building it for nothing?" (John Fenton, cited in Waghorne 1999: 123). See also Wood (1980: 280, 286).

5. Vertovec cites Clifford Geertz's similar observations about Muslims living in Morocco and Indonesia. Living on the margins of the Islamic world, they experience a shift between " 'religiousness and religious-mindedness,' between being held by religious convictions and holding them" (Geertz quoted in Vertovec 2000: 149).

6. *Miruthangam* drums are about two-and-a-half feet long, made from a hollowed tree trunk roughly one foot in diameter. The drum has two playing surfaces, one at each end, made from animal skin and held tightly by leather thongs. A round patch made from iron filings and rice paste creates a special resonance on one of the playing surfaces.

7. Hinting that this clash of intergenerational expectations is due to a change not simply in culture but also in era are similar trends in North American Christian communities. Reginald Bibby discusses the waning of mainline Christian denominations in spite of the population's widespread belief in God, an afterlife, and the supernatural. He notes that "religious organizations without adequate programs aimed at young people, such as Sunday schools and teen groups, are asking for annihilation" (1993: 311). According to Bibby, the church must cater to people looking for spiritual answers, not church involvement (296).

8. Aiya gives a three-part explanation for the application of *vibhuti* ash. First, ash contains nitrogen, phosphorous, and potassium, elements present in the body at trace levels. When worn they slowly infuse the skin to replenish these elements, which, in turn, help prevent vertigo. Second, ash is a reminder of the inevitable destination of all bodies and, when worn, helps the devotee keep worldly aspirations in perspective. Third, the wearing of *vibhuti* ash is associated with Śiva and Śaivism.

Aiya's explanation for the wearing of *kumkum* is also threefold. First, the red powder is made from lime (calcium hydroxide) and turmeric. When mixed, the resulting chemical reaction gives *kumkum* cleansing properties. Second, *kumkum* worn on the skin regularly crumbles; by placing it between the eyebrows the crumbling reminds the wearer to maintain a devotional focus. Third, the person wearing *kumkum* between the eyebrows cannot be hypnotized—a concern for some living in village Sri Lanka—since the red dot breaks the gaze of the person attempting to cast the hypnotic spell.

9. Devi Parvati's association with the temple's Rājarājeśwarī *mūrti* predates Aiya's. See chapter 7 for the full story.

10. In Raymond Williams's study of South Asian immigrant religion in the United States, he mentions the Hindu summer camp phenomenon. He notes two particularly successful summer camps, one of which, at the time of his writing, was

directed by Devi Parvati from the Poconos. He describes her as "an American woman convert to Hinduism who is particularly well-equipped to help these American children of Hindu parents make the transition between East and West" (1988: 46).

11. The Durgā temple in the Toronto area is popular among young women praying for future husbands, and features a Tamil ritual in which an inverted lime is filled with ghee and lit. The Aiyappan temple is popular among young men preparing for pilgrimage to the Aiyappan shrine in Kerala, India. The temple guides participants in a regimen of bodily discipline and prayer and has earned a reputation for helping troubled young men reform their lives. Diana Eck describes innovations at a Detroit temple where widespread youth involvement contrasts with the tendency, in other temple contexts, for young people to "flee to the parking lot with their frisbees" (2001: 130). Eck describes the skit, "Hanuman meets Superman," performed by the temple youth, and suggests that an "imaginative, creative bridge building had taken place to link the ritual and mythic world of Hindu India and the suburban world of Detroit, Michigan" (130).

12. Although it seems that lukewarm youth involvement at temples has much to do with inadequate information about traditional practices, there are other rationales, as well. For instance, a twenty-seven-year-old Canadian Sri Lankan man told me that he had little interest in temples although they were everywhere in Toronto. He said that Rush was one of the few places that did not feel to him like a business. His mother interjected that she regularly visits a number of temples in Toronto yet was happy to come to Rush because she could convince her son and daughter to accompany her.

13. Traditional temples, particularly Vedic south Indian temples like Rush, consistently bar women from playing priestly leadership roles. There are exceptions to this rule; one of note are the women trained by Kerala's goddess/guru Ammachi (Amritanandamayi) to perform the role of priest or *pūjāri* in specially consecrated south Indian temples. Ammachi's aim to train and establish women priests at temples seems to be part of her interest in providing female role models that will encourage change in a male-oriented system. See Raj (2004).

Generally speaking, one of the most visible religious roles available to women is that of guru. Although gurus are usually male, some of the most famous and esteemed guru/saints have been, particularly by the twentieth century, female. Ammachi's contemporary following spans the globe (see Amritaswarupananda (1993) and Raj 2004; forthcoming), and Ānandamayī Mā, a Bengali woman, was one of the best-known guru saints of the twentieth century (see Hallstrom 1999, 2004; Mukerji 1989). For more on an array of female gurus, see Pechilis (2004). For female saint-poets from the *bhakti* tradition, see Kher (1979), Mukta (1994), and Ramanujan (1983). For a general overview of women's leadership in religious roles in Hindu traditions, see Narayanan (1999).

Khandelwal's (1997) article features female ascetics in north India and argues that beneath the presumed male orthodoxy, *sannyāsa* is gendered as feminine. On the seemingly oxymoronic quality of Hindu female renunciation, see also Denton (1991), King (1984), and Ojha (1981). Pearson's (1996) work on female asceticism within conventional householder roles further complicates the issue.

14. The fact that temple women gladly embrace leadership roles is consistent with Indian women's legacy of leadership and organization in the secular sphere,

both in India and in North America (see Agnew 1993). Leonard argues that South Asian women are not only largely responsible for embodying and transmitting "tradition" they also play a key part in the process of adaptation and change (1993).

15. Three south Indian temples that encourage female palanquin bearers during their festivals are the Pittsburgh temple, the Mīnākṣī temple in Toronto, and, very recently, the temple in Ashland, Mass.

16. The *kālasam* pot typically contains water, turmeric, cloves, perfume, and devotees' gold ornaments (to be returned as *prasādam* after the *abhiṣekam*). Most important, the liquid is infused with power from mantras chanted during ritual.

17. The ten directions include the eight cardinal directions plus above and below. The corresponding deities are Indra in the east, Agni in the southeast, Yama in the south, Nirudhi in the southwest, Varuṇa in the west, Varu in the northwest, Kubera in the north, Iśan in the northeast, Brahmā above, and Viṣṇu below. Also invoked into nine of the shells are the nine planetary deities.

18. For a brief description of the conch as a ritual implement as well the mechanics of its worship, see Buhnemann (1988: 128–130).

19. *Swahā*, chanted only during fire rituals, is one of five *antas*, or endings, tacked onto the end of a mantra, giving it power. Aiya likens *antas* to stamps on an envelope; without them, the envelope/mantra cannot reach its destination.

20. The worship of Śrīvidyā's goddess Tripurasundarī was also adopted by the monastic orders at Kāñcīpuram and Śṛṅgiri established, according to tradition, by Śāṇkara, the father of Advaita Vedānta. These *maṭhs*, run by powerful Śaṇkarācāryas, are centers of learning that promote the egalitarian view that the innermost self—regardless of caste or gender—is identified with the universal *Brahman* or Divinity. In spite of this, Vedāntic *maṭhs* are often socially conservative and tend to divest "social, economic, and political relations of any fundamental significance" (Yocum 1992: 89–90; see also Larson 1989). Exceptions to this trend are currently emerging, however. See Cenkner (1992).

21. "The Madhvanaths" refers to Madhvanath and his wife, Gnanpurani, the same people who distributed Aiya's *Śrī Vidyā* books from their home in Chennai (see chapter 4).

22. My thanks to Sudharshan for these examples of Toronto temple changes, prompted by the Rush temple, corroborated by others inside and outside the temple community. Further examples of prompted change I will leave for Sudharshan to address in future work.

23. Vertovec discusses this dual or paradoxical nature of diaspora consciousness, caught between place and nationality (2000: 146–148). According to James Clifford, "Diaspora consciousness lives loss and hope as a defining tension" (1994: 312).

24. Vertovec similarly describes tensions at British diaspora temples: "Most of these conflicts have stemmed fundamentally from personality clashes among prominent members, politicking with the local Hindu 'constituency' for support of rival would-be leaders, and arguments over the proper means of collecting and spending finances—all phenomena, indeed which are known to almost any kind of public organization in control of resources of one kind or another" (2000: 129).

25. Originally Indian temples were built and maintained by kings. During the colonial period, the British government assumed this role by setting up temple trusts both independent of and affiliated with state governments. This system is still in use

today. Diaspora temples are normally run by a temple board made up of appointed and elected trustees and supported by hundreds of individual contributors (Waghorne 1999: 119).

26. The most widely anticipated tensions arising at guru-led ashrams involve disputes over succession of leadership after the guru dies (see Gold 1988: 35–75; Harris 1994; McKean 1996: 2, 18, 47–48, 54). Obviously this has not yet been an issue at Rush, though devotees express concern over what will happen when Aiya is no longer at the helm.

27. In contrast to Rush temple trends, Ashis Nandy proposes that Hinduism in diaspora naturally becomes more exclusive, hegemonic, and brahmanical (cited in Vertovec 2000: 152).

28. Ultimately, the Rush temple confounds Weber's distinctions between prophetic and unprophetic religions and leaders. Although Rush's promotion of an ethical structure in lieu of an ecclesial hierarchy fits Weber's prophetic category, its emphasis on ritual aligns it with his unprophetic designation ([1922] 1958: 78). Weber differentiates prophet and priest, in that the former gleans authority from personal revelation and charisma whereas the latter's comes from an established tradition (46). Because Aiya both breaks with and conforms to tradition, he fits neither category. While he is a layperson usurping a priestly role, he is also a Śrīvidyā *upāsaka* who claims an ancient lineage with full support from his guru.

29. For descriptions of similar instances in which gurus take on their disciples' negative karma, see Babb (1986: 66) and Vail (1985: 129–131).

CHAPTER 6

1. To accommodate more people, Aiya eventually moved the Friday evening story sessions to Saturday evenings.

2. *Vibhuti tripundaram* is the three-lined mark of Śiva made from *vibhuti* ash paste and applied, in this instance, on the top segment of the *lingam.*

3. The name Kannappa, which Śiva gives to Thinnan to stop him from gauging out his eye, combines the word for eye (*kanna*) and the word for father (*appa*) as a form of respect.

4. This story is an origin tale for the Kālahasti (Kāḷatti) temple in Andhra Pradesh near the Tamil Nadu border. Devotees understand the *lingam* present in the temple today to be the same one out of which Śiva emerged to bless Thinnan. The same story is told in Shulman (1980: 135).

5. This process of deciding which traditions to maintain or drop, reflecting in some ways distinctions between culture and authentic religion, is a natural part of diaspora adaptation (Vertovec 2000: 151–152; see also Knott 1986: 46; Pocock 1976: 363; and Williams 1988: 191).

6. In his book on the Sri Lankan Tamil diaspora in Norway, Fuglerud makes a similar observation. As he sees it, Sri Lankan Tamils carry out "family/caste competition through the medium of 'Western' status criteria like cars, houses, and conspicuous consumption" (1999: 113). Fuglerud also describes ostentatious houses and ritual events as providing opportunities for the display of wealth and status (113–114).

7. The questionable idea that materialism and consumerism are necessarily

Western inventions is something that Indian participants of the Independence movement promoted stridently. The positioning of Indian (Eastern) spirituality in opposition to Western materiality is part of an Orientalist equation several centuries old, still operating in India as well as in Europe and North America. See Said (1978), Inden (1986, 1990), and Dempsey (2001: 18–51). The fact that Aiya sometimes connects consumerism with the West—as do the bulk of his listeners at the temple—is therefore not surprising.

8. Milton Singer also discusses selective assimilation by noting the various effects of British-influenced industrial capitalism on the religious practices of elite industrial leaders in south India. He is particularly interested in how elite Indians worked to preserve tradition amid interactions with British colonizers (1972: 322). See Srinivas (1966), Kopf (1969), and Irschick (1969).

9. Thanks to Vijitha for cheerfully steering visitor after visitor in my direction during the summer of 2002. People always seemed willing to talk with me, but I am sure I would have had far fewer conversations if it were not for her ice-breaking introductions.

10. Although a growing number of adherents argue that Hinduism as a tradition can be neatly identified as a homogenous entity, there are others who argue that there are many ways to be Hindu, its complexity eluding tidy definition. Intrinsic to the debate is the question of who indeed is claiming to define or speak for Hinduism. For a selection of twelve scholarly perspectives and opinions, see the thematic issue "Who Speaks for Hinduism?" in the *Journal of the American Academy of Religion* 68/4 (2000).

11. Fred Clothey discusses the trend within south Indian diaspora groups in which ritual orthopraxy is increasingly gaining importance. He reasons that this gives increased status and power not only to rituals but to their associated communities (1992: 129–130). See also Bharati (1980: 25). Arguing for similar trends within both the north and south Indian diaspora, see Ashis Nandy (1990: 102–104).

Angrosino's (1983) study of the South Asian diaspora suggests that U.S. and British communities stress orthodoxy more than do their Caribbean, Southeast Asian, Pacific rim, and African counterparts. Religious practices in the latter communities—particularly in the Caribbean—tend to be more localized, directed at lower-caste traditions, and less concerned with laws of purity and pollution, probably because the Indian ethnic populations include few brahmans. Contributing to this is the tendency, observed by William Safran, that myths of homeland return tend to weaken when Indians are either a majority (as in Fiji) or a dominant minority (as in Trinidad and Tobago and Guyana) (1991: 89–90).

12. Tying one's hair back in the temple seems to be prescribed more in south than in north India, more in rural than in urban areas. In south India, some woman secure only the front of their hair and let the rest flow freely. Since the Rush temple is concerned less with female symbolism than with sanitation, women (and men) with long hair must tie it back completely—into a ponytail, a braid, two braids, or bun. For alternative paradigms in which bodily binding reflect issues of control over and power of Sri Lankan Tamil women, see David (1980). For a discussion of the connection between female restraint and auspicious power in ancient Tamil Nadu, see Hart (1973).

13. For a description of how Indian menstrual taboos have different meanings within the separate grids of purity/pollution and auspiciousness/inauspiciousness, see Marglin (1985).

14. Aiya here is referring to restrictions prescribed in the *Laws of Manu*, written in Sanskrit around the first century CE.

15. The fact that a woman is polluting and therefore harmful to cremation rites can be expressed in various and vague terms. Whitney Kelting, who works with Jain communities in Maharashtra, notes that pregnant women are most strictly barred from attending cremation ceremonies. Her deduction is that super-auspiciousness may be more an issue than pollution (personal communication). This seems consistent with Aiya's contention that women are most vulnerable when between the ages of eighteen and twenty-three. Paul Courtright notes that cremations in which *sati* is performed—when a widow immolates herself along with her deceased husband—are not off limits to women, since the auspiciousness of the *sati* event overrides the potential danger and inauspiciousness of the cremation (personal communication). For more on the issue of *sati* and female auspiciousness, see Harlan (1992).

16. Pratap Kumar notes that South African Tamil women diverge from tradition in a number of ways. Somewhat similar to their South Asian urban, north Indian, and North American counterparts, they routinely ignore menstrual taboos and accompany family members to crematoriums. Breaking even more dramatically from tradition is their insistence on wearing their wedding *tāli* after their husbands die. The common rationale, different from Aiya's, is that it marks the woman's eternal connection with her husband (rather than with the goddess). Women in South Africa commonly argue that since their husbands gave them their *tāli*, no one has any right to take it away (personal communication).

17. There are eleven *mahā abhiṣekam* substances. Each is poured onto Śrī Rājarājeśwarī, followed by a bucket full of water. In order of appearance they are: milk, yogurt, ghee (clarified butter), honey, *pañcamṛt* (five types of chopped fruit mixed with jaggery, sugar crystals, and honey), fruit juice, young coconut milk, turmeric, *vibhuti*, sandalwood, and rosewater. Also, at some point, water from the creek below the temple, Kāśī, will be poured on the *mūrti* as well.

CHAPTER 7

1. For a survey of influences of Indian religions upon North American culture ranging from the nineteenth-century Transcendentalists through late twentieth-century pop assimilation, see Tweed and Prothero (1999).

2. The Śriṅgeri jagadguru, Abhinava Vidyateertha, died in 1989. His funeral was a major national event attended by Prime Minister Rajiv Gandhi. Although the jagadguru was unusually approachable—as Glen Yocum put it, he "went to extraordinary lengths to be accessible to his devotees" (1992: 83)—he nevertheless subscribed to laws of purity and pollution and to brahmanical caste values (Yocum 1992: 85–87; Singer 1972: 341). Given his adherence to tradition, along with his exalted position as jagadguru, his willingness to recognize and assist Euro American Hindus is quite remarkable.

3. Because Hindu renouncers have already undergone ritual death to the world,

they are not cremated, as is standard practice for nonrenunciate Hindus, when they die.

4. For a lengthier discussion of temple growing pains, see chapter 9.

5. Many scholars understand the *Devī-Bhāgavata Purāṇa* to have been written in stages, making a definitive date for the text elusive at best. See C. Mackenzie Brown (1990).

6. Jonathan Z. Smith touches upon a similar issue in his description of early Christian and pre-Christian practices in which newly built centers deliberately replicated older ones (1987: 75). He argues that Christianity eventually replaced its emphasis on location with an emphasis on annual seasons associated with Christian narratives (96–117).

7. "Burned-Over District" began as a pejorative term, coined by skeptics and later adopted by participants.

8. See Bhardwaj (1990: 222–223).

9. Another fairly recent means for transferring South Asian sacrality to new lands is through ancient architectural styles. Beginning in the early 1970s, North American immigrant communities often tried to blend into their surroundings by worshiping in rented halls and renovated buildings and churches. Newly built temples were often well camouflaged within their neighborhoods. It was not until the early 1990s that traditional Indian architecture was widely adopted as a means for expressing pride and authenticity. The first two Hindu temples built from the ground up in the United States are exceptions. The Shri Venkateshwara temple in Pittsburgh, consecrated June 1977, and the Ganesh temple in Flushing, Queens, consecrated July of the same year, are replicas of existing south Indian temples (Leonard 1997: 112).

10. The *Āgamas* and *Vastu Śāstras* specify animals that are best suited to be prior inhabitants of temple grounds. Most preferred for constructing temples are places where elephants have lived (*kuñjarastanam*), then horses (*aśvastanam*), then cows (*gostanam*).

11. See Buhnemann (1988: 113–15) for a description of a more extensive *saṅkalpam.*

12. Bhardwaj also notes a new, more elaborate, route developing from Toronto/Montreal to the Kāśī Temple in Flint, Michigan to Balaji and the HTGC in Chicago, to New Vrindaban, the Shri Venkateshwara temple outside Pittsburgh, and return via Niagara Falls (1990: 225).

13. Bhardwaj posits that temples best situated for pilgrimage are in remote areas that are nonetheless easily accessible. Since pilgrimage marks a break with hurried daily life, rural terrain often evokes a certain topographical otherness. Easy access naturally facilitates the process of travel. The fact that the Rush temple is nestled in hilly farm country just off Interstate 90 and close to Niagara Falls makes it an ideal pilgrimage destination.

14. The temple has since installed small, softly lit solar-powered lights by each shrine, making the need for an evening festival trek obsolete.

15. This is a rather strange sequence of events. People have different opinions as to why the priest did not finish his mission and deliver the Devī to the Toronto temple. Some speculate that his interests were more financial than spiritual.

16. Akka is the Tamil term for elder sister.

17. When I asked Aiya to say more about Akka's relationship to divinity, he explained that divinity manifests in human beings in proportion to the amount of goodness in the world at the time. During deluded times, if divinity were to fully manifest, people would be overwhelmed by its power. As such, Akka has human feelings and thoughts; the difference between her and us is that the goddess is constantly working through her. Akka can, at will, tap into a cosmic understanding, something that the rest of us, to varying extents, only get a fleeting glimpse of.

18. *Bhumi pūjā* is the worship of the earth, typically performed on land where a temple is to be built. Aiya had been planning to perform the *pūjā*, but was waiting for clearance from the town council first.

19. For more on Rush city politics and obstructions to temple construction, see chapter 8.

20. The deity Akka is believed to embody, Akhilāndeśwarī, further connects her to the Rush *pīṭham*. In one of Rājarājeśwarī's local legends, related to me by Aiya, two Tamil goddesses emanate from the implements she holds in her hands: Mīnākṣī from Madurai emerges from the five flowery arrows in her right hand, and Akhilāndeśwarī from Tiruvānaikaval from the sugarcane bow in her left. Rājarājeśwarī, ruler of the universe, delegates certain authorities to these goddesses. Mīnākṣī becomes prime minister and Akhilāndeśwarī the commander-in-chief of the armed forces. Akhilāndeśwarī leads 640 million deities in the Hindu pantheon and so, as Aiya put it, "You can imagine the reverence we feel when that deity herself [in the form of Akka] walks into our temple."

Brooks mentions that Akhilāndeśwarī sometimes wears earrings with the *śrī-cakra* on them, and thus is associated with the Śrīvidyā tradition and its goddesses (1992: 48, 72).

21. Avyāja Karuṇā Mūrti is one of the names for the goddess in the *Lalitāsahasranāmam*.

CHAPTER 8

1. The first recorded South Asian immigrant arrived in the United States in 1820, although it was not until the beginning of the twentieth century that more than 275 people came in a single decade (Williams 1988: 14).

2. Most South Asian immigrants during this period were Sikh Punjabi men who farmed in California, often marrying into the Mexican community. See Karen Leonard (1992).

3. Aiya and Amma's daughter was ten when they moved to the Rochester area, and was the only Asian in her school. According to Aiya, she was teased terribly at first, so he coached her to give a speech that he paraphrased as follows: "I'm ten years old; I've lived Africa; I've traveled to India. I've seen places and people and cultures that you guys will never even hope to see. You have a problem with that? By saying these things to me you're showing me what you don't know. I can only feel sorry for you." Charu's speech, according to Aiya, helped stave off the school bullies.

4. There are, of course, exceptions to this trend, the most significant being ISKCON, or International Society for Krishna Consciousness, otherwise known as the Hare Krishnas. Although ISKCON has appealed to North American sensibilities, it still highlights devotion to a deity, in this case Krishna. It is thus more like a diaspora

Hindu temple than an ashram that focuses primarily on a guru and his or her teachings. For more on Hinduism as adopted and reinterpreted by non-Indians, see Tweed and Prothero (1999).

5. Milk offerings are sometimes specified by scriptural injunction to be simply "from a cow." According to ritual purists, this means unadulterated, unpasteurized milk.

6. For a similar agricultural event at the Ashland Massachusetts temple, see Eck (2001: 91).

7. Kerala and Goa, whose populations are roughly 25 and 30 percent Christian, respectively, are the Indian states with the largest percentage of Christians.

8. The Ganesh temple in Flushing offers a similar interreligious display. Its official medallion is marked with symbols from five major world religions (Richardson 1985: 36).

9. I have written about this tendency for interreligious mixing in south India. Although practitioners usually maintain clear and regular denominiational allegiances, many visit powerful places of worship—regardless of their religious affiliation—during festival occasions or in special times of need (Dempsey 2001; see also Dempsey 2002).

10. I do not recount this story since, as the reader might suspect, I have chronicled many more miracles than I have room to include in this book. It is pertinent here that other interreligious miracle stories help demonstrate how Aiya's crossover experience is not unique. Particularly moving is Jeya's account of being in dire straits in Spain, facing and praying to Mary at Lourdes, and, as he sees it, receiving immediate and miraculous deliverance.

CHAPTER 9

1. A source of mystery for many is the fact that the Park Circle and Rush temples have typically drawn devotees from Syracuse, Buffalo, and Toronto and only very few from Rochester. Rochester has had its own community temple since 1993, perhaps partially explaining the pattern, but Buffalo and Syracuse also have their own temples. Some speculate that the Rush temple's tantric tradition is daunting for potential devotees, as is the fact that Aiya is not brahman. The Sri Lankan focus may lessen the appeal for others. Nonetheless, as non-Sri Lankan devotees continue to commute from Syracuse, Buffalo, and locales even further away, the puzzle of Rochester's continuing noninvolvement persists.

2. Kathy had earlier heard about the temple through her grandparents' neighbor. Their daughter visited Guruji's temple while in India and, during one of Kathy's visits to her grandparents in Rochester, the two women swapped stories about India. The woman also informed Kathy about Aiya, Guruji's disciple, who had a temple in the area.

3. TM, or Transcendental Meditation, was developed and promoted by Maharishi Mahesh Yogi, an Indian-born guru. TM became widely popular outside India in the 1970s after it was endorsed by the Beatles and by football star Joe Namath. The main TM center that runs retreats and workshops is in Iowa.

4. Another instance in which a dream led someone to the Rush temple involves a Hungarian woman who told Vish Uncle her story during the 2002 *pratiṣṭhā*. In

1997, before the temple was built, she stayed with friends in Rochester while en route from Buffalo to Syracuse and had a vivid dream about a south Indian temple situated in a barn. She had been to India and had learned Tamil, so she was intrigued. Yet no one she asked seemed to know of such a place. Five years later she was back in Rochester and, inquiring again about a Hindu barn temple, was directed to Rush. Vish Uncle recalled her excitement not only about finding the temple but also about timing her visit so well, during the *pratiṣṭhā* weekend.

5. Kalyanasundaram took over Mataji's orphanage after she died.

6. During the summer of 2003, Amma agreed to be formally interviewed. By then I was finishing this book, wrapping up loose ends and collecting photographs, and did not have my tape recorder with me. We sat together on the floor in the small house near the temple and talked for over an hour about the joys and challenges of temple life and the path that lead her to religious commitment. While Amma talked, I did my best to take notes.

CONCLUSION

1. The Sanskrit compositions attributed to this man, named Mukar, are called the *Mukapañca Sathi.*

2. Supporting the notion that intercultural research should be transformative on a variety of levels, Satya Mohanty notes that cultural interpretation should be performed in such a way "that the interpreter and her analytical apparatus might be fundamentally challenged and changed by the material she (and it) are attempting to 'assess' " (1989: 10–11).

3. One must also grant that "everyday realities" are culturally constructed as well. As such, cross-cultural psychologists have noted that the self within mainstream European and North American contexts, for instance, in contrast with Indian contexts, tends to be more individually than relationally understood (see Roland 1988).

4. Both postmodern ethnography and Advaita philosophy insist upon the blurring of self/other distinctions; both also admit that knowledge of the other (or of divinity) is not readily or easily accessible. They do differ significantly, however, in their stated goals. Aiya encourages students to engage their inner village idiots, to invest hard work in religious practices, and, with Devī's blessings, to capture the Moment. Ethnographers, on the other hand, typically not only view such complete knowledge of the other as elusive but even doubt its existence to begin with.

5. John Thatamanil similarly writes about the ways in which Advaita Vedānta offers important strategies for approaching his scholarly work. In contrast to Western notions of a singular, self-contained personhood (see Taylor 1984: 130), Thatamanil, an Indian Christian, proposes that Advaita's very different notion of self helps support genuine engagement in theological systems outside one's "own."

6. For a discussion of the ways in which anthropologists and scholars of religion describe intersections between established space, society, and time as offering opportunities for religious expression and definition, see the Introduction.

7. Related to the idea that ethnographic intimacies help question conventional dichotomies, Sara Suleri argues that the study of colonial intimacies can help to break down imperial binarisms. She posits that postcolonial theorists' tendency to reify and allegorize otherness can affect scholarly investigation by silencing it. The ignorance

this produces, she argues, is equally if not more problematic than silence itself. She insists that the alterist construction of the Other as unknowable is one that results in "a repetetive monumentalization of the academy's continuing fear of its own ignorance" (1990: 12). For a similar argument against overly rigid constructions of colonial and postcolonial difference and power dynamics, see Ashis Nandy (1983). Also see also Dempsey (2000; 2001: 85–87) for a discussion of this conundrum and its relationship to ethnography.

8. On a slightly different but related note, Edward Said's *Beginnings* maintains that the moment of human creativity within the task of writing takes place at the beginning. It is not a completely original moment (Said asserts that origins belong to divinity), but one that combines agency with repetition. As he cautiously puts it, beginnings "verify evidence of at least some innovation—of *having begun*" (1975: xiii).

Bibliography

Abu-Lughod, Lila. 1991. "Writing against Culture." In *Recapturing Anthropology,* ed. Richard Fox. Santa Fe: School of American Research Press, 137–162.

Agnew, Vijay. 1993. "Feminism and South Asian Immigrant Women in Canada. In *Ethnicity, Identity, Migration: The South Asian Context,* ed. Milton Israel and N. K. Wagle. Toronto: University of Toronto Centre for South Asia Studies, 142–164.

Amritaswarupananda, Swami. 1993. *Mata Amritanandamayi: Life and Experiences of Devotees.* Kollam, Kerala: Mata Amritanandamayi Mission Trust.

Angrosino, M. V. 1983. "Religion among Overseas Indian Communities." In *Religion in Modern India,* ed. G. R. Gupta. New Delhi: Vikas, 357–398

Babb, Lawrence. 1986. *Redemptive Encounters: Three Modern Styles in the Hindu Tradition.* Berkeley: University of California Press.

Badone, Ellen. 1990. "Introduction." In *Religious Orthodoxy and Popular Faith in European Society,* ed. Ellen Badone. Princeton: Princeton University Press, 3–23.

Balasubramanian, ed. 2000. *Advaita Vedanta.* Volume 2 part 2 of *History of Science, Philosophy and Culture in Indian Civilization,* ed. D. P. Chattopadhyaya. New Delhi: Centre for Studies in Civilization.

Ballard, Roger. 1994. *The South Asian Presence in Britain.* London: Hurst.

Baumann, Martin. 1995. "Conceptualizing Diaspora: The Preservation of Religious Identity in Foreign Parts, Exemplified by Hindu Communities outside India." *Temenos* 31: 19–35.

Baumer, Bettina. 1990. "The Guru in the Hindu Tradition." *Studies in Formative Spirituality* 2/3: 341–353.

Bell, Catherine. 1997. *Ritual: Perspectives and Dimensions*. New York: Oxford University Press.

Bharati, Agehananda. 1980. "Indian Expatriates in North America and New-Hindu Movements." In *The Communication of Ideas*, ed. J. S. Yadava and Vinayshil Gautam. New Delhi: Concept, 245–255.

Bhardwaj, Surinder. 1990. "Hindu Deities and Pilgrimage in the United States." In *Pilgrimage in the United States*, ed. Gisbert Rinschede and Surinder Bhardwaj. Berlin: Dietrich Reimer Verlag, 211–228.

Bhattacharyya. 1982. *History of the Tantric Religion: A Historical, Ritualistic and Philosophical Study*. New Delhi: Manohar.

Bibby, Reginald. 1993. *Unknown Gods: The Ongoing Story of Religion in Canada*. Toronto: Stoddart.

Bilmoria, Purushottama. 1996. *Hindus and Sikhs in Australia*. Canberra: Australian Government Publishing Service.

Boff, Leonardo, and Clodovis Boff. 1987. *Introducing Liberation Theology*, trans. Paul Burns. New York: Orbis Books.

Bourdieu, Pierre. 1977. *Outline of a Theory of Practice*, trans. Richard Nice. Cambridge: Cambridge University Press.

Brettell, Caroline. 1990. "The Priest and His People and the Contractual Basis for Religious Practice in Rural Portugal." In *Religious Orthodoxy and Popular Faith in European Society*, ed. Ellen Badone. Princeton: Princeton University Press, 55–75.

Brodie, Fawn. 1976. *No Man Knows My History: The Life of Joseph Smith the Mormon Prophet*. New York: Alfred A. Knopf.

Brooks, Douglas Renfrew. 1992. *Auspicious Wisdom: The Texts and Traditions of Śrīvidyā Śākta Tantrism in South India*. Albany: State University of New York Press.

Brown, C. Mackenzie. 1990. *The Triumph of the Goddess: The Canonical Models and Theological Vision of the Devī-Bhāgavata Purāṇa*. Albany: State University of New York Press.

Brown, Karen McCarthy. 1991. *Mama Lola: A Vodou Priestess in Brooklyn*. Berkeley: University of California Press.

Brown, Robert. 1998. "Expected Miracles: The Unsurprisingly Miraculous Nature of Buddhist Images and Relics." In *Images, Miracles, and Authority in Asian Religious Traditions*, ed. Richard H. Davis. Boulder, Col.: Westview, 23–35.

Buchignani. 1980. "Accommodation, Adaptation, and Policy: Dimensions of the South Asian Experience in Canada." In *Visible Minorities and Multiculturalism: Asians in Canada*, ed. Victor Ujimoto and Gordon Hirabayashi. Toronto: Butterworths, 121–150.

Buhnemann, Gudrun. 1988. *Pūjā: A Study in Smārta Ritual*. Leiden: E. J. Brill; Vienna; Gerold.

Burghart, Richard. 1983. "Renunciation in the Religious Traditions of South Asia." *Man* 18: 635–653.

Burke, Peter. 1994. *Popular Culture in Early Modern Europe*. 2nd ed. Hants, England: Scholars Press.

Butterfield, Stephen. 1994. *The Double Mirror: A Skeptical Journey into Buddhist Tantra*. Berkeley: North Atlantic Books.

Case, Margaret. 2000. *Seeing Krishna: The Religious World of a Brahman Family in Vrindaban.* New York: Oxford University Press.

Cenkner, William. 1992. "The Sankaracarya of Kanchi and the Kamaksi Temple as Ritual Center." In *A Sacred Thread: Modern Transmission of Hindu Traditions in India and Abroad,* ed. Raymond Williams. Chambersburg, Penn.: Anima, 52–67.

———. 1983. *A Tradition of Teachers: Śankara and the Jagadgurus Today.* New Delhi: Motilal Banarsidass.

Clifford, James. 1997. *Routes: Travel and Translation in the Late Twentieth Century.* Cambridge: Harvard University Press.

———. 1994. "Diasporas." *Cultural Anthropology* 9: 302–308.

Clifford, James, and George E. Marcus. 1986. *Writing Culture: The Poetics and Politics of Ethnography.* Berkeley: University of California Press.

Clothey, Fred. 1992. "Ritual and Reinterpretation: South Indians in Southeast Asia." In *A Sacred Thread: Modern Transmission of Hindu Traditions in India and Abroad,* ed. Raymond Williams. Chambersburg, Penn.: Anima, 127–146.

Cobb, John, and David Griffin. 1976. *Process Theology: An Introductory Exposition.* Philadelphia: Westminister Press.

Courtright, Paul. 1985. "On this Holy Day in My Humble Way: Aspects of *Pūjā.*" In *Gods of Flesh/Gods of Stone: The Embodiment of Divinity in India,* ed. Joanne Punzo Waghorne and Norman Cutler. Chambersburg, Penn.: Anima, 53–68.

Coward, Harold. 2000. "Hinduism in Canada." In *The South Asian Religious Diaspora in Britain, Canada, and the United States.* Eds. Harold Coward, John Hinnells, and Raymond Brady Williams. Albany: State University of New York Press, 151–172.

Coward, Harold, and David Goa. 1987. "Religious Experiences of the South Asian Diaspora in Canada." In *South Asian Diaspora in Canada: Six Essays,* ed. Milton Israel. Ontario: Multicultural Historical Society.

Cutler, Norman. 1987. *Songs of Experience: The Poetics of Tamil Devotion.* Bloomington: University of Indiana Press.

Daniel, Valentine. 1996. *Charred Lullabies: Chapters in an Anthropography of Violence.* Princeton: Princeton University Press.

David, Kenneth. 1980. "Hidden Powers: Cultural and Socio-Economic Accounts of Jaffna Women." In *The Powers of Tamil Women,* ed. Susan Wadley. Foreign and Comparative Studies/South Asian Series, no. 6. Syracuse: Maxwell School of Citizenship and Public Affairs, Syracuse University, 93–136.

Davis, Richard. 1998. "Introduction: Miracles as Social Acts." In *Images, Miracles, and Authority in Asian Religious Traditions,* ed. Richard Davis. Boulder, Colo.: Westview, 1–22.

———. 1997. *Lives of Indian Images.* Princeton: Princeton University Press.

Dempsey, Corinne. 2002. "Lessons in Miracles from Kerala, South India: Stories of Three 'Christian' Saints." In *Popular Christianity in India: Riting between the Lines,* ed. Selva Raj and Corinne Dempsey. Albany: State University of New York Press, 115–140.

———. 2001. *Kerala Christian Sainthood: Collisions of Culture and Worldview in South India.* New York: Oxford University Press.

———. 2000. "The Religioning of Anthropology: New Directions for the Ethnographer-Pilgrim." *Culture and Religion* 1/2: 189–210.

Denton, Lynn Teskey. 1991. "Varieties of Hindu Female Asceticism." In *Roles and Rituals for Hindu Women,* ed. Julia Leslie. Madison, N.J.: Fairleigh Dickinson University Press, 211–231.

Devlin, Judith. 1987. *The Superstitious Mind: French Peasants and the Supernatural in the Nineteenth Century.* New Haven: Yale University Press.

Doshi, Sacheta. 1996. "Divided Consciousness amidst a New Orientalism: South Asian American Identity Formation on Campus." In *Contours of the Heart: South Asians Map North America,* ed. Sunaina Maira and Rajini Srikanth. New York: Asian American Writers' Workshop, 201–213.

Douglas, Mary. 1966. *Purity and Danger: An Analysis of Conceptions of Pollution and Taboo.* London: Routledge and Kegan Paul.

———. 1968. "The Social Control of Cognition: Some Factors in Joke Perception." *Man* 3: 361–376.

Driver, Tom. 1991. *The Magic of Ritual: Our Need for Liberating Rites that Transform Our Lives and Our Communities.* New York: HarperCollins.

Eck, Diana. 2001. *A New Religious America: How a "Christian Country" Has Now Become the World's Most Religiously Diverse Nation.* San Francisco: HarperCollins.

———. 1981. *Darśan: Seeing the Divine Image in India.* Chambersburg, Penn.: Anima.

Eliade, Mircea. 1964. *Shamanism: Archaic Techniques of Ecstasy.* Princeton: Princeton University Press.

———. 1958. *Patterns in Comparative Religion,* trans. Rosemary Sheed. New York: Sheed and Ward.

———. [1957] 1987. *The Sacred and the Profane: The Nature of Religion,* trans. Willard R. Trask. San Diego: Harcourt Brace.

Ewing, Katherine Pratt. 1997. *Arguing Sainthood: Modernity, Psychoanalysis, and Islam.* Durham, N.C.: Duke University Press.

Freedberg, David. 1989. *The Power of Images: Studies in the History and Theory of Response.* Chicago: University of Chicago Press.

Fuglerud, Øivind. 1999. *Life on the Outside: The Tamil Diaspora and Long-Distance Nationalism.* London: Pluto.

Geertz, Clifford. 1968. *Islam Observed: Religious Developments in Morocco and Indonesia.* Chicago: University of Chicago Press.

Gold, Daniel. 1995. "Guru's Body, Guru's Abode." In *Religious Reflections on the Human Body.* ed. Jane Marie Law. Bloomington: Indiana University Press, 230–250.

———. 1988. *Comprehending the Guru: Towards a Grammar of Religious Perception.* Atlanta, Ga.: Scholars Press.

Goldberg, Ellen. 2002. *The Lord Who Is Half Woman: Adhanārīśwara in Indian and Feminist Perspective.* Albany: State University of New York Press.

Griffin, David Ray. 1997. *Parapsychology, Philosophy, and Spirituality: A Postmodern Exploration.* Albany: State University of New York Press.

Gupta, Akhil, and Ferguson, James. 1992. "Beyond 'Culture': Space, Identity, and the Politics of Difference." *Cultural Anthropology* 7: 6–23.

Gupta, Ranjit Sen. 2000. *Pranayama: A Conscious Way of Breathing.* New Delhi: New Age Books.

Gutiérrez, Gustavo. 1973. *A Theology of Liberation.* Maryknoll, New York: Orbis Books.

Hallstrom, Lisa Lassell. 2004. "Anandamayi Ma: The Bliss-filled Divine Mother." In *The Graceful Guru: Hindu Female Gurus in India and the United States,* ed. Karen Pechilis. New York: Oxford University Press, 85–118.

———. 1999. *Mother of Bliss: Ānandamayī Mā (1896–1982).* New York: Oxford University Press.

Handelman, Don. 1990. *Models and Mirrors: Towards an Anthropology of Public Events.* Cambridge: Cambridge University Press.

Harlan, Lindsey. 1992. *Religion and Rajput Women: The Ethic of Protection in Contemporary Narratives.* Berkeley: University of California Press.

Harris, Lis. 1994. "O Guru, Guru, Guru." *New Yorker,* November 14, 92–109.

Hart, George. 1973. "Women and the Sacred References in Ancient Tamilnad." *Journal of Asian Studies* 32: 233–250.

Hawley, John Stratton, and Mark Juergensmeyer. 1988. *Songs of the Saints of India.* New York: Oxford University Press.

Hume, David. [1777] 1975. "On Miracles." In *Enquiries Concerning the Human Understanding.* Oxford: Clarendon Press.

———. 1748. *Philosophical Essays Concerning Human Understanding.*

Inden, Ronald. 1990. *Imagining India.* Oxford: Basil Blackwell.

———. 1986. "Orientalist Constructions of India." *Modern Asian Studies* 20: 401–446.

Irschick, Eugene. 1969. *Politics and Social Conflict in South India: The Non-Brahman Movement and Tamil Separatism, 1916–1929.* Berkeley: University of California Press.

Israel, Milton. 1994. *In the Further Soil: A Social History of Indo-Canadians in Ontario.* Toronto: Organization for the Promotion of Indian Culture.

James, William. 1958. *The Varieties of Religious Experience: A Study in Human Nature.* New York: Mentor Books.

Johnson, Curtis. 1989. *Islands of Holiness and Rural Religion in Upstate New York, 1790–1860.* Ithaca: Cornell University Press.

Judith, Anodea. 1987. *Wheels of Life: A User's Guide to the Chakra System.* St. Paul, Minn.: Llewellyn.

Kane, S. 1994. *The Phantom Gringo Boat: Shamanic Discourse and Development in Panama.* Washington, D.C.: Smithsonian Institute Press.

Kendall, Laurel. 1988. *The Life and Hard Times of a Korean Shaman: Of Tales and the Telling of Tales.* Honolulu: University of Hawaii Press.

Khandelwal, Meena. 1996. "Walking a Tightrope: Saintliness, Gender, and Power in an Ethnographic Encounter. *Anthropology and Humanism* 21/2: 111–134.

———. 1997. "Ungendered *Atma,* Masculine Virility and Feminine Compassion: Ambiguities in Renunciant Discourses on Gender." *Contributions to Indian Sociology* 31/1: 79–107.

Khanna, Madhu. 1979. *Yantra: The Tantric Symbol of Cosmic Unity.* London: Thames and Hudson.

Kher, B. G. 1979. "Maharashtrian Women Saints." In *Women Saints: East and West,* ed. Swami Ghananand and John Stewart-Wallace. Hollywood, Calif.: Vedanta Press, 58–63.

King, Ursula. 1984. "The Effect of Social Change on Religious Self-Understanding: Women Ascetics in Modern Hinduism." In *Changing South Asia: Religion and Society*, ed. K. Ballhatchet and D. Taylor. London: School of Oriental and African Studies, 69–83.

Knott, Kim. 1986. *Hinduism in Leeds: A Study of Religious Practice in the Indian Hindu Community and Hindu-Related Groups*. Leeds: Community Religions Project: University of Leeds.

Kondo, Dorinne. 1986. "Dissolution and Reconstitution of the Self: Implications for Anthropological Epistemology." *Cultural Anthropology* 1: 74–88.

Kopf, David. 1969. *British Orientalism and the Bengal Renaissance: The Dynamics of Indian Modernization 1773–1835*. Berkeley: University of California Press.

Lane, Belden. 2002. *Landscapes of the Sacred: Geography and Narrative in American Spirituality*. Expanded edition. Baltimore: Johns Hopkins University Press.

Larson, Gerald. 1989. " 'Conceptual Resources in South Asia for 'Environmental Ethics.' " In *Nature in Asian Traditions of Thought: Essays in Environmental Philosophy*, ed. Baird Callicott and Roger T. Ames. Albany: State University of New York Press.

Leach, Edmund. 1976. *Culture and Communication*. Cambridge: Cambridge University Press.

Leonard, Karen Isaksen. 1997. *The South Asian Americans*. Westport, Conn.: Greenwood.

———. 1993. "Ethnic Identity and Gender: South Asians in the United States." In *Ethnicity, Identity, Migration: The South Asian Context*, ed. Milton Israel and N. K. Wagle. Toronto: University of Toronto Centre for South Asia Studies, 165–180.

MacDaniel, June. 1992. *Making Ethnic Choices: California's Punjabi Mexican Americans*. Philadelphia: Temple University Press.

———. 1989. *The Madness of the Saints*. Chicago: University of Chicago Press.

Marglin, Fredérique Apfel. 1985. "Female Sexuality in the Hindu World." In *Immaculate and Powerful: The Female in Sacred Image and Social Reality*, ed. Clarissa Atkinson, Constance Buchanon, and Margaret Miles. Boston: Beacon, 9–60.

McAfee Brown, Robert. 1993. *Liberation Theology: An Introductory Guide*. Louisville, Ky.: Westminster/John Knox Press.

McElroy, James. 1974. "Social Reform in the Burned-Over District: Rochester, New York, as a Test Case, 1830–1854." Ph.D. dissertation, SUNY Binghamton.

McKean, Lise. 1996. *Divine Enterprise: Gurus and the Hindu Nationalist Movement*. Chicago: University of Chicago Press.

Miller, David. 1976. "The Guru as the Center of Sacredness." *Studies in Religion* 6/5: 527–533.

Mohanty, J. N. 2000. *Classical Indian Philosophy*. Lanham, England: Rowman and Littlefield.

Mohanty, Satya. 1989. "Us and Them: On the Philosophical Bases of Political Criticism." *Yale Journal of Criticism* 2/2: 1–31.

Mukerji, Bithika. 1989. "Sri Anandamayi Ma: Divine Play of the Spiritual Journey." In *Hindu Spirituality: Vedas through Vedanta*, ed. Krishna Sirraman. New York: Crossroads, 392–413.

Mukta, Parita. 1994. *Upholding the Common Life: The Community of Mirabai.* Delhi: Oxford University Press.

Muller-Ortega, Paul Eduardo. 1997. "Shaktipat: The Intiatory Descent of Power." In Douglas Renfrew Brooks, Swami Durgananda, Paul E. Muller-Ortega, and William K. Mahony, *Meditation Revolution: A History and Theology of the Siddha Yoga Lineage.* Fallsburg, N.Y.: Agama, 407–444.

Mullin, Robert Bruce. 1996. *Miracles and the Modern Religious Imagination.* New Haven: Yale University Press.

Nandy, Ashis. 1990. "Dialogue and the Diaspora: Conversation with Nikos Papstergiadis." *Dialogue and the Diaspora* 11: 99–108.

———. 1983. *The Intimate Enemy: Loss and Recovery of Self under Colonialism.* Delhi: Oxford University Press.

Narayan, Kirin. 1993a. "How Native is a 'Native' Anthropologist?" *American Anthropologist* 95: 671–686.

———. 1993b. "Refractions of the Field at Home: American Representations of Hindu Holy Men in the 19th and 20th Centuries." *Cultural Anthropology* 8/4: 476–509.

———. 1989. *Storytellers, Saints, and Scoundrels: Folk Narrative in Hindu Religious Teaching.* Philadelphia: University of Pennsylvania Press.

Narayanan, Vasudha. 2000. "Diglossic Hinduism: Liberation and Lentils." *Journal of The American Academy of Religion* 68/4: 761–780.

———. 1999. "Brimming with Bhakti, Embodiments of Shakti: Devotees, Deities, Performers, Reformers, and Other Women of Power in the Hindu Tradition." In *Feminism and World Religions,* eds. Arvind Sharma and Katherine Young. Albany: State University of New York Press, 25–77.

———. 1992. "Creating the South Indian 'Hindu' Experience in the United States." In *A Sacred Thread: Modern Transmission of Hindu Traditions in India and Abroad,* ed. Raymond Williams. Chambersburg, Penn.: Anima, 147–176.

———. 1985. "*Arćāvatāra*: On Earth as He Is in Heaven." In *Gods of Flesh / Gods of Stone: The Embodiment of Divinity in India,* ed. Joanne Punzo Waghorne and Norman Cutler. Chambersburg, Penn.: Anima, 53–68.

Ojha, Catherine. 1981. "Feminine Asceticism in Hinduism: Its Tradition and Present Condition." *Man in India* 61/3: 254–285.

Padoux, André. 1996. "The Tantric Guru." In *Tantra in Practice,* ed. David Gordon White. Princeton: Princeton University Press, 41–51.

Pandolfo, Stefania. 1997. *Impasse of the Angels: Scenes from a Moroccan Space of Memory.* Chicago: University of Chicago Press.

Parry, Jonathan. 1985. "The Aghori Ascetics in Benares." In *Indian Religion,* ed. Richard Burghart and Audrey Cantlie. London: Curzon Press, 51–1.

Pearson, Anne MacKenzie. 1996. *"Because It Gives Me Peace of Mind": Ritual Fasts in the Religious Lives of Hindu Women.* Albany: State University of New York Press.

Pechilis, Karen, ed. 2004. *The Graceful Guru: Hindu Female Gurus in India and the United States.* New York: Oxford University Press.

Peterson, Indira Viswanathan. 1989. *Poems to Śiva: The Hymns of the Tamil Saints.* Princeton: Princeton University Press.

Pocock, D. F. 1976. "Preservation of the Religious Life: Hindu Immigrants in England." *Contributions to Indian Sociology* 10/2: 341–365.

Raj, Selva. Forthcoming. "Passage to America: Ammachi, the Transnational Mother." In *Gurus in America,* ed. Cynthia Humes and Tom Forsthoefel. Albany: State University of New York Press.

———. 2005. "Transplanting Tradition: Syro-Malabar Catholics on American Soil." *Chakra: Tidskrift for Indiska Religioner* April 2005: 130–146.

———. 2004. "Ammachi: Mother of Compassion." In *The Graceful Guru: Hindu Female Gurus in India and the United States,* ed. Karen Pechilis. New York: Oxford University Press, 203–218.

Ramanujan, A. K. 1983. "On Women Saints." In *The Divine Consort: Rādhā and the Goddesses of India,* ed. John Stratton Hawley and Donna M. Wulff. Berkeley: Berkeley Religious Studies Series, 316–24.

———. 1981. *Hymns for the Drowning: Poems for Viṣṇu by Namālvār.* Princeton: Princeton University Press.

———. 1975. *Speaking of Śiva.* London: Penguin Books.

Rangaswamy, M. A. Dorai. 1990. *The Religion and Philosophy of Tēvāram.* Madras: University of Madras.

Richardson, E. Allen. 1985. *East Comes West: Asian Religions and Cultures in North America.* New York: Pilgrim.

Roland, Alan. 1988. *In Search of Self in India and Japan: Toward a Cross-Cultural Psychology.* Princeton: Princeton University Press.

Rosaldo, Renato. 1989. *Culture and Truth: The Remaking of Social Analysis.* Boston: Beacon.

Safran, William. 1991. "Diasporas in Modern Societies: Myths of Homeland and Return." *Diaspora: A Journal of Transnational Studies* 1: 83–99.

Said, Edward. 1978. *Orientalism.* New York: Vintage Books.

———. 1975. *Beginnings: Intention and Method.* New York: Basic Books.

Sharma, Arvind. 2000. "Who Speaks for Hinduism? A Perspective from Advaita Vedanta." *Journal of the American Academy of Religion* 68/4: 751–760.

Sheth, Pravin. 2001. *Indians in America: One Stream, Two Waves, Three Generations.* New Delhi: Rawat.

Shulman, David Dean. 1980. *Tamil Temple Myths: Sacrifice and Divine Marriage in the South Indian Śaiva Tradition.* Princeton: Princeton University Press.

Singer, Milton. 1972. *When a Great Tradition Modernizes: An Anthropological Approach to Indian Civilization.* New York: Praeger.

Smart, Ninian. 1987. "The Importance of Diasporas." In *Gilgul: Essays on Transformation, Revolution and Permanence in the History of Religions,* ed. S. Shaked, D. Shulman, and G. G. Stroumsa. Leiden: E. J. Brill, 288–297.

Smith, Brian K. 2000. "Who Does, Can, and Should Speak for Hinduism?" *Journal of the American Academy of Religion* 68/4: 741–750.

Smith, Jonathan Z. 1987. *To Take Place: Toward Theory in Ritual.* Chicago: University of Chicago Press.

Srinivas, M. N. 1966. *Social Change in Modern India.* Berkeley: University of California Press.

Suleri, Sara. 1990. *The Rhetoric of English India.* Chicago: University of Chicago Press.

Tambiah, Stanley Jeyaraja. 1992. *Buddhism Betrayed? Religion, Politics and Violence in Sri Lanka.* Chicago: University of Chicago Press.

———. [1986] 1991. *Sri Lanka: Ethnic Fratricide and the Dismantling of Democracy.* Chicago: University of Chicago Press.

Taylor, Mark. 1984. *Erring: A Postmodern A/Theology.* Chicago: University of Chicago Press.

Thatamanil, John. 2000. "Managing Multiple Religious and Scholarly Identities: An Argument for a Theological Study of Hinduism." *Journal of the American Academy of Religion* 68/4: 791–804.

Thistlethwaite, Susan, and Mary Engel, eds. 1998. *Lift Every Voice: Constructing Christian Theologies from the Underside.* 2nd ed. Maryknoll, N.Y.: Orbis Press.

Turner, Edith. 1992. *Experiencing Ritual: A New Interpretation of African Healing.* Philadelphia: University of Pennsylvania Press.

Turner, Victor. [1969] 1995. *The Ritual Process: Structure and Anti-Structure.* New York: Aldine de Gruyter.

Tweed, Thomas, ed. 1997. *Retelling U.S. Religious History.* Berkeley: University of California Press.

Tweed, Thomas, and Prothero, Stephen, eds. 1999. *Asian Religions in America: A Documentary History.* New York: Oxford University Press.

Urban, Hugh. 2001. *The Economics of Ecstasy: Tantra, Secrecy, and Power in Colonial Bengal.* New York: Oxford University Press.

Vail, Lise. 1985. "Founders, Swamis and Devotees: Becoming Divine in North Karnataka." In *Gods of Flesh / Gods of Stone: The Embodiment of Divinity in India,* ed. Joanne Punzo Waghorne and Norman Cutler. Chambersburg, Penn.: Anima, 122–140.

Van der Veer, Peter. 1988. *Gods on Earth.* London: Athlone.

Vertovec, Steven. 2000. *The Hindu Diaspora: Comparative Patterns.* London: Routledge.

Waghorne, Joanne Punzo. 1999. "The Hindu Gods in Split-Level World: The Sri Siva-Vishnu Temple in Suburban Washington, D.C." In *Gods of the City,* ed. Robert Orsi. Bloomington: Indiana University Press, 103–130.

Weber, Max. [1922] 1958. *The Religion of India: The Sociology of Hinduism and Buddhism.* Glencoe, Ill.: Free Press.

Williams, Raymond. 1992. "Sacred Threads of Several Textures." In *A Sacred Thread: Modern Transmission of Hindu Traditions in India and Abroad,* ed. Raymond Williams. Chambersburg, Penn.: Anima, 228–257.

———. 1988. *Religions of Immigrants from India and Pakistan: New Threads in the American Tapestry.* Cambridge: Cambridge University Press.

———. 1986. "The Guru as Pastoral Counselor." *Journal of Pastoral Care* 40/4: 331–440.

Wood, Marjorie. 1980. "Hinduism in Vancouver: Adjustments in the Home, the Temple, and the Community." In *Visible Minorities and Multiculturalism: Asians in Canada,* ed. Victor Ujimoto and Gordon Hirabayashi. Toronto: Butterworths, 277–288.

Woodward, Kenneth. 1990. *Making Saints: How the Catholic Church Determines Who Becomes a Saint, Who Doesn't and Why.* New York: Touchstone.

Yocum, Glenn. 1992. "The Coronation of the Guru: Charisma, Politics, and

Philosophy in Contemporary India." In *A Sacred Thread: Modern Transmission of Hindu Traditions in India and Abroad,* ed. Raymond Williams. Chambersburg, Penn.: Anima, 68–91.

Younger, Paul. 2002. *Playing Host to Deity: Festival Religion in the South Indian Tradition.* New York: Oxford University Press.

Index